The Last of the Chiefs

Alasdair Ranaldson Macdonell
of Glengarry 1773–1828

BRIAN D OSBORNE

Argyll
publishing

First published 2001
Argyll Publishing
Glendaruel
Argyll PA22 3AE
Scotland
argyll.publishing@virgin.net

The author has asserted his moral rights.

British Library Cataloguing-in-Publication Data.
A catalogue record for this book is available from the British Library.

ISBN 1 902831 27 6

Origination
Cordfall Ltd, Glasgow

Printing
Bell & Bain Ltd, Glasgow

CONTENTS

ACKNOWLEDGEMENTS

It is a pleasure to be able to acknowledge, in even so impersonal a manner as this, my immense debt to a wide range of individuals and institutions built up in the process of writing this book.

As no full life of Glengarry has previously been written I have been more than usually dependent on original materials and sources and I am deeply grateful for the courtesy and professionalism of the librarians and archivists of the Aberdeen University Directorate of Information Systems and Services, Department of Special Collections and Archives; the British Library; the Clan Donald Centre Library; East Dunbartonshire Libraries; Edinburgh City Libraries; Eton College; Glasgow City Libraries; Glasgow University Library; the Highland Council Library Service; the National Archives of Scotland (The Scottish Record Office); the National Library of Scotland; Oxfordshire Archives; Perth & Kinross Libraries; the Scottish Catholic Archives and the Scottish National Portrait Gallery.

Individuals to whom I am indebted include the late Air Commodore Æneas R Macdonell of Glengarry, CB, DFC; the Rt. Rev. Gerard Mark Dilworth, OSB, MA PhD, FSA (SCOT.) the former Abbot of St. Benedict's Abbey, Fort Augustus and James Irvine Robertson whose admirable life of Glengarry's rather more amiable contemporary David Stewart of Garth, *The First Highlander,* provided both an example and much food for thought.

My friends have suffered much in the course of writing this book and have, perforce, become somewhat more knowledgeable about Alasdair Ranaldson Macdonell than they might have wished. In particular I am grateful to Kevin Goldie for his help with various legal questions and to Ronnie Renton for his willing and expert assistance with Gaelic matters and for his translations of the poems of Allan MacDougall. My friend and colleague Alan Reid undertook the thankless task of reading the manuscript chapter by chapter and making helpful and detailed suggestions for its improvement and clarification. My grateful thanks are due to all. The responsibility for any mistakes and shortcomings in the final text however rests with the author.

Brian D Osborne
February 2001

A NOTE ON NAMES

Most of the branches of Clan Donald spell their name MacDonald – literally the son of Donald. From the seventeenth century, when Æneas, the ninth chief of Glengarry, was raised to the peerage by Charles II on his restoration, the Glengarry branch has however used the spelling of Macdonell or MacDonell. While the version with a capital D is probably preferable the other version, Macdonell, has been adopted in the text of this book as this was the form used by Alasdair Ranaldson. No attempt has however been made to standardise the spelling where original documents or other books have been quoted and thus MacDonald, MacDonell and M'Donell will all be found.

In many documents Macdonell is referred to as Alexander, in others as Alasdair or Alastair. Alexander is not, of course, an English translation of the Gaelic Alasdair, but an English equivalent. There was, and remains, a fashion in the Highlands for English Christian names drawn from classical sources – thus Alasdair Ranaldson Macdonell's son was called Æneas, an English (or more precisely, Latin) version of the Gaelic Aonghas. The preferred form in the present text is Alasdair, but, as in the case of the surname, other versions will appear in sources cited and no attempt has been made to standardise.

His second Christian name – Ranaldson – was a traditional one in his family in tribute to the progenitor of the houses of Glengarry and Clanranald, Ranald (or Raghnall) of the Isles who flourished in the late fourteenth century.

The chiefs of Highland clans, in addition to conventional surnames and Christian names, use a traditional patronymic, often derived from the founder of their house, thus the chiefs of Clan Campbell are known as MacCailean Mòr – the Son of Great Colin. The MacDonalds of Clanranald were known as Mac Mhic Ailein – the Son of Alan's Son. The chiefs of Glengarry were, in the same manner, known as Mac Mhic Alasdair (or Mac 'ic Alasdair) – the Son of Alasdair's Son, a reference to the fifteenth century fourth chief and first to possess the lands of Glengarry.

After such complexities it is something of a relief to rely on the long-established Scottish custom of referring to a landowner by the title of his property and this was indeed the most usual means of referring to our subject, simply as 'Glengarry'. Unfortunately this simple appellation was confused, later in his life, by his claim to the chiefship of Clanranald and his habit of signing himself 'Alasdair Ranaldson Macdonell of Glengarry and Clanranald' or 'of Clanranald and Glengarry'.

Introduction

A lasdair Ranaldson Macdonell died in 1828, leaving behind little but debts and a trail of argument, controversy and on-going litigation. He never occupied any major offices of state, wrote nothing of significance, and failed in what was probably the dearest desire of his heart – to have the family peerage restored. Debts forced the sale of much of the once vast family lands shortly after his death and by the middle of the century, with the sale of Knoydart, the Glengarry estate was reduced to a ruined castle and a mausoleum. The case for writing, or reading, a biography of such an unsuccessful and ill-fated man may perhaps seem unclear.

However Macdonell was both an unusually interesting man and lived in interesting times. His life and career illustrate many of the most significant features of Highland life at the end of the eighteenth and beginning of the nineteenth centuries. His activities in raising troops to fight in the French wars, his estate management policies, his establishment of the Society of True Highlanders, his devotion to tradition (even to the point of maintaining a personal bard, and a blind one at that), his feuding with the Commissioners for the Caledonian Canal – all cast light on the changes in the Highlands in Macdonell's day and illustrate the significance of these changes in the way of life of the Highlanders.

Macdonell's immense capacity for contradiction and seeming lack of any deep capacity for self-awareness or self-criticism allowed him to simultaneously promote sheep-farming and the clearance philosophy while promoting the ancient Highland customs and traditions which the new patterns of estate management were inevitably doomed to destroy. Similarly he could sell ground and timber to the Caledonian Canal, take a leading part in the celebration of the opening of the Canal, attack the Canal Company's workmen when the Canal was being built and after it was opened sue the Commissioners because in his view the 'passage boats and smoking steam vessels' using the Canal breached the privacy of what he considered a private waterway. To add a final twist to the tale, his wife was a shareholder in one of these 'smoking steam vessels' and Glengarry himself did not disdain to travel on them; indeed his death resulted from a trip on the *Stirling Castle* steam ship.

In his own day Glengarry was seen as an eccentric aberration, as the 'Last of the Chiefs', as a man born out of his proper time. His Gaelic sobriquet was 'Alasdair Fiadhaich' – Wild Alasdair or Fierce Alasdair, which does convey something of the light in which he was seen by contemporaries.

When Henry Raeburn painted the great portrait of him around 1812 he depicted him in a consciously archaic setting with targe and broadsword on the walls of some idealised baronial hall and with Glengarry holding an old-fashioned rifle with an octagonal barrel. Glengarry is, at first sight, a commanding and imposing figure, but there is also, on closer examination, a sense of distance almost amounting to insecurity in the pose. Glengarry does not meet the artist's or the viewer's eye, he looks out of the picture, as it might be to some distant focus of desire. This is hardly an accidental pose. Raeburn's portraits combine technical excellence with a high degree of psychological insight – his subjects might have been drawn from 'society' but no one could accuse Raeburn of being merely a 'society portraitist'. His work goes below the skin, below the tartanry, below the accoutrements of *sgian dubh* and pistol, to show a man, proud in his position, traditional in his outlook and alienated from his contemporary environment.

What Henry Raeburn saw in his Edinburgh studio, and depicted in what is one of the great Scottish portraits, Walter Scott, from longer and deeper knowledge of Glengarry, wrote about both in fiction and in his diaries and private correspondence. To the Irish novelist Maria Edgeworth he wrote of Glengarry's 'wild and fierce' character and of his 'kind, honest and warm heart', while in his diary for 26 February 1826 he reflected:

> I had a call from Glengarry yesterday, as kind and
> friendly as usual. This gentleman is a kind of Quixote in
> our age, having retained, in their full extent, the whole

feelings of clanship and chieftainship, elsewhere so long abandoned. He seems to have lived a century too late, and to exist, in a state of complete law and order, like a Glengarry of old, whose will was law to his sept.

Scott, it is generally considered, drew heavily on Glengarry in his portrayal of the Jacobite chief Fergus Mac-Ivor in *Waverley*. In Chapter XIX he wrote of his fictional creation:

> Had Fergus Mac-Ivor lived sixty years sooner than he did, he would, in all probability, have wanted the polished manner and knowledge of the world which he now possessed; and had he lived sixty years later, his ambition and love of rule would have lacked the fuel which his situation now afforded.

Fergus Mac-Ivor, 'Vich Ian Vohr', of Glennaquoich, Scott suggests, lived in his proper age – an age which would see the end of the old Highlands in the blood and shot of Culloden and in the destruction of the traditional Highland polity in the aftermath of the Jacobite rising.

Alasdair Ranaldson Macdonell, 'Mac Mhic Alasdair', of Glengarry (and laird of Glenquoich) lived in an age in which he was not at ease. For all his retention of so much of the trappings of a traditional chief, such as his 'tail', or retainers, the age of the Highland warrior chief had gone, the reason for the familial relationship between clan chief and clansman had gone, to be replaced by a cash connection. Fergus Mac-Ivor was able to sustain and support (albeit with some judicious cattle reiving and blackmailing) the full complement of followers and keep open house for his dependants. In Chapter XVI his follower, Ewan Dhu, tells Edward Waverley of the proper accompaniments of chiefly state, of Vich Ian Vohr's tail:

> . . . there is his *hanchman*, or right-hand man, then his *bhaird*, or poet; then his *bladier*, or orator, to make harangues to the great folks whom he visits; then his *gilly-more* or armour-bearer, to carry his sword, and target, and his gun; then his *gilly-casflue*, who carries him on his back through the sikes and brooks; then his *gilly-comstraine*, to lead his horse by the bridle in steep and difficult paths; then his *gilly-trusharnish*, to carry his knap-sack; and the piper and the piper's man, and it

may be a dozen young lads beside, that have no
business, but are just boys of the belt to follow the laird,
and do his honour's bidding.

Glengarry, brought up from his earliest days with a profound
conviction of the high place to which he had been born and the
dignity and worth of a clan chief, attempted to maintain this
splendid, archaic state in an age when its relevance was gone and
when his fellow Highland chiefs counted their wealth in sheep
and in pounds and guineas accumulating to their credit in Forbes
or Coutts bank rather than, as in days of old, in long rent-rolls and
the number of armed men they could raise from their estates.
Supporting this lifestyle proved to be too severe a strain on his
finances, despite the considerably increased income he was able
to extract from his estate by ending traditional tenancies.

Much of the difficulty in which Glengarry found himself
throughout his life, from his duel and trial for murder, the problems
of his military career, his quarrels and litigation with neighbours
and tenants, his feuding with the Caledonian Canal, can surely be
traced to this overweening pride of lineage and birth, unchecked
by considerations of policy or practicality. Scott reflected on his
friend's character in his diary:

> Warm-hearted, generous, friendly, he is beloved by those
> who know him, and his efforts are unceasing to show
> kindness to those of his clan who are disposed fully to
> admit his pretensions. To dispute them is to incur his
> resentment, which has sometimes broken out in acts of
> violence which have brought him in collision with the
> law . . . The number of his singular exploits would fill a
> volume; for, as his pretensions are high, and not always
> willingly yielded to, he is every now and then giving rise
> to some rumour. He is, on many of these occasions, as
> much sinned against as sinning; for men, knowing his
> temper, sometimes provoke him, conscious that
> Glengarry, from his character for violence, will always be
> put in the wrong by the public.

It is perhaps strange that so famous, or so notorious, a figure,
whose life was colourful and controversial, whose death was
appropriately flamboyant, who played at least a walk-on part in
some of the great events of his period, and who is the subject of a

genuinely iconic Scottish portrait, should not have previously been thought worthy to 'fill a volume.'

The lives of typical figures, of men and women representative of their age, can of course be interesting and revealing and can allow valuable insights into that age. Surely, however, the life of a maverick, an eccentric, can also be of interest not only for what it says about the maverick, but about the times in which he lived and which he kicked against. It is not necessary to like or admire a figure (although there was much that was likeable and admirable in Glengarry) to gain interest and enjoyment from reading, or writing, his biography and I hope that readers will share my enjoyment in exploring the life and times of Colonel Alasdair Ranaldson Macdonell 15th Chief of Glengarry, 'Mac Mhic Alasdair', the Last of the Chiefs.

CHAPTER 1

The Royal Visit

'Auld England held him lang and fast;
And Ireland had a joyfu' cast
But Scotland's turn is come at last –
Carle, now the King's come'

Edinburgh was perhaps not Glengarry's most natural setting. The fifteenth chief of Clan Macdonell was certainly much more comfortable in his Highland homes at Invergarry and Knoydart where his taste for traditional Highland customs and the loyalty of his retainers could both be more easily enjoyed. Edinburgh was the location of the lawyers who dealt with his increasingly tangled financial affairs and it was the seat of the Court of Session where he had become a regular litigant. It was also in Edinburgh that he had stood trial for murder at the High Court of Justiciary in 1798.

In a normal August he would have been in the north, enjoying country pastimes and preparing for the great Highland games with which he normally celebrated his birthday on 15th September. But 1822 was never going to be normal. The visit of George IV to Edinburgh in August 1822 was a major event for Scotland and the Scottish capital, if only because the last reigning monarch to visit Scotland had been Charles II in the middle of the seventeenth century. Charles had been crowned at Scone on 1st January 1651, in the midst of the Civil War, but after his Restoration in 1660 never revisited Scotland. Charles's brother the Duke of York, later James VII & II, had spent some time in Scotland before his brief reign. After coming to the throne neither he, nor any subsequent sovereign of Great Britain, had thought it safe or appropriate to visit their Northern Kingdom. Indeed the only prince of the House of Hanover who had been to Scotland had been George II's son, William, Duke of Cumberland, the victor of Culloden: known as 'the butcher' for his enthusiastic disposal of Highlanders after the Battle of Culloden in 1746, this was hardly the most auspicious of precedents.

However by the 1820s the Jacobite threat had ended; the last plausible Jacobite claimant to the throne, Henry Benedict, Cardinal York had died in 1807, apparently reconciled to the Hanoverian succession. As the full title of Walter Scott's immensely successful first novel *Waverley, or 'Tis Sixty Years Since,* suggests, Jacobitism was a business which was now buried safely in the past. George IV had come to the throne in 1820 after a long Regency and had made a successful visit to Ireland in 1821, as Scott's celebratory poem indicates. The way was now clear for a visit to Scotland.

Sir Walter Scott was conscripted as the stage-manager of the Royal Visit by the Lord Provost of Edinburgh. Scott, seeking to reconcile Highlands and Lowlands, Jacobite and Hanoverian, and with a poet's romantic eye for spectacle, included a huge Highland element in his plans for the visit. This was perhaps not surprising. Scott had, to a previously unprecedented extent, celebrated the Highland element in Scottish history and Scottish society. In poems such as *The Lady of the Lake* (1810) and *The Lord of the Isles* (1815) and in his first two novels *Waverley* (1814) and *Rob Roy* (1818) he had substantially and enduringly shaped the way Scotland and the wider world viewed the Highlands and Highlanders.

Highlanders might be very well in the pages of *Waverley* or singing a stirring boat-song in *The Lady of the Lake* but not everyone accepted happily the Royal Visit's emphasis and the implication that the Highlands and Highlanders were appropriate symbols and representatives of Scotland. Even in Scott's own family circle, his son-in-law and future biographer, John Gibson Lockhart, had more than a few reservations. He notes in his *Life* of his father-in-law:

> It appeared to be very generally thought, when the first programmes were issued, that the Highlanders, their kilts, and their bagpipes, were to occupy a great deal too much space in every scene of public ceremony connected with the King's reception. With all respect and admiration for the noble and generous qualities which our countrymen of the Highland clans have so often exhibited, it was difficult

to forget that they had always constituted a small, and
almost always an unimportant part of the Scottish
population; and when one reflected how miserably their
numbers had of late been reduced in consequence of the
selfish and hard-hearted policy of their landlords, it
almost seemed as if there was a cruel mockery in giving so
much prominence to their pretensions. But there could be
no doubt that they were picturesque. . . [1]

Much of Lowland Scotland shared Lockhart's view. Generations of suspicion of Highlanders, fuelled by memories of cattle-reiving, the Highland Host quartered on the Lowlands in the religious conflicts of the 1680s, the Jacobite risings and the religious divisions between the largely Catholic and Episcopalian Highlands and the predominantly Presbyterian Lowlands was a legacy which was not easily overturned by sixty years of tranquility and some romantic poetry.

One figure who had no doubts about the part that the Highlands should play in celebrating the King's coming was Colonel Alasdair Macdonell of Glengarry. Glengarry was certainly 'picturesque' and his behaviour also fitted Lockhart's condemnation of 'selfish and hard-hearted' Highland landlords, but such matters were lost sight of in the excitement of the Royal Visit. Glengarry felt that he should have a major role to play in the King's visit, not only as the chief of an ancient and powerful Highland clan and as a descendant of the Lords of the Isles, but as the head of a society of Highland gentlemen. His friend Scott, however, did not find a role for Glengarry's Society of True Highlanders in his tartan pageant.

Glengarry had formed the True Highlanders at a meeting at Inverlochy, near Fort William, in June 1815 as a:

. . . pure Highland Society, in support of the true Dress,
Language, Music and Characteristics of our illustrious and
ancient race in the Highlands and Islands of Scotland,
with their genuine descendants wherever they may be. [2]

Inverlochy was, of course, the site of the great victory in 1641 of the Highland and Irish Royalist army under Montrose and Alasdair MacDonald over the Covenant forces led by Argyll. As such it was a place dear to the heart of Clan Donald and an evocative and significant location for Glengarry to choose to launch a Society devoted to recapturing the glorious past and preserving a fast-vanishing Highland way of life.

The Society flourished. It recruited no less than ninety-seven members at its inaugural meeting, the proceedings of which were entirely conducted in Gaelic. All chiefs of clans who joined were to become Vice Presidents and the President or *Ceann Suidhe* was to be elected each year from among these chiefs/Vice Presidents. The Society in its first few years saw many of the principal Highland figures enlisting under Glengarry's leadership – men such as the Dukes of Atholl and Argyll, MacKenzie of Seaforth, Robertson of Struan and MacDonald of Clanranald. After a couple of years as *Ceann Suidhe* Glengarry stood down in favour of MacKenzie of Seaforth and took the title of *Fear Bunachar* or Founder.

In October 1815 the Society had appointed Ewan MacLachlan (1773-1822), the distinguished Gaelic poet and librarian of King's College, Aberdeen, as its Gaelic Secretary and, in a post-war outburst of reconciliation, elected Maréchal Jacques Étienne Joseph Alexandre MacDonald (1765-1840), Duc de Tarente, the descendant of an exiled Scots Jacobite who had become one of Napoleon's most distinguished generals, as an Honorary Member.

This eminently respectable body, selective in its membership, earnest in some of its attempts to investigate and preserve Highland and Gaelic culture, was in Glengarry's view ideally suited to play a leading role in the celebrations surrounding the King's visit. It was, however, not the only Highland society – there was, based in Edinburgh, the Celtic Society. This had been formed in 1820 by David Stewart of Garth, the amiable soldier-author of *Sketches of the Highlanders*, and William Mackenzie of Gruinard. The Celtic Society had as its President not one of the great Highland chiefs but the Borderer Sir Walter Scott. Although it included in its membership representatives of many ancient and aristocratic Highland families, it also took in enthusiastic lowlanders – like Scott – and included many Edinburgh professional men. There was some degree of overlap between the two Societies; Stewart of Garth was an early member of the True Highlanders and Glengarry had joined the Celtic Society. However the Celtic Society's lack of ethnic purity and aristocratic exclusiveness proved to be unappealing to Glengarry. Scott obviously did not share Glengarry's views about the Celtic Society and wrote in a major role for it in the arrangements for the Royal Visit. As a result Glengarry was obliged to appear simply as the head of a Highland clan and any otherwise uncommitted members of the True Highlanders who wished to take part appeared as part of his 'tail' and not as a separate formed body.

Scott involved Stewart of Garth with him in the arrangements for the celebrations. Colonel Stewart, a distinguished soldier, had just recently won considerable praise for his comprehensive account of the Highland Clans and Regiments and his combination of military authority and literary distinction proved to be of considerable assistance in regulating the competing claims of the Highland component of the visit. Scott was at the centre of all the planning as Lockhart records:

> Ere the green-room in Castle Street [Scott's Edinburgh
> house] had dismissed provosts, and bailies, and deacon-
> conveners of the trades of Edinburgh, it was sure to be
> besieged by swelling chieftains, who could not agree on
> the relative positions their clans had occupied at
> Bannockburn, which they considered as constituting the
> authentic precedent for determining their own places,
> each at the head of his little theatrical *tail*, in the line of the
> King's escort between the Pier of Leith and the Canongate.

Lockhart goes on to tell how Stewart of Garth, commanding the Celtic Society, also:

> . . . had a potential voice in the conclave of rival
> chieftains, – and, with the able backing of this honoured
> veteran, Scott succeeded finally in assuaging all their
> heats, and reducing their conflicting pretensions to terms
> of truce, at least, and compromise. [3]

Lockhart's depiction of the Highland chiefs squabbling over precedence does, despite his fairly obvious anti-Highland bias, convey something of the spirit which imbued Glengarry, whose proud boast was that Clan Donald had fought on the right of the line at every Scottish battle from Bannockburn in 1314 to Falkirk in 1746. This privilege had been denied them at Culloden – and everyone knew what had happened there.

The lengths to which Scott had to go to smooth over the prickly sensitivities of the Highland chiefs is suggested by his composition, in the midst of making all the arrangements, of a second part of twenty-three verses to his ballad, *Carle, now the King's come!* The first part of this appeared with eighteen verses (one of which is quoted at the head of this chapter) but the daily papers around August 12th carried Scott's well-intentioned, if not particularly poetically accomplished, attempt to flatter the participants and to keep his touchy Highlanders on board:

> Cock o' the North, my Huntly bra',
> Where are ye wi the Forty-twa,
> Ah! waes my heart that ye're awa',
> Carle, now the King's come!

> But yonder come my canty Celts,
> With durk and pistol at their belts,
> Thank God, we've still some plaids and kilts,
> Carle, now the King's come!

> Lord, how the pibrochs groan and yell,
> MacDonell's tae'en the field himsel',
> MacLeod comes brankin' o'er the fell,
> Carle, now the King's come! [4]

The compromises and truces which Scott and Garth engineered were at best surface deep – in a very long two-part letter which Glengarry addressed to the *Edinburgh Observer* after the Royal Visit was over he rehearsed Clan Donald's historical precedence and, noting that the Drummond and Sutherland contingents were lead by English peeresses, observed that this offence to the national pride had only been agreed to by a public-spirited overcoming of every selfish and personal idea in the greater interest of welcoming the King.

The procession from Leith to Holyrood, as finally agreed, organised and compromised, blended the State and the Celtic components in a remarkable and innovative way. There certainly had never been seen so many Highlanders in Edinburgh since Charles Edward Stuart had entered the city in 1745.

Three trumpeters Mid-Lothian Yeomanry Cavalry
Squadron Mid-Lothian Yeomanry
Two Highland Pipers
Captain Campbell and Tail of Breadalbane
Squadron Scots Greys
Two Highland Pipers
Col. Stewart of Garth and Celtic Society
Sir Evan MacGregor and Tail of MacGregor
Herald
Marischal Trumpets & Grooms
Marischal Esquires
Knight Marischal
Marischal Rear-Guard of Highlanders
Sheriff
Sheriff Officers
Deputy Lieutenants
Two Pipers
General Graham Stirling and Tail
Barons of Exchequer
Lord Clerk Register
Lords of Justiciary and Session
Lord Lieutenant (Marquis of Lothian)
Two Heralds
Glengarry
Æneas Glengarry
Tail of Glengarry
Herald Trumpeters
White Rod
Lord Lyon Depute
Lord High Constable
Heralds
Squadron Scots Greys
Vice Chamberlain & Comptroller of Household
Treasurer of Household & Equerry
Archers THE KING Archers
Master of the Horse & Groom of the Stole
Sir Thomas Bradford
Squadron Scots Greys
Three Clans of Highlanders
Two Squadrons of Mid-Lothian Yeomanry
Grenadiers of 77th Foot
Two Squadrons 3rd Dragoon Guards
Band, and Scots Greys. [5]

As will be seen Alasdair Macdonell had managed to obtain
for himself and his heir Æneas, a fourteen year old schoolboy, the

places of honour among the Highland contingents – being nearest before the King and next to the great Officers of State such as the Lord Lyon and the Lord High Constable. Clan Donald's privilege of the right of the line had been well defended. Indeed Glengarry had done even better than the order of march suggests, for twelve gentlemen of the Clan, under the command of their Chief, had been given the honour of guarding the Royal Carriage until the King entered it, whereupon the privilege of close escort devolved to the Royal Company of Archers. This might have been thought place and prominence enough for anyone, but Glengarry added in his own, private, unscripted, welcome to the King by galloping forward to meet and greet him.

An English visitor to Edinburgh at this spectacular moment in its history was the poet George Crabbe, the clergyman author of the East Anglian epic poem *The Borough*. Crabbe was an acquaintance of Scott's who had taken up Sir Walter's earlier invitation to come north and found that his visit coincided with his sovereign's. Crabbe suffered a degree of culture-shock in tartan-mad Edinburgh – Lockhart reflected that:

> . . . he had never for one moment conceived that the same island, in which his peaceful parsonage stood, contained actually a race of men, and gentlemen too, owning no affinity with Englishmen, either in blood or in speech, and still proud in wearing, whenever opportunity served, a national dress of their own, bearing considerably more resemblance to an American Indian's than to that of an old-fashioned rector from the Vale of Belvoir. [6]

Crabbe's reaction to all this tartan splendour is indicated in his journal entry, written after a dinner at Scott's on 15th August:

> . . . there met at the sumptuous dinner, in all the costume of the Highlanders, the great chief himself, and officers of his company. This expresses not the singularity of appearance and manners – the peculiarities of men all gentlemen, but remote from our society – leaders of clans – joyous company. Then we had Sir Walter Scott's national songs and ballads, exhibiting all the feelings of clanship. I thought it an honour that Glengarry even took notice of me, for there were those, and gentlemen too, who considered themselves honoured by following

in his train . . . I conversed at dinner with Lady
Glengarry, and did almost believe myself a harper, or
bard, rather – for harp I cannot strike; and Sir Walter was
the life and soul of the whole. [7]

There is, of course, no more inherent improbability in a Suffolk-
born poet and clergyman feeling himself a Celtic bard than in
George IV reinventing himself as a kilt-wearing Stuart. Well might
the Duke of Atholl describe the period of the King's visit as the
'one and twenty daft days.'

Edinburgh enjoyed the unprecedented activity and the sight
of the more or less peaceful invasion of several hundred kilted
Highlanders. As the *Scots Magazine* reported:

The inhabitants were astonished by the number of
dazzling equipages that rolled along the streets, and the
multitudes of inquisitive faces that crowded the
pavements. In this moving multitude, the brave
Highlanders were conspicuous objects, and their fine
martial appearance served agreeably to diversify, and
greatly to heighten the interest of this animated scene. [8]

Few Highlanders were more conspicuous than Glengarry, an
imposing figure, as his portraits suggest, the more imposing when
accompanied, as he took pains to be on every possible occasion,
by his 'tail' or retinue of attendants. For this occasion he had, in
addition, swept into his court as many of the gentlemen of the
Macdonell clan as he could – his brother Colonel James and his
kinsmen of the cadet branches of the House of Glengarry. He and
James were presented to the King at a levée held on 17th August
at Holyrood, a somewhat mass production event in which almost
2000 gentlemen kissed the hand of their sovereign at a rate,
calculated by a member of the Archer bodyguard, of fifteen a
minute. The Macdonells' sponsor on this 'splendidly and
numerously attended' occasion was the Duke of Montrose.

As part of the entertainment for the King's stay a production
was arranged for the 27th August of the play *Rob Roy*, recently
adapted by William Murray from Scott's novel. *Rob Roy* was, in
1822, at the start of its immensely successful nineteenth century
run as the 'Scottish National Drama' and its performance had been
specially requested by the King. George IV was a devoted admirer

of Scott's work and had offered him the Poet Laureateship in 1813. Scott was also offered a baronetcy in 1818 although he did not actually receive the honour until 1820 as one of the first acts of the new King's reign. Lockhart quotes an account of the Royal visit to the theatre:

> The boxes were filled with the rank, wealth, and beauty of Scotland. In this dazzling galaxy were observed the gallant Sir David Baird, Colonel Stewart of Garth, Glengarry, the Lord Provost, and Sir Walter Scott; each of whom, as he entered, was greeted with loud acclamations. [9]

It is noteworthy that the writer, James Ballantyne, had no hesitation in putting Glengarry in this select group of public figures who were greeted by the crowds with 'loud acclamations.' Stewart of Garth and Sir David Baird were military heroes of the Napoleonic Wars; Sir Walter was a unique national figure; the Lord Provost, William Arbuthnott, was the Lord Provost and had, just three days before, been made a baronet by the King at a dinner in Parliament-Hall. Glengarry's place in this assemblage perhaps owed more to his effrontery than to his accomplishments, but his inclusion shows the willingness of society to take him at his own assessment. A reporter for the *Edinburgh Observer* also noted this group of distinguished persons who received the plaudits of the crowd and described Glengarry as 'that truly noble representative of the Highland Chieftain.' [10]

The Royal Visit might have been tailor-made for Glengarry – it provided a platform from which he could perform and the Scott-fanned obsession with tartanry and the Highlands created a context in which Glengarry's own Celtic obsessions and tireless campaign for self-advancement seemed more, if not entirely, normal. Not only did George IV appear in 'national costume' but his friend and travelling companion, the London Alderman Sir William Curtis, with less excuse than the King, appeared at the royal levée in Stuart tartan. At the Civic Banquet the King, after proposing a toast to the new Baronet, Lord Provost Arbuthnott, moved on to propose another toast:

> His Majesty again rose and said, 'Gentlemen, I trust you will all do justice to a toast, in which I feel a very great interest. I shall simply give you, All the chieftains and all

the clans of Scotland, and may God bless the Land of
Cakes!' [11]

The designation of Scotland as 'the Land of Cakes' had been
popularised by Burns but its origins go back at least to the
seventeenth century and, of course, refer to the staple oatcake,
rather than to any more delicate work of the baker or pâtissier.
The hand of Sir Walter, as royal script writer, may perhaps be
detected. In any event the King's toast to Scotland, given in the
heart of its very Lowland capital, was particularised to a toast to
Highland Scotland.

After the King left the Civic Banquet at nine to return to
Dalkeith Palace (where he was obliged to stay with the Duke of
Buccleuch because of the dilapidated state of the Palace of
Holyrood) the party continued with an almost endless round of
toasts until nearly midnight. One toast was to:

> The Chieftains and Clans who have come forward on the
> present occasion to grace His Majesty's Court,
> particularly Glengarry, Sir Ewen MacGregor, the Earl of
> Breadalbane, Lady Gwydir [Drummond] and the
> Marchioness of Stafford [Sutherland]

Glengarry rose to reply to this toast.

> Glengarry returned thanks for himself and Sir E
> Macgregor, remarking, whenever His Majesty should
> require their services, either to grace his Court, or to
> defend his throne, the Highlanders would ever be found
> ready to stand forth in honour or defence. [12]

The report does not make clear exactly why Glengarry chose only
to respond on behalf of himself and MacGregor. Breadalbane was,
of course a Campbell, and Clan Donald and Clan Campbell were
traditional rivals, with much grounds for ill-blood other than
Inverlochy and Glencoe. It might also have appeared presump-
tuous for the untitled Glengarry to reply on behalf of an Earl who
was presumably present – although a self-effacing modesty does
not seem particularly characteristic of the Macdonell chief. The
ladies mentioned would, of course, not have been at the Banquet,
and could not respond on their own behalf and it might have
seemed appropriate for Glengarry to have included them in his
remarks. However the ladies in question were the heads of those

clans with English chieftains and whose command by other than the male descendants of the rightful line on the occasion of the Royal Visit had, as we have seen, caused Glengarry great distress.

The King left Edinburgh on the 29th August, after knighting the artist Henry Raeburn and commanding him to come to London to paint his portrait. The visit had been an enormous success, the King having been in equal measure impressed with Edinburgh and with the people of Scotland. Even the not-untypical Edinburgh haar which managed to coincide with the King's visit to the Castle failed to dampen his enthusiasm for the view – indeed the general opinion was that the 'incumbent gloom' added to the 'wild and most romantic effect.' In any event the King was reported to have exclaimed to his attendants:

> This is wonderful! What a sight! [13]

His Scottish subjects were equally to the King's taste. At the end of his first day in Edinburgh he said to Thomas Graham, Lord Lynedoch, who had been Wellington's deputy in the Peninsula campaign:

> I have often heard the Scots called a proud nation – they may well be so – they appear to be a nation of gentlemen.

Robert Peel, the Home Secretary, who had accompanied the King north, wrote a letter of thanks to Scottish Officers of State expressing the King's approbation of the arrangements and thanks for the success of the visit. He also wrote at the King's particular command to Scott:

> . . . conveying to you individually his warm personal acknowledgements for the deep interest you have taken in every ceremony and arrangement connected with his Majesty's visit, and for your ample contributions to their complete success.

> His Majesty well knows how many difficulties have been smoothed, and how much has been effected by your unremitting activity, by your knowledge of your countrymen and by the just estimation in which they hold you.

> The King wishes to make you the channel of conveying to the Highland chiefs and their followers, who have

given to the varied scene which we have witnessed so
peculiar and romantic a character, his particular thanks
for their attendance, and his warm approbation of their
uniform deportment. [14]

Scott, dutifully copied the Home Secretary's letter to the
various Highland chiefs. Glengarry, never one to do things by
halves, decided to publish the letter in the daily press. As he wrote
to Scott from Aberdeen on 4th September:

. . . I coincide with you in thinking that it will afford the
gentlemen of my escort and all the other Highlanders
concerned much real pleasure, but, as my friends the
True Highlanders have scattered in many directions,
some to England, Ireland and Dumfries-shire (on
business and pleasure) others to the Highlands, while a
few, like myself are visiting about, previous to returning
to our native mountains – I say, under all these
circumstances, I considered it my Duty, to lay your
agreeable communication with its honourable
testimonial before the Public, as the surest & far the most
expeditious means of getting at all the Gentlemen
concerned, who will not fail to notify to their followers,
that most gracious acknowledgement, transmitted
through you by the Secretary of State of the esteem and
approbation of their Sovereign. [15]

Which was all very satisfactory and the entire visit could be
put down as a success. Yet Stewart of Garth would write to Sir
Walter a year later reflecting that:

Had it not been for Glengarry the King's visit would
have passed without an angry word or unpleasant
feeling. . .[16]

Apart from his intrusiveness at the arrival of the King, and if
the King did not object there was little anyone else could do about
that piece of ill manners, the real problem came after His Majesty
was safely back on board the *Royal George*. Glengarry wrote an
extremely long, extremely offensive and extremely ill-judged letter
to the *Edinburgh Observer* – so long that it had to be published in
two episodes. In the first part he rebuked the *Observer* for
attributing a poem about the Royal Visit to Miss Macdonell. This
he felt was bad form – publishing a lady's name in the public press,
and in addition the writer was a daughter of Macdonell of Scotus,

currently residing in England. Citing the author as 'Miss Macdonell' without further geographical or territorial designation would, he felt, lead throughout the length of Scotland to an assumption that the writer had been his daughter Miss Elizabeth Ranaldson Macdonell. He continued with the matter referred to earlier about the priority of Clan Donald and the shocking breach of standards occasioned by the Sutherland and Drummond contingents coming under the command of Englishmen. The second instalment was to be much, much worse.

The issue of the *Edinburgh Observer* of Thursday 5th September gave over almost two broadsheet columns of typically small nineteenth century print to Glengarry's tirade. After rehearsing the shame of the Sutherlands and Drummonds being represented by English peers, he attacked Clan Campbell for being always opposed to the general policy of the clans, reminded his readers of his own ancient name and fame then moved on to the substance of his letter, an uninhibited attack on the gentlemen of the Celtic Society. He described them as:

> . . . an incongruous assemblage of all ranks, that have no one common bond of union among them. They neither speak the language, nor know how to put on correctly the garb of the 'Gael'; and yet, *without possessing the blood or the manly frame* of that interesting race, or any other ostensible cause whatever, they barefacedly *masked themselves* in the Highland garb, and trusting to the cloak of this *assumed character,* in their tartans and with eagle plumes in their bonnets, *the distinctive mark of the chieftain of old!* This novel and non-descript body, stopping at nothing which could be accomplished by a brazen effrontery, and those borrowed plumes, (of which, as in the fable of the daw, they are about to be stripped) unwarrantably pushed itself forward under those *false colours.* – 1st, To the charge of the regalia of Scotland, over which, *for a few days,* they mounted guard, like private soldiers, (of not a very soldierly cast); 2dly, They presented themselves to the King, in numbers, at the levee at Holyrood; and, 3rdly, They took up a position on the sands at Portobello, among the Highlanders, whom his Majesty was *most graciously* pleased to express a desire of seeing upon that ground on the day of the review. *Lastly,* I have been told (though I do not

positively know it, as I kept myself and my friends quite
aloof from them) that they contrived to draw lots with
the representatives of the four Highland clans, subject
that day to the Duke of Argyle's orders, for their place
among them. If this really happened, it was carrying the
farce too far, as upon that; and the having had a
temporary charge of the regalia of Scotland, they may, in
their modesty, at some future time, lay claim to a right to
these honours, in conjunction with those to whom that
right especially belongs. [17]

One problem that Glengarry might have considered about
launching such an attack on the Celtic Society was that he himself
was a member of this 'incongruous assemblage'. He explained that
when the Society was founded four of the five leading members
were in fact members of his own Society of True Highlanders, and
the fifth was Sir Walter Scott, whom he was kind enough to pass
as an honorary Highlander, being:

> . . . the pride of his country, with whom we would all
> delight to associate, though the Highlands could not
> claim him for a mountaineer, either by birth or
> hereditary male descent; and though, consequently, he
> was inadmissible (from the strict rules of the Society,) as
> a member of our truly Highland fraternity. . .

Under the attraction of these names Glengarry had joined the Celtic
Society and even attended one of their dinners:

> . . . I never saw so much tartan *before*, in my life, with *so
> little Highland material.*

He now publicly wished to withdraw his name from the Society,
for the reason that, although:

> There may be some very good and respectable men
> amongst them . . . their general appearance is assumed
> and fictitious, and they have *no right to burlesque the
> national character or dress of* Highlanders.

He went on to complain that he had been:

> . . . much disgusted, repeatedly, by seeing both the belted
> plaid, and the shoulder plaid, disfigured and caricatured
> by the members of that Society *in public*, who wear
> improperly, (very likely through ignorance), and in many
> instances bedaubed with gold or silver lace, like what

> footmen wear occasionally on their liveries, but quite
> different from the ancient and warlike garb of
> Caledonia's mountain race.

Not only did the Celtic Society not know how to wear Highland dress and had usurped the position he would have wished for the True Highlanders, they seemed to Macdonell to let absolutely anyone join:

> I believe there are some broken Highlanders on their list,
> belonging to almost every clan in the Highlands, *my own
> not excepted.* I have seen a mulattoe, a Jew – son to the
> vendor of the Balm of Gilead, and some other foreigners
> equally preposterous, appear in the George's Street
> Assembly Rooms, with scarfs almost down to their heels. .
> .

After a long digression on clan history and the iniquities of the Celtic Society allocating plant badges to clans in a manner unauthorised by tradition he wound up by recalling that when the first reports of the King's visit had circulated he had written:

> . . . to most of the few noblemen and gentlemen, who like
> myself then stood upon the list of the Celtic Society as
> well as that of the True Highlanders, explaining my
> disapprobation of the measures adopted by the body, so
> improperly assuming our national dress; I have not,
> therefore, any hesitation to remark, as I have now done,
> since no gentler hint was sufficient to restrain them,
> having observed to all with whom I corresponded upon
> that subject, that it was impossible for true Highlanders
> to associate with such a body or convention of people,
> open to all nations, and to all religions; and, as their
> example of assuming the dress is frequently followed,
> *upon Sundays,* by many of the shop boys of Edinburgh,
> not calculated to add either dignity or decency to the
> garb of the Gael, the line must now be strictly drawn,
> *otherwise* the national character of the Highlander must
> be tarnished, nay, demoralized in such hands.

A. Rn. MacDonell

These were wounding and deliberately immoderate words. Accusing them of setting an example to the shop boys of Edinburgh was hardly temperate and his reference to 'a body or convention of people' was probably a much more deliberate insult than it may seem to the modern reader. The term 'convention' had been popularised by the French Revolutionaries and was widely adopted in Britain by radical reformers – to be described thus can hardly have been pleasant to a Tory gentleman like Sir Walter Scott.

It can have come as little surprise to Macdonell that an Extraordinary General Meeting of the Celtic Society was called, through the columns of the *Edinburgh Observer*:

> ... to consider a motion for the expulsion of Alexander M'Donnell, Esq. of Glengarry, as the author of a libel on the Society, not less atrocious for its numerous misrepresentations, than for the malignant jealousy it exhibits. [18]

This, it need hardly be said, drew another letter from the angry Glengarry which, in part, observed:

> I would not have meddled with any of them, so long as they left me and my highlanders to stand or fall by the merit or demerit of our own act; but as long as I carry a St Andrew about me, in the warlike garb of my ancestors, I shall not be bearded by the best man among them, who may choose to put himself forward as their champion, *propria persona*. Though I do not think it worthwhile to ask (as I undervalue that *frothy effusion*, proceeding from such an authority) who suggested the motion of which I am thus generously apprised, but, at the same time, *assassin like*, stabbed at me from *behind a curtain*, by calling my statement 'misrepresentations,' and papering my open, and, at least, manly conduct, with this term of 'malignant jealousy'. . . [19]

A 'St Andrew' is presumably a reference to an Andrea Ferrara broadsword. Glengarry suggested that 'malignant jealousy' might more appropriately be attributed to the Celtic Society – or at least to that faction which authorised the publication of the call for his expulsion. Of course, whether he was expelled or not was something of a non-issue. In his letter he had indicated his desire to withdraw his name from the Celtic Society's membership.

Stewart of Garth's view was that, Glengarry excepted, the Royal visit had passed without an angry word. Glengarry had certainly succeeded in souring the event and its aftermath. It is a tribute to Glengarry's supreme insensitivity that he continued to visit and correspond with Sir Walter Scott on apparently friendly terms after having so comprehensively and personally attacked both the Society of which Sir Walter was President and the events which he had organised. Doubtless he felt that having made laudatory remarks about Scott and accepted him as a Highlander *honoris causa* his other remarks would not cause offence. It is equally a tribute to Scott's remarkable generosity of spirit that he did not instantly cut off all relations with Glengarry.

CHAPTER 2

Mac Mhic Alasdair

'ni h-eibhneas gan Chlainn Domhall'
'it is no joy without Clan Donald'

When Alasdair Ranaldson Macdonell was born on 15th September 1773 he did not simply become the heir to a major Highland estate. He entered into a great dynastic tradition and into a potentially leading role in a once-powerful family whose members had for centuries ruled much of the Highlands and Islands.

The Macdonells of Glengarry were one of the nine major branches of Clan Donald. All of Clan Donald proudly traced their descent from Somerled, the twelfth century warrior leader, who won control of the western isles from the Norse and established himself as *Ri Innse Gall*, King of the Isles of the Norsemen. More distantly and mythically Clan Donald traced their origins back to Conn of the Hundred Battles, High King of Ireland. However it was Somerled's grandson, Donald of Islay, who died in 1249, who gave his name to the clan. During the Wars of Independence one of Donald's grandsons, Angus Og, was an early and loyal follower of King Robert the Bruce and Clan Donald was appropriately rewarded with lands in Lochaber formerly held by the Comyn family, unsuccessful contenders for the Crown, as well as lands in Mull and Tiree held by the MacDougall clan, allies of the Comyns.

As the years went on what became recognised as the Lordship of the Isles – the title was claimed from the fourteenth century under John of Islay but only officially recognised by the Crown in the fifteenth century – would embrace a huge sweep of the West Coast of Scotland. By the death of Angus Og's son, John of Islay, in 1386 the Lordship in the Hebrides extended from Lewis south to Islay (with the exception of Skye) as well as the mainland coast and much of the interior from Knoydart, Moidart and Loch Oich in the North through Ardnamurchan, Morvern, Lorne, Knapdale to Kintyre in the South. The power and scope of the Lordship were significantly increased when one of John of Islay's sons married an Antrim heiress and with her brought a large part of Northern Ireland into the family. John's heir, Donald, the 2nd Lord of the Isles, by marriage to the heiress of the Earldom of Ross, laid the foundation for his son, Alexander, to become Earl of Ross and so to incorporate vast areas of the Central Highlands and the island of Skye in the Lordship.

The nine distinct and principal branches of Clan Donald give a good indication of the spread and significance of the clan and the overarching Lordship to which they all paid some form of fealty. Apart from the main branch, the Lords of the Isles, with their power base in Islay, the other branches were the MacIains of Ardnamurchan, the MacDonalds of Glencoe, the MacDonalds of Clanranald, the Macdonells of Glengarry, the MacDonalds of Sleat, the Earls of Antrim, the MacDonalds of Dunnyveg and the Glens, and the MacDonalds of Keppoch. In the course of time some of these chiefly lines became extinct – as did the Lordship itself.

The branch which became known as Glengarry traces its origins back to Ranald, the son of John of Islay and his first wife, Amy MacRuarie. In a politically inspired move John later was to divorce Amy to marry Margaret Stewart, a princess of the Royal house. John was succeeded in the Lordship by Donald the eldest son of this second marriage, while Ranald inherited the lands of the MacRuarie lordship of Garmoran – including Moidart, Morar, Knoydart, Ardgour, Eigg, Rum, the Uists and Harris. Ranald was the progenitor of two of the great branches of Clan Donald. From his first son, Allan, sprang the Clan Ranald and from his second son, Donald Ranaldson who died in 1420, came what would become the Glengarry branch.

In the middle of the fifteenth century the 4th Chief, Alexander, known in the Gaelic as *Alasdair Na Coille* – Alasdair of the Woods – seems to have been the first of the family to possess the lands of Glengarry, and it is from this Alexander or Alasdair that the Chiefs of Macdonell take their patronymic of *Mac Mhic Alasdair* – the son of the son of Alasdair.

In a state like Scotland, which was weakened by wars with England, by a series of regencies and child kings, it was perhaps to be expected that the great land owning families should become powerful and unruly subjects. It was especially probable in the case of the Lords of Isles whose control of the sea bound together the island and coastal lands of their Lordship but who were in turn isolated from Lowland Scotland by geography and, increasingly, language.

The Lords of the Isles grew to become, at best, somewhat conditional vassals of the Scottish kings. John the 1st Lord had supported Edward Balliol in his English-backed attempt to win back the Scottish crown from the House of Bruce. Donald, the 2nd Lord, in 1411, had marched a Highland and Island army to Harlaw in Aberdeenshire to defend his wife's claim to the Earldom of Ross. Alexander the 3rd Lord was twice imprisoned by James I and the 4th and last Lord of the Isles proved to be perhaps the most troublesome of his line. He had rebelled against James II in 1452 and in 1462, during the minority of James III, signed the Treaty of Westminster Ardtornish with Edward IV of England and the Earl of Douglas. The two Scottish lords agreed that in the event of a successful invasion of Scotland by Edward they would divide all Scotland north of the Forth between them, leaving the South to Edward, and rule their lands as vassals of the English King. They accepted pensions from the English King in exchange for signing away the integrity and autonomy of the Scottish state which their ancestors had fought with Bruce to defend.

As a consequence of such conduct, which went beyond the tolerable behaviour of even the most over-mighty subject or normal baronial unruliness to clear and outright treason, John's titles of Lord of the Isles and Earl of Ross were forfeited in 1475. On the promise of good behaviour the Lordship was restored in 1476 (although the Earldom of Ross remained in the possession of the Crown). However under James IV, who took a vigorous policy towards the Highlands, the Lordship was finally suppressed in 1493.

The Lordship was however not simply a succession of piratical petty kings exercising arbitrary power beyond the reach of a weak central government. A Council of the Isles, drawing representatives from the various classes of chiefs and landowners, met at Loch Finlaggan in Islay and a new Lord of the Isles was invested with religious ceremony and great feasting. Under the Lordship Gaelic culture flourished. Hereditary families of poets, musicians, lawyers, and doctors flourished and were supported by the Lordship. Craftsmanship in wood and metal and stone flourished and remnants of this can be seen today in, for example, the great Crosses of Iona, Islay and Oronsay and in monumental stones at Kilmartin and Kilmichael Glassary in mid-Argyll.

All this was, of course, long in the past when Alasdair Ranaldson was born. However the reputation and memory of the Lordship remained strong in Gaeldom and the sentiments expressed in the sixteenth century poem preserved in the *Book of the Dean of Lismore* held true for many years after:

> It is no joy without Clan Donald
> it is no strength to be without them;
> the best race in the round world:
> to them belongs every goodly man.

If the Lordship was still an emotional, if not a political, reality then the issue of which of the remaining branches of Clan Donald was to be regarded as pre-eminent and the true heir to the Lordship was a live issue and this was to become one of Alasdair's obsessions. His campaign to gain recognition for the House of Glengarry is discussed later in Chapter 10.

Less distantly in the past was the Civil War of the mid seventeenth century and the Jacobite campaigns of the first half of the eighteenth century. Clan Donald had fought on the Royalist side under Montrose and his lieutenant Alasdair MacDonald of Colonsay. When in 1645 the Royalist forces defeated the forces of the Covenanters under Argyll at Inverlochy, the Bard of Keppoch, Iain Lom, sang of the victory of his side in a bloody praise song that could have been written for a fifteenth century Lord of the Isles and which reveals how much of ancient clan rivalry underlay the political and religious differences that ostensibly fuelled the conflict.

The Glengarry of the day, Æneas, or Aonghas, the 9th Chief,

had been a loyal supporter of the Royalist cause right up to the end of armed resistance to the Commonwealth. Charles II, in exile, had promised Æneas that he would restore to him Clan Donald's long-forfeited Earldom of Ross. When restored, the King reneged on this promise and created him a Lord of Parliament with the title of Lord Macdonell and Aros, in the most limited form possible, that is with succession limited to the heirs male of his body. Æneas died childless, the peerage died with him, the lands and name of Glengarry passed to a cousin, Ranald of Scotus. The issue of the family peerage was another subject that was to occupy much of Alasdair Ranaldson's time and energy.

By the period of the Jacobite risings the Macdonells of Glengarry were one of the most significant of the anti-Hanoverian clans. Traditional in their Catholicism they were natural supporters of the Stuart cause. Owning a broad swathe of land from the Great Glen west to Knoydart and North Morar the clan lands were centrally placed and populous and Glengarry support would be crucial in any Jacobite rising. *Alasdair Dubh* (Black Alasdair), the 11th Chief, organised a loyal address to George I on his accession to the British throne which was signed by over a hundred clan chiefs and heads of families in the Highlands, but for all that, the Glengarry family loyalty to the House of Stuart was hardly in doubt. Although clan historians, and Alasdair Ranaldson in his peerage petition, claimed that the slighting of this loyal address at Court was the reason for the 1715 Rising there can be no doubt that somewhat more substantial motives were at work – not least international power politics. In any event *Alasdair Dubh* came out with his clansmen and fought at Sheriffmuir. For his services he was in 1716 granted a peerage, as Lord Macdonell, by the exiled Old Pretender, James VIII of Scotland and III of England in the eyes of the Jacobites. In the ill-fated rising of 1719 the Chief of Glengarry played no overt part, although 150 men of the clan fought at Glenshiel.

John, the 12th Chief, whose life embraced the 1745/46 Jacobite rising was unfit to lead the clan, and his eldest son *Alasdair Ruadh* (Red Alasdair) was an officer in the French army. The Glengarry contingent in the '45 was thus commanded by John's second son, Æneas. The cash income from the Glengarry estates might not have been huge – in 1761, for example, it was only £761. What was more important was that the clanlands could muster substantial numbers of fighting men and in 1745 a Glengarry regiment of 500 men was swiftly raised and fought through the campaign up to the eventual disaster at Culloden. Æneas was killed, in an accidental shooting incident, after the Battle of Falkirk in January 1746. Alasdair had attempted to come to Scotland to join the Prince and the Jacobite cause but the ship he was travelling in from France was captured by a British man of war and he spent a year and a half in the Tower of London.

Alasdair succeeded to the chiefship in 1754. He is generally accepted to be the Highland chief who became a Hanoverian spy in and around Jacobite circles in France and Scotland. Andrew Lang (1844 -1912) in two volumes *Pickle the Spy* and *The Companions of Pickle* outlined the case for this identification. Alasdair died unmarried and was succeeded in 1761 by his nephew, Duncan, the 14th Chief. Duncan was the father of Alasdair Ranaldson, the subject of this biography. When Duncan had inherited the estates his trustees attempted to solve the debt problem his uncle had left by selling the North Morar estate to Fraser of Lovat. North Morar had been among the earliest holdings of the family, part of the ancient MacRuarie lands of Garmoran.

This long family history stretching from the glory of the Lordship of the Isles to the tragedy of Culloden was part of the formation of Alasdair Ranaldson's character. He was steeped in family history and in the history of the Highlands. Sir Walter Scott wrote appreciatively of him in his journal:

> To me he is a treasure, as being full of information as to
> the history of his own clan, and the manners and
> customs of the Highlanders in general. [1]

Glengarry was indeed generous with information about the history of his family in particular and Clan Donald in general. He regretted, for example, that he had been unable to brief Scott adequately on clan matters, especially the falsely presumed precedence of Clanranald, when Scott was writing his epic poem *The Lord of the Isles*.

> Did I not feel I was too late for your present work I
> would willingly hand you an acknowledged anecdote of

one of my ancestors, a Lord of the Isles, trusting to your indulgence, if it has already reached your well-informed ears. Tho' I will first observe my regret that you seem impressed with a belief that Clanranald (i.e. MacDonald of Moidart 'The Captain of Clanranald') is of legitimate extraction, and no less so that it does not appear to have reached you that the Glengarries were the Chiefs of Clanranald which is the oldest branch of the whole clan.[2]

Scott fully reciprocated this spirit of genealogical enquiry and passed on to Glengarry any matters of family interest that came his way. In 1816 he wrote to say:

. . . I have now in my possession . . . an original letter from Charles II to General Middleton in which he acknowledges himself bound by promise to give Glengarry the Earldom of Ross but excuses himself on account of the Act of Annexation. . . The letter is dated Cologne 6 Jany. 1654/5 and says many polite things of Glengarry's services. I think it may be interesting to you to know that your family at all times maintained their claim to the Earldom and were not therein opposed by the counter claims of any other family but only by the State jealousy which would interfere to prevent the reestablishment of so great an authority as was possessed by the Earls of Ross.

It is perhaps difficult to visualise a young man being brought up into such a tradition who would not have harboured some ideas of his own importance and of the high position to which he had been born. Older and wiser heads, and the rough and tumble of daily life would, in most cases, have moderated these views and forced at least a surface compliance with the values and standards of a more modern age. It was Glengarry's misfortune to be brought up in an isolated setting, without exposure to companions of his own class outwith his own family group, and in what was a peculiarly difficult household.

His father Duncan was not a strong character but his mother, Marjory Grant of Dalvey, more than made up for her husband's weakness of character. She came from another old Highland family and she seems to have been determined to restore the Glengarry family fortunes and to this end took a very aggressive line in the management of the estate. Marjory had brought with her the very useful dowry of £2,000 which went some way to facilitating her plans. Charles Fraser-Mackintosh, a nineteenth century historian of the Highlands, wrote of Marjory:

> . . . her great rise in social importance moved her at once to strive with success to clear off the debts, to raise the rents and generally to aggrandise the position of the Glengarry family. [3]

Much of the land was occupied by the tacksman class, the clan gentry, who sublet land to minor tenants and cottars. Many of the tacksmen held land by wadset, having long-term possession of the land as mortgage security against cash loans to the Chief. Under the urging of Marjory, Duncan Macdonell attempted, with considerable success, to buy out this type of holding and replace them with tenancies at a newly negotiated price. Many of the chief men of the clan were unwilling to embrace this change of status and there was a substantial emigration of the wadsetters and their closest followers to New England.

There had been, in the traditional political and social structure of the Highlands, a clear role for these tacksmen. The clan gentry had formed the officer corps for the clan regiments and had formed an advisory group around the chief, able to furnish a temporary commander if the chief was too old or too young to take the field in time of war. The post-Culloden pacification of the Highlands had removed this role and the reduced status of tenant farmer was not an attractive substitute.

The coming of the large low-country sheep into the Highlands also drove the process of change. Sheep had been raised in the Highlands for centuries, but these were small, hardy beasts which could forage for a living on rough hill ground. The imported sheep needed winter grazing on low ground, land that was already occupied by small tenants and cottars. The large scale raising of the Cheviot or Blackface sheep was incompatible with the small-scale subsistence farming practised in the Highlands to this time.

The large population sustained by small-scale farming had been a matter of pride to the traditional clan chief, who measured his importance by the number of men of military age he could raise from his lands. In a settled and peaceful Highlands cash income was becoming more significant than a long muster roll.

In 1782 the first sheep farmer from the Borders was planted in Glen Quoich, then directly managed by Glengarry. A series of evictions took place on the Glengarry estates in 1785, 1786 and 1787. In 1786 around 500 people emigrated from Knoydart led by their priest, Father Alexander Macdonell of Scotus, and settled in what is now Ontario.

Marjory Macdonell was given the Gaelic sobriquet of *Marsalaidh Bhinneach* or light-headed Marjory and her light-headedness or high-handedness continued after Duncan's largely unmourned death in 1788. She was one of the curators or trustees appointed to run the estate during the minority of her son along with a number of Grant relations and some of the Macdonell gentry. William MacDonald of St Martin's, a Writer to the Signet, and long-standing adviser to the Glengarry family was another trustee. His letter book is still extant and reveals how impossibly difficult Marjory Macdonell must have been to deal with.

Although the estate was now much more profitable than it had been there were still financial problems – for example money had been borrowed to buy back the forfeited Barrisdale estate and payment to this account would soon be required. In December 1788 MacDonald wrote to Marjory Macdonell:

> As you declined any conversation with me on business when I had the last opportunity of waiting on you I am obliged to apply in this manner by letter which I hope you'll forgive. [4]

He went on to list the matters of pressing business that required attention. These included the Exchequer seeking payment for the Barrisdale estate, arrears of stipend for the parish minister of Kilmonivaig and payments towards the building of Inverness jail. He concluded:

> I trust that you'll see the propriety of a meeting to adopt some plan of a regular administration during the minority.

However in January he was again forced to write:

> Pardon my troubling you in this manner by letter as you do not incline to speak to me on any business for I have

> no intention to offend. I am again applied to from
> Exchequer for the Barrisdale money.

A day later he confided to another curator, John Buchan, a fellow Writer to the Signet, that he was concerned about the administration of the Glengarry estate and that he felt:

> . . . awkward when applied to by any person in relation
> to business in which the Glengarry family is concerned.

In February 1789 he was again remonstrating with Marjory over the Treasury's demand for payment of the Barrisdale money:

> I am not permitted any other mode of communication
> with you on family affairs other than by correspondence
> I must request your attention to this matter.

Part of the problem seems to have been that Marjory took the advice of Buchan to the exclusion of the rest of the curators and MacDonald remonstrated with her on this practice:

> Pardon me for observing that however attentive Mr.
> Buchan may be to your directions the real interest of
> Glengarry's family requires regular proceedings and
> joint measures for as things go at present disorder &
> confusion must ensue in the long run however good
> your intentions.

He also remonstrated with Buchan on their shared responsibilities as professional men and curators.

Marjory would appear to have called meetings of the curators at inconvenient times, without due notice and generally behaved in a high-handed fashion. In 1791 MacDonald writing to a lawyer in Inverness regretted:

> . . . nor can I pretend to give instructions as the Lady and
> Mr. Buchan only manage the rents and estates.

This position had arisen when, in April 1790, at a meeting of the curators, the Minor, as Alasdair Ranaldson was referred to in the legal documents, insisted on the appointment of his mother as Factor on the estate. This in effect made her the manager of the estate and strengthened her hand to carry out the policies she wished. William MacDonald's views on this may be deduced from his comments above.

Fraser-Mackintosh's view of the raising of Alasdair Ranaldson was that his mother had made a bad job of bringing him up, due to her shortcomings of character – a judgement which there seems to be very little reason to dissent from.

Glengarry seems to have been a headstrong youth who undoubtedly grew into a difficult, highly-opinionated and at times irrational man. The circumstances of his birth and education, his mother's influence, his succession to the estate at an early age, combined with his natural tendencies must all be seen as factors contributing to the formation of the mature Glengarry. The tragedy of the mature Glengarry was that throughout his life he seemed unable to learn from life's experiences and rise above these influences.

CHAPTER 3

Oxford

. . . an amiable young gentleman. . .

In October 1790, aged 17, Alasdair and his younger brother Lewis, matriculated as undergraduates at University College, Oxford; Alasdair under the Anglicised form of his name – Alexander. No members of the Glengarry family of an earlier generation had gone to Oxford for their education and the decision, presumably taken by the boys' mother with the assent of their curators, is indicative of a growing tendency among Scottish gentry families in the period to secure an English education for their sons. Such an education was seen as a better way to fit a young man of good birth for a career in the British state than education at home, at a Scottish school or a Scottish university.

However, the bald statement that Alexander and Lewis matriculated at University College on 12th October also highlights a very significant change in the Glengarry family. As we have seen, the family were traditionally Catholic and many writers have assumed that Alasdair had been reared in, and remained in, that faith. However the legal disabilties Catholics suffered at the time meant that as a Catholic he could not have been granted the King's Commission in March 1793 (the Scottish Catholic Emancipation Act was not introduced in the House of Commons until April that year). Admission, as a Roman Catholic, to Oxford would have been equally impossible for him then and for many years thereafter. Oxford University was an exclusively Anglican institution and all those matriculating were required to subscribe to the Thirty Nine Articles, the definitive statement of Anglican beliefs drawn up in 1571. Indeed this insistence on Anglican conformity drove many English Protestant dissenters to seek their higher education at Scottish universities and would, in the nineteenth century, lead to the establishment of new non-sectarian institutions such as the University of London and Owen's College, Manchester. Had Macdonell been a practising Roman Catholic, or if indeed he had been anything other than a member of the Church of England or its sister Episcopal Church in Scotland he could not have, in good conscience, matriculated at Oxford.

Macdonell's religion has been a matter of much confusion. His daughter Louise relates, in one of two articles on her father published in *Blackwood's Magazine* in the 1890s, how in her recollection he went from being a Presbyterian to become an Episcopalian.

> Our mother, as a daughter of Sir William Forbes of Pitsligo, always was an Episcopalian, and continued so till her death in 1840. She mentioned that she never was more surprised than when our father first spoke of having an infant baptised into the Episcopal Church; and of joining it himself. Stupidly none of us asked why he did so. We all knew that this must have taken place between 1809 and 1812, because our brother was baptised by a Presbyterian and Jemima by an Episcopalian minister; but so far as we were concerned his Presbyterian customs continued, for on Sunday evenings we had to repeat to him as formerly psalms or paraphrases, not collects, &c, out of the English Prayer-book. There was an Episcopalian chapel about two and a half miles from the house, which we understood was built by our father and a lady whose name we never heard. [1]

While Louise's evidence suggests that Glengarry had been a Presbyterian until he decided to adopt his wife's denomination this would have been incompatible with his attendance at Oxford. To add to the confusion Louise Macdonell also notes in her earlier article [2] that the tutor employed for her brother was a divinity student and a future parish minister of Kilmonivaig (the parish which included Glengarry House). It may well be that Macdonell took a somewhat relaxed attitude to denominational matters – an Episcopalian at Oxford and a Presbyterian in the Highlands – at least until around 1809 when the evidence for his Episcopal connection seems good. Alasdair's father had married outwith the Catholic faith into the Grant family, who came from a strongly

Episcopalian area, and if he took a decision to convert from Catholicism, or to have his children brought up as Protestants, then the easiest step to take would surely have been to the Scottish Episcopal Church rather than the more extreme transition to the Church of Scotland. In the period Louise Macdonell was writing about there were very few Episcopalians in the Kilmonivaig parish and it seems perfectly possible that Macdonell conformed to the religious practices of his countryside – somewhat in the same way as, many years later, Queen Victoria, Defender of the Faith and Head of the Church of England happily attended Presbyterian services at Crathie when staying at Balmoral.

Part of the reason for the assumption that Alasdair Macdonell was a Roman Catholic is his association, which will be examined in more detail in the next chapter, with the proposed raising of an exclusively Catholic Regiment in 1794, which was planned to be under his command, his close association with a Catholic priest, the Rev. Alexander Macdonell, and the overwhelmingly Catholic composition of the Glengarry Fencibles when that regiment was raised later in 1794. However, a comment on Glengarry by the Roman Catholic Bishop George Hay, at the time of the proposed raising of a Catholic Fencible Regiment, does suggest that Glengarry was not a co-religionist of the Bishop. The Bishop said:

> He is an amiable young gentleman, and I hope will one day be an honour and support to his Country and to his Religion. [3]

This observation is also quoted in Norman MacDonald's *The Clan Ranald of Knoydart and Glengarry*, but here the word 'his' is omitted before religion, which of course makes a considerable difference. Had the Bishop spoken of Glengarry being 'an honour . . . to religion' it is hard to believe that he would have meant anything other than Roman Catholicism, however the phrase 'an honour . . . to his religion' does distance Glengarry's religion from the Bishop's.

That Glengarry had a sympathetic view towards Catholics is undeniable and understandable. Despite his own upbringing most of the those around the household when he was growing up at Invergarry would have been Catholic and as the head of a predominantly Catholic clan it was seen a natural move for him to be at the head of a Catholic regiment. Indeed, for a time, he actually seems to have considered joining the faith of his fathers. In February 1794 the Rev. Alexander Macdonell wrote to Bishop Hay that Glengarry was:

> . . . following instructions to become a Catholic but is hesitating in order to avoid it being considered an act of his youthful impetuosity and bad council. [4]

His intention to join the Catholic Church was not carried through, although his friendship with the Rev. Alexander Macdonell continued and he considered himself sympathetic and supportive towards Roman Catholics. For example, a letter from Glengarry to Bishop Chisholm, in 1803, when his relationship with the Rev. Alexander Macdonell had become strained, spoke of 'his former friendship towards Catholics would soon be the reverse' unless the Bishop acted to suspend Macdonell from his duties. [5]

Macdonell's attendance at University College was somewhat spasmodic, at least as far as it can be traced from the College Buttery Books [6] which record the expenditure in his name for food and drink. Like many undergraduates of the period Macdonell never took a degree and he combined a connection with University College which lasted until April 1795 with a demanding military career. He is recorded as being present, in Forres, at a muster of the Grant Fencibles on 4th June [7] and also incurring expenditure in the Buttery Book in the week of 7th June. Whether this represents much hard travelling between Oxford and the Highlands, shaky record keeping in the orderly office of the Grant Fencibles or shaky record keeping in University College is now impossible to determine. Certainly in the second half of 1793 matters are somewhat less confused – Glengarry had six months absence with leave from his Regiment. He appears regularly during this period in the College Buttery Books which form our only documentary evidence for his stay in Oxford. He neither distinguished or disgraced himself sufficiently to feature in the College Register – the contemporary equivalent of a minute book.

Lewis, who had gone up to Oxford with Alasdair in 1790, drops out of the College records in November 1792, which is consistent with a decision taken at the first meeting of the curators on their father's estate to be held after the death of their mother. This took place on 13 December 1792. At this meeting Alasdair, still only 19 and a minor, but clearly already a forceful character announced that Lewis should go into the Army and the third brother, James, who had gone to Cambridge, be 'educated for a mercantile line', while Somerled, the fourth brother should be:

> . . . got into the Royal Navy, his name put in the Books as a midshipman for some time and that the Loan should be encreased to £1500 for purchasing an Ensigncy in the Army for Lewis. [9]

Somerled had not yet reached his twelfth birthday, which was not unusually young for a lad to be enrolled as a midshipman in that period. However, what seems to have been proposed is that a common deception should be entered into. Somerled would have his name entered on the books of a ship commanded by a friendly officer thus enabling him to acquire, in theory if not in reality, the necessary sea-time to allow him to sit his lieutenant's examination at the earliest date.

James, despite Alasdair's plans for his mercantile career, in fact went into the army, joining his brother in the Strathspey Fencibles when they were raised in 1793 and would go on to have an exceptionally distinguished career ending up a full General and a Knight Grand Cross of the Order of the Bath. James also became famed as one of the heroes of Waterloo, as a Lieutenant Colonel commanding a battalion of the Coldstream Guards, he was in charge of the Guards detachment sent to hold the key strong point of the Chateau of Hougoumont

A commission was purchased for Lewis in the 19th Foot (1st Yorkshire North Riding Regiment) and he appears in the 1794 *Army List* with an Ensign's commission dating from 31st January 1793. The 1795 *Army List*, the last in which he appears, shows Lewis as a Lieutenant, with seniority from 14th December 1793, suggesting that another promotion step had been purchased. *Alumni Oxoniensis* indicates that Lewis died a Captain in the army – and as the 19th Foot includes among its battle honours Flanders 1794-95 it is likely that Lewis died in this campaign. Somerled went to sea and died, a Lieutenant in the Royal Navy, while serving at Curaçao in the West Indies.

Alasdair's remarkable dominance of the curators, indicated by his efficient disposal of his brothers' careers, was not a new phenomenon. At a meeting held on 17th April 1790, when Alasdair was only 16, the minute records that Lady Glengarry (that is Marjory Macdonell his mother) was appointed as factor on the Estate 'at the insistence of the Minor'.

Indeed one of the curators on the estate, William MacDonald of St Martins, seemed to fear for the nature of the heir to the estate. In July 1793 he wrote of Alasdair:

> I dread his getting into bad hands. Perhaps he may pull up and come to reason, for it grieves me to see the representative of that family running into folly, and must soon involve him. [10]

MacDonald's view was, much later, echoed by Charles Fraser-Mackintosh, a late nineteenth century historian of Inverness-shire, who concluded that Alasdair had been:

> . . . alternately crossed and petted, so that before his mother's death, and especially thereafter before attaining his majority, young Glengarry's temper and disposition showed itself as most overbearing. [11]

If Alasdair did not get a degree at Oxford he certainly acquired some of the social skills and graces expected of an eighteenth century gentleman. His daughter Louise records that he was an accomplished fencer. She wrote in her reminiscences of her father:

> At Cambridge, my uncle [James] was so expert that he drove his teacher back into a corner. The latter was naturally annoyed at this, and said no one had ever done so, 'except that fellow at Oxford they call Glengarry,' to which our uncle remarked, 'My brother, sir.' [12]

CHAPTER 4

Colonel of Fencibles

. . . the inviolable attachment of a numerous tribe of faithful Highlanders. . .

In January 1793, the French National Assembly declared war on Great Britain, and involved Britain in a European, indeed a world war which would last, with one brief pause, for over twenty years. Britain, as usual, found herself ill-prepared for war. A national distaste for taxation and fear of standing armies meant that after every war savage retrenchment in the armed forces was the order of the day. Regiments raised for the emergency were broken up or disbanded, seamen were discharged and the bulk of the Fleet scrapped or laid up.

In 1793 the usual urgent steps were taken to put the nation on to a war footing, and one of these steps was the enlargement of the army. Expeditionary forces were to be sent to the Low Countries and to the West Indies, but to find troops for these theatres meant stripping the country of regular units. The threat of invasion and the danger of civil disturbance demanded that a substantial army presence had to be retained in Great Britain and Ireland.

New regular battalions were raised but the Government also took the step of raising second-line regiments for home defence. These regiments of fencible infantry and yeomanry cavalry were full-time soldiers voluntarily enlisted for the duration, paid, equipped, trained and organised on the same lines as regular units. While they would not always reach the levels of training and efficiency which could be expected of long-serving regular forces they were emphatically not a part-time local militia, or a 'home guard', of World War II variety, or a Territorial Army on the modern pattern with a commitment limited to weekly drills and annual camps. The articles of engagement of the fencible regiments raised in Scotland permitted them to be employed in any part of Scotland, but prohibited their deployment to England, except in the event of an actual invasion. In no event were they to serve outwith Great Britain.

In February 1793 the Government issued orders for the formation of fencible regiments – seven Scottish regiments were raised in that year, mostly from the Highlands where, despite all the changes since the last Jacobite rising, the military tradition was still strong. In the Highlands a military career was still seen as an honourable occupation, unlike some other areas where the army was considered an employment of last resort. There is much evidence that the standard of behaviour among the Highland regiments was remarkably high and the harsh discipline imposed in other units was generally not known or needed in these regiments. The speed with which Highland fencible regiments were formed, while perhaps owing something to economic motives, is also testimony to the continuing attractions of soldiering to the Highlanders.

The normal process was that a major local landowner made an offer to raise a regiment, of which he would become Colonel. In this process he would look to his neighbours, kinsmen and fellow landowners to assist and to take commissions as regimental or company officers. Instructions were issued as to the categories of men who were to be enlisted and the time scale that was to be allowed for completion of their companies. Demarcation of recruitment areas was agreed with those raising fencible regiments in neighbouring districts.

Sir James Grant of Grant, who was one of the curators on Glengarry's estate appointed to look after his interests during his minority (it will be recalled that Glengarry's mother was a Grant of the Dalvey family, a cadet branch of the Grants of Grant), was the first to offer to raise a regiment and by 1st March was able to issue recruiting instructions to his potential officers, whose commissions ranked from that date. [1] Sir James wished the unit to be called 'The Grant Regiment of Fencible Highlanders', reflecting the clan basis of the unit, but for some reason this changed in some paperwork to 'Grant's Fencibles', a more personal designation to which the Government expressed objections and a compromise title of 'The First or Strathspey Regiment of Fencible Highlanders' was adopted, although some references still continued to be made to the 'Grant Fencibles'.

The clan nature of the Strathspeys was very evident. Of the twenty-nine officers who mustered in June for the embodiment of the Regiment no fewer than eighteen bore the name Grant, and others, like the Lieutenant Colonel, Andrew Cumming, Sir James's brother-in-law, were related to the Grant family. One of his company commanders was the young Glengarry.

Glengarry was still only nineteen years of age when he received a Captain's commission, which carried with it the obligation to raise at least forty men towards his company's total strength of seventy-one. He was given command of the 3rd battalion company of the Regiment. In all the Strathspeys would field six line or battalion companies and two flank companies, the Grenadier company and the Light Infantry company, a strength of 568 all ranks plus a Headquarters echelon – Adjutant, Quartermaster, Surgeon, etc.

Glengarry raised his entire company from the family estates, and had his fifteen year old brother James as his Lieutenant and, perhaps to ensure a Grant presence, was assigned one James Grant as Ensign. In strict practice Glengarry's men, who were Roman Catholics, should not have been enlisted. At this time recruits were still obliged to sign, or make their mark on, a form of attestation which commenced:

> I . . . do make Oath, that I am a Protestant, and by Trade
> a . . . and to the best of my Knowledge and Belief was
> born in the Parish of . . . in the County of . . . and that I
> have no Rupture, nor ever was troubled with Fits; that I
> am nowise disabled by Lameness or otherwise, but have
> the perfect use of all my Limbs. . .'

Roman Catholicism was, theoretically, as serious an obstacle to serving one's country in time of war as a 'Rupture' or 'Fits'. This, of course, had the effect of reducing the potential military resource of the Highlands to a considerable extent.

The religious affiliation of the Highland clans at this period is more complex than is sometimes thought. There were probably more clans which were predominantly Episcopalian than clans which were predominantly Roman Catholic, and many, particularly in the far North and Argyll were Presbyterian. However some of the most numerous clans, including the Gordons and many branches of Clan Donald, were overwhelmingly Catholic and, as such, legally barred from serving in the armed forces of their country without renouncing their faith.

Having raised his company, Glengarry, who was still of course an undergraduate at University College, Oxford, obtained leave of absence from his military duties for six months from June 1793.[2] To judge from the entries in the College Buttery Books he was fairly consistently in residence at Oxford during that period.[3] He returns to the Regimental Muster Roll at Christmas 1793 and is recorded as being present with the Regiment from then until he resigned his commission in the Strathspeys in May 1794.[4]

The passing of the Scottish Catholic Emancipation Act in June 1793 made it possible for an oath of allegiance to the Crown to be taken in the form:

> I A.B. do hereby declare, That I do profess the Roman
> Catholick Religion: I A.B. do sincerely promise and
> swear, that I will be faithful and bear true allegiance to
> his Majesty King George the Third. . .'[5]

This permitted the enlistment of Roman Catholics into the armed forces, without either causing offence to their conscience by obliging them to declare themselves Protestants, or illegality on the part of the recruiting officer.

On 26th February 1794 a meeting was held at Fort Augustus attended by, among others, Glengarry, the Rev. Alexander Macdonell, a priest of Highland origins and of some unexplained, distant kinship to Glengarry, and John Fletcher of Dunans, a prosperous convert to Catholicism. Father Macdonell, who had trained at the Scots College in Valladolid and had returned to Scotland in 1787 to serve in Badenoch had received permission to leave this charge and to go to Glasgow to look after the many displaced Catholic Highlanders who had settled there. The cotton mills in the Glasgow area were, in the early 1790s, short of labour and Highlanders cleared from the glens were a useful source of manpower. Father Macdonell proved an effective leader of this community and persuaded the Protestant, if pragmatic, manufacturers of the city to fund a chapel and contribute towards a stipend for a priest and served his Highland Catholic flock as interpreter and clergyman. The war acted as a check on the export of cotton and the prosperity of the industry and many of the Highlanders were thrown out of employment and were obliged to enlist in the regular army or the Fencibles. Prior to June 1793 this, of course, obliged them to deny their Catholicism.

The idea of the formation of a Catholic regiment was probably Father Macdonell's. In a brief history of the Glengarries written for the *Canadian Literary Magazine* in 1833 the Rev. Macdonell certainly claimed the credit (the 'Missionary' he refers to is, of course, himself):

> At this crisis the Missionary conceived the idea of getting these unfortunate Highlanders embodied as a Catholic corps in his Majesty's service, with his young Chief, Macdonell of Glengarry, for their Colonel. [6]

John Fletcher of Dunans wrote to Lord Advocate Robert Dundas following the Fort Augustus meeting and expressed the feeling of the meeting that:

> . . . in order to express their warm attachment to His Majesty's person and Government in return for the special Indulgences they had lately met with. They find it their duty to make offer to His Majesty of raising a Catholic Regiment – Alexander Macdonell Esquire of Glengarry to be in command. [7]

Robert Dundas was faced with something of a difficulty on receipt of this document. True, there was no longer a legal barrier to Catholic enlistment, but there were political problems. Father Macdonell later wrote to Bishop Hay, who had not been enthusiastic about the scheme and had tried to stop Macdonell's involvement in it:

> The Lord Advocate was satisfied but said Catholic proposals were declined for fear of irritating the dissenters. [8]

The Lord Advocate's sentiments would have been shared by

Bishop Hay who followed a low profile policy of discretion and minimising opportunity for interdenominational conflict.

However attractive the idea of another fencible regiment and tapping the Catholic Highlands for manpower might be to the Government, Protestant opinion had to be kept mind of. There was another dimension as well: the Duke of Gordon had raised a fencible regiment among his, largely Catholic, tenantry, and there was a perceived danger that an overtly Catholic regiment might be more attractive to Catholic volunteers. The Dowager Duchess of Gordon was keen to see the Glengarry proposal turned down to protect her son's interests and lobbied against the creation of an exclusively Catholic regiment.

In March 1794 the authorities sought to obtain fencible reinforcements from Scotland and proposed drawing 500 men from each of four Scottish fencible regiments and shipping them to The Nore to help defend the English coast against threatened invasion. Such a proposal was quite contrary to the terms of engagement of the men and required delicate handling. Scottish troops had a particular dislike of being shipped, rather than marched, out of Scotland – their fear being that once they were on board a transport ship there was no knowing where they might end up.

When, on 17th March, the Strathspeys were given news of this request to volunteer their services furth of Scotland they had just arrived at Linlithgow, having marched there from Glasgow through areas where political unrest was endemic. Sir James Grant addressed his men and made it known that he expected them to volunteer for service in England. However, as he wrote the next day to the Commander in Chief in Scotland, Lord Adam Gordon:

> They all declared to a man they were resolved not to go
> by sea, and some of them, particularly in the Macdonell
> company, said they would not go by land . . . [9]

The Macdonell company seems to have been the focus for much unrest in the Regiment – their status as an entirely Catholic company in a Protestant unit was a divisive one and one which could hardly avoid making for tension. If, as seems probable, word had spread of their company commander's intention to raise his own regiment and perhaps leave them stranded in a doubly alien environment, England and a Protestant unit, this was hardly likely to make them feel easier about the situation.

A few days later Colonel Grant made another appeal to his men, with even more discouraging results. He reported to the Commander in Chief:

> To my regret and astonishment, Captain Macdonell's whole company and some of the Grenadiers, the Cols., Lt. Cols. and Major's broke off from the field without any orders, ran away, and took possession of the castle, where the ammunition was lodged, broke it up and distributed it amongst them, and, when the Adjutant and Capt. Macdonell went over to them, made them prisoners, where at present they remain. . . Captain Macdonell's company has ever been the bane of the discipline and good order of the regiment. . .

Grant's reference to the Colonel's, Lieutenant Colonel's and Major's companies reflects the then current practice of three of the line companies being nominally commanded by the three senior field officers of the battalion. The other companies were commanded by Captains.

Macdonell, however one may question his command skills, and the old military maxim that there are no bad troops only bad officers comes to mind, clearly did not lack courage in going to reason with his armed and mutinous troops. Although the other companies proved to be more open to persuasion, the Macdonell company remained obdurate and refused to march out of Scotland unless there was an actual invasion.

Glengarry left the Regiment, with his company still in open rebellion. He travelled to London with Fletcher of Dunans and the Rev. Alexander Macdonell to press the case for a Catholic fencible regiment in Whitehall and at Court. They carried with them a wide-ranging degree of support:

> The Manufacturers of Glasgow furnished them with the most ample and honorable testimonials of the good conduct of the Highlanders during the time they had been in their works, and strongly recommended that they should be employed in the service of their country.[10]

Back in Scotland the black sheep of the Strathspey Regiment continued to cause Grant much heartache. While most of his men were now under command and willing to go to England the spirit of disaffection had been awakened, was alive, and was worrying. Writing to Robert Dundas on 14th April he said:

> About 380 private soldiers exclusive of sergeants and corporals have declared their readiness to march to England when His Majesty please. At the same time such is the effect the Macdonell Company's example may have, tho' they are very much enraged against them at present, that I cannot pledge myself for a certainty of no change of sentiment. [11]

Glengarry's visit to London proved unproductive, at least in the short term. The offer of a Catholic regiment was turned down. On 2nd May he wrote to Grant:

> The circumstances of my coming of age in September next makes me desirous of withdrawing at present from military life that I may have the more leisure to examine into the state of my affairs and see in what situation they are. [12]

On 8th May the Regimental muster roll of the Strathspey Fencibles records Glengarry's resignation of his commission. [13] His letter is, at best, disingenuous. Had he had his way and been given letters of service to raise a Catholic fencible regiment in February or March he would have been even more deprived of leisure to look into the state of his affairs.

The Catholic fencible regiment was not a politically acceptable proposition. However, three months after he resigned his commission in the Strathspeys, Letters of Service were issued to Glengarry. These, dated 14th August, a month and a day before his twenty-first birthday, authorised him to raise the First Fencible Regiment of Glengarry Highlanders, and commissioned him as Colonel of the Regiment. His military experience at this point was fourteen months as a company commander in the Strathspeys – a good proportion of which time he spent on leave of absence at Oxford. The highly experienced, sixty-six year old Commander in Chief in Scotland, Lord Adam Gordon, described Glengarry around this time as ' a young chieftain composed of vanity and folly' [14] and it is difficult to see what, apart from his name and position, he had to offer as a military commander.

Inevitably a regiment raised predominantly in Glengarry's country would be overwhelmingly Catholic, and it is impossible to believe that the Government, or its Scottish managers like Robert Dundas, did not know this. However, they probably thought that the avoidance of the word Catholic in the regimental title would avoid inflaming extreme Protestant opinion, and they may have hoped that Glengarry would be reasonably discreet about his recruitment. However discretion was hardly Glengarry's strong suit and later in 1794 Bishop John Chisholm, Vicar Apostolic of the Highland Diocese, would write to Bishop Hay:

> Glengarry goes on as well as he can with his Regiment
> and tells the Catholics everywhere he is to have a
> Catholic chaplain. [15]

The Catholic chaplain was of course the Rev. Alexander Macdonell who, despite being bound by his 'mission oath', taken at Valladolid in 1779, to serve for life in the Scottish mission field, managed to persuade his superiors to accept the *fait accompli* of his decision to join the Glengarry Fencibles. By so doing he became the first Catholic chaplain in the British army since the Reformation. A fellow priest, Angus Chisholm, made the sardonic comment on Macdonell's abandonment of his charge:

> Here lies Sandy tall
> A politician and that is all

Macdonell was to have a major role in the creation and formation of the Glengarry Fencibles and served with them until the Regiment was disbanded in 1802. After this, disappointed in their hopes of finding land to settle on in Scotland, many of the former members of the Regiment planned to emigrate and Father Macdonell was instrumental in obtaining grants of land in Upper Canada and indeed emigrated with the former Glengarries and in due course became the first Bishop of Upper Canada. Chisholm's comment has a certain truth – there is no doubt that Father Macdonell enjoyed mixing in political circles and his brief account of the Glengarry Fencible's service in Ireland from 1798 is remarkably self-serving – the Chaplain did this, the Chaplain did that:

> The Chaplain, upon this and all other occasions,
> accompanied the Regiment to the field with a view of
> preventing the men from plundering, or committing any
> act of cruelty upon the country people. [16]

Quite how contentious an issue the creation of a Catholic regiment might be is shown by a letter from the Earl of Fife to the Secretary for War, Henry Dundas, in October 1794. The Duke advised Dundas:

> . . . About three weeks ago a tenant's son of mine here, a
> Mr. Macdonald, a Roman Catholick who lives at
> Newcastle, came to me with a Priest who lives on my
> estate here, and who I had never spoken to, altho' I
> allowed him every indulgence, they said they came to
> solicit my protection and aid to raise a Regt. of Roman
> Catholick Fencibles for Glengarry, I told them I would
> take no concern, that all people that were willing to go,
> were free. My friend, the Priest, was first educated a
> Baker at Banff and after that went to learn Priesthood, as
> a better way to make bread, his name is Cattanach. All
> the Roman Catholicks here are Jesuits, the Priests had
> 'till lately some allowance from foreign societies, that is
> now at an end, they must therefore have their support
> intirely on keeping the poor people in a state of
> ignorance and disruption, which I have always
> considered as a great misfortune. I humbly think the
> arming of a distinct Roman Catholick Regt. a very
> dangerous measure, the allowing them to enlist in a
> Protestant Corps is a very different matter. . . [17]

The Earl's hostility to Catholic priests is fairly clear and his suspicions of an armed Catholic force equally obvious. Glengarry's Fencibles were of course not exclusively Catholic and not Catholic in regimental title. Fife's reaction to the earlier plan to raise an overtly Catholic regiment would presumably have been even more hostile.

Recruitment for the new Regiment went on during the autumn of 1794 both in Inverness-shire and in and around Glasgow. There were however difficulties as the Rev. Alexander Macdonell advised Henry Dundas, Secretary for War, on 20th October:

> Though hard necessity compelled many of Glengarry's
> vassals and adherents to scatter over the whole face of

the country and some of them even to quit the Kingdom after they despaired of the success of his application to employ them together in the service of their sovereign, still he and his friends have been till now very successful in recruiting and have already upwards of 300 men, they would have been by this time near completed but for a report for some weeks back in circulation that new fencible corps are to be raised on the same footing with his, whose colonels (it is said) are allowed 10 guineas of bounty money and leave to draft 200 men out of the other fencible regiments. By this Col. Macdonell's recruiting is quite obstructed here for some time back. His having put himself under your protection from the first of this undertaking and your goodness to the party that supports him make both him and them rely with full confidence on the continuation of your countenance, and hope that you'll procure the same advantages to him as those other new colonels get, at least leave to get his own men drafted out of the Grant Fencibles which would enable him to have his Regt. in the course of a few weeks ready for inspection and be the means of rendering them in a very short time fit for service. [18]

Macdonell, in his opening sentence, is of course referring to the frustrated plan for a Catholic regiment. A bounty of £3.3.0 had been paid to each recruit in the Strathspey Fencibles, and presumably a similar bounty was offered in the Glengarry Fencibles, so the rumours of ten guineas in new regiments, would have acted as a serious disincentive to recruitment. The notion of Glengarry claiming his own followers out of the Strathspey Fencibles, which Macdonell floated to Dundas, proved to be a source of considerable dispute, at a period of some difficulty for Grant and his unit.

The Government had launched in September 1794 a further round of creation of fencible regiments, this time with wider terms of engagement which would permit them to be used anywhere in Great Britain, the Channel Islands or Ireland, and the suggestion was floated that existing fencible regiments, with more limited and thus, less useful, terms of engagement, might be raided for men to make up the new wave of regiments. Men transferring from the older units, such as the Strathspeys, would get an additional bounty of five guineas. While the Glengarry Fencibles were raised under the 'Scotland only' terms of service the unit as a whole, under the persuasion of the Chaplain, volunteered for wider service on the same terms as the post-September 1794 units.

Sir James Grant was advised at the end of September by one of his officers, Captain John Grant that:

> It is now beyond a doubt that Glengarry and his Priest have gone to Stranraer. [19]

Stranraer was the area in which the Macdonell company of the Strathspey Fencibles was, at that time, billeted. Glengarry and his Chaplain were evidently off on a poaching mission.

Glengarry, anxious to complete his Regiment, understandably looked with possessive eyes on the seventy-odd men he had recruited into the Strathspeys and who, however much of an awkward squad they might be in their present unit, could be a trained and experienced cadre for the new one. He confided his ambitions to Henry Dundas in a letter of 27th October 1794:

> . . . I brought about a hundred men into the Grant's Fencibles, all my own Tenants and Sons who followed me from mere attachment, you cannot therefore be surprised if I should have every inclination to have as many of them or any others out of that Regt. as would chose to follow me to the number permitted by the Government – which would be the means not only of completing but also of disciplining the Regt. in a very short time. [20]

It may be thought strange for this form of direct communication to have been entered into between a regimental commander and the Secretary for War. However in part this is due to the administration of the army being less formal and bureaucratic than we can readily imagine today. For example Glengarry's letter to Dundas, later created the 1st Viscount Melville, did not enter into the War Office archives but was retained by Dundas when he left office and forms part of the Melville archive, now held by the Archives of Scotland. The other explanation is that Glengarry, on gaining permission to raise his Regiment, seems to have felt himself to have become a recipient of Dundas's patronage and, in a very eighteenth century way, considered that this created a continuing special relationship between him and the house of Dundas, a relationship which he would exploit at every opportunity. Thirty years later he would write to Henry Dundas's son, the 2nd Viscount Melville, as part of long-running campaign to have the Macdonell peerage restored, and observe:

> . . . having since 1794 regarded your house as my patron which (during the lifetime of your worthy father) never failed; I am unwilling to attribute a less friendly disposition to his Noble Son, the present Viscount. [21]

The poaching trip to Stranraer was successful. On 27th October 1794 72 members of the Strathspey Fencibles, mostly bearing the name Macdonell, wrote to their 'Most Honoured and Renowned Colonel' to assure him that:

> . . . it is our most earnest and ardent wish to follow you to any part of the earth his Majesty may order you to lead us. We seek no Bounty or other recompense from Government but the satisfaction of being under your banners and sharing with you every danger in the service of our King and Country as it was our attachment to you alone that made us forsake our friends and families . . . our forefathers pertained to your forefathers and we wish to pertain to you that we may in like manner receive protection from you. [22]

This touching expression of clan loyalty went on to address a sensitive area of relationship between Glengarry and his tenantry. The signatories to the letter state:

> Indeed we expect to enjoy those possessions which our ancestors so long enjoyed under your ancestors though now in the hands of strangers – as we do not wish that you should lose by us we shall give as high Rent as any of your lowland Shepherds ever gave and we shall all become bound for any one whose circumstances may afford you room to mistrust us . . .

This letter, with its assertion of the troops desire to resettle after the War in their native Glengarry country, might have been thought somewhat critical of their Colonel, Alasdair Macdonell. There had been an introduction of sheep into the Glengarry estate in 1782, although onto land then in the proprietor's hands rather than onto tenanted land. However there were significant clearances in 1785 and subsequent years. These took place under his father's stewardship of the estate and during the period of Alastair's minority. He had only entered into full and unfettered management of the estate in September 1794. The Macdonells in the Strathspey Fencibles might have hoped that the young laird would have a more sympathetic approach, or at least a more romantic approach and prefer the traditional Highland wealth of a long rent-roll and ample reserves of fighting men to the modern fashion for cash from mutton and wool and money in the bank. Their faith in their young Chief was shared by Father Macdonell (who may well have drafted the letter for them) because he had written as early as February 1794 to Bishop Hay:

> Glengarry might provide land for every man in his
> Regiment and so soon as he has it in his power he says
> he'll show to the whole world that he prefers men to
> sheep. All the men that are with him in the Fencibles
> rest perfectly satisfied that he'll make good his
> promise to see them comfortably settled in Glengarry.
> Their attachment to him is beyond anything you can
> conceive and not a day passes without he gives some
> new mark of his to them. [23]

However much Sir James Grant might resent losing an eighth of his force he must also have felt that he would be well rid of this focus for much of his Regiment's dissension and unrest. Glengarry headed north to Castle Grant to see his distant kinsman, former guardian and ex-Colonel to negotiate the transfer of his clansmen. His letter to Dundas also played its part and Grant received a request from Henry Dundas to let Glengarry have the men he had personally recruited and by 25th December 76 non-commissioned officers and private soldiers had left the Strathspeys to swell the ranks of the Glengarry Fencibles. [24]

However not all of Glengarry's recruitment measures were quite so firmly based on reciprocal feeling of patriarchal sentiment and clan loyalty. On 29th November 1794 he wrote to his factor in Knoydart:

> Enclosed you have a list of small tenants belonging
> to my Knoydart property – their leases being expired
> by Whitsunday first – and having refused to serve
> me, I have fully determined to warn them out, and
> turn them off my property, without loss of time; and

as this is the first order of the kind I have given you
since I came of age, I have only to add that your
punctuality and expedition on the present occasion
will be marked by me. . .[25]

Glengarry was thus making a very direct connection between his tenants willingness to serve him in his Regiment, either personally or, in the case of the female and older tenants, by means of a relative and their continuing to occupy their land. Twenty-eight tenants are named in Glengarry's letter, but many of these tenants had sublet ground to cottars and these cottars were to be evicted along with the tenants. Indeed the cottar class seems to have been particularly reluctant to enlist because the factor is instructed:

Their cottars must be particularly specified, as they have
a great number of them that refused.

Enlistment in the Laird's regiment was not always a popular option as an incident in June 1795 indicates. A deserter, Duncan Cameron, was being escorted back to face military justice when the escort was set upon by, among others, Dugald Bane Macphee, John McMillan, Alexander Macphee and John McMillan Jnr. of Shenavallie, in the parish of Kilmallie, Inverness-shire. These four were prosecuted at the circuit Justiciary Court in Inverness for assembly in a riotous and tumultuous manner and violently resisting and deforcing an officer or soldier.

The details of the charge give an excellent account of the incident, although some mysteries remain. For example, was it simply coincidence that Glengarry was on hand to witness the incident? The 'other gentleman' mentioned in the charge was almost certainly Coll MacDonald of Dalness, a Writer to the Signet, and Glengarry's man of business – he was cited as a witness by the Crown along with Glengarry, a merchant in Fort William and the Corporal who was escorting Duncan Cameron. Was the presence of Glengarry and his lawyer in Knoydart connected with clearance of tenants from the land, and thus likely to inflame local feeling?

Corporal Gillies, Glengarry Fencibles, assisted by a
man appointed for that service was escorting Duncan
Cameron a deserter belonging to that Regiment from

Knoidart, where he was apprehended, to the Garrison
of Fort William in passing through the farm of
Shenavallie aforesaid he was attacked by a lawless
and disorderly mob of men and women, armed with
sticks and stones, headed by the same persons above
complained upon who in consequence of a previous
concert were in wait to rescue the said deserter, and
who upon the appearance of the said Corporal Gillies,
made up to him in a most violent and outrageous
manner, and with threats and imprecations declared
that they were resolved to prevent the said Duncan
Cameron being carried out of Glendessary and were
determined to take the lives of all such as should
attempt to oppose them; that notwithstanding the
remonstrances of Colonel Macdonnel of Glengarry, as
also of another gentleman who happened to be then
present and their repeated assurances that no injustice
should be done to the said Duncan Cameron, the said
riotous and disorderly mob, headed as above
mentioned, made up to the said deserter, laid hold of
him, and forcibly carried him off, and after having
done so behaved in a most outrageous manner
brandishing their sticks over the head of Colonel
Macdonnel and threatening violence to him and those
along with him. [26]

What is clear from this incident is that the traditional patterns
of Highland loyalty and clan deference were breaking down. It is
inconceivable that in an earlier generation the Knoydart tenants
would have threatened violence to their chief – but in an earlier
generation their chief would not have turned off his tenants in
favour of sheep.

The final mystery in the case is that, despite the Crown citing
four credible witnesses, and trial being set for the Autumn Circuit
on 12 Sept 1795 the papers are marked 'Diet deserted', indicating
that the case had been abandoned by the Crown.

However, by fair means or foul, Glengarry got his regiment
together. At the beginning of March 1795 he wrote, from Glengarry
House, to Henry Dundas that returns from various parts of the
Highlands had been delayed due to stormy weather but he was
now in a position to advise him that the Regiment would number
600 rank and file. He went on:

Notwithstanding the severity of the storm and the
difficulty of marching men thro' the Highlands I shall
make every exertion to have the whole assembled at
Kilmarnock, the present Headquarters, by the 25th inst.
As I am convinced that the Regt. how soon it is formed
will be ordered out of Scotland I would be happy to
know our destination as soon as possible in order that I
may have my own affairs arranged so as to enable me to
accompany them where ever they are ordered. [27]

By the first week in April he was able to inform Dundas that
his Regiment was now virtually complete apart from some twenty
recruits expected from the Islands and was quartered at
Kilmarnock. Glengarry felt that the spirit of his instructions had
been to produce a good corps of 'real Highlanders':

In this I have been tolerably successful – about 550 of
them are real Highlanders and the rest such as are
recruited in common in the West Country – I have
neither English nor Irishmen among them, so that they
may be called a real Scotch Regiment and I hope they
will prove themselves worthy of the appellation. [28]

He went on to remind Dundas that he had managed to secure
the Regiment's agreement to extend their service outside Scotland
without any reward from the Government – in other words he
and his men did not receive the extra bounty that later fencible
regiments were enjoying. Furthermore he reminded Dundas that
he had :

met with great opposition in my recruiting operations
where I had no reason to expect and where I am sure I
did not deserve any, and which I can only attribute to the
interested views of certain individuals.

The first Muster Roll of the Glengarry Fencibles, dated 1st April
1795, shows a unit then comprising 1 colonel, 1 major, 5 captains,
8 lieutenants, 6 ensigns, 1 adjutant, 1 surgeon, 28 sergeants, 10
drummers or fifers, and 540 rank and file. Thirty four others were
absent on recruiting duties, six were sick and four had died.
Macdonell had been able to nominate his officers, and while many
were from Clan Donald, there was a leavening of experienced
officers with previous service. His second in command, the
Lieutenant Colonel, was to be Charles MacLean, a Captain in the

Argyleshire Regiment; the next most senior officer, the only Major allowed to a regiment at this time, Matthew Macalister, had been a Lieutenant in the East India Company's army. Three of the Captains commanding companies had seen service, Archibald Fraser was a half-pay lieutenant from the 78th Regiment, Alexander Macdonald was a Lieutenant of the Bengal Artillery and Archibald MacLachlan had served as a Lieutenant in the former Argyleshire Fencible Regiment. The Adjutant, James Macnab transferred from the Breadalbane Fencibles, and the Quartermaster, responsible for much of the administration of the Regiment, was a regular from the 42nd Regiment, the Black Watch. [29]

The Chaplain, as noted above, was Alexander Macdonell. The establishment of the Regiment also called for a Presbyterian Chaplain, but there is no record of this post being filled. As late as 27th May 1795 Glengarry was still writing to Dundas about Macdonell's appointment: the notion of a Roman Catholic chaplain was clearly causing some problems in the Horse Guards, the army headquarters in London. [30] HRH the Duke of York, Frederick Augustus, the second son of George III, as Commander in Chief had to approve all officer appointments, a requirement that would later pose considerable personal problems for Glengarry.

By July 1795 the Regiment had marched to Newcastle and the muster roll completed there shows a nominal strength of 630 rank and file, 22 drummers and fifers, 31 sergeants, 8 ensigns, 12 lieutenants, 7 captains, major, lieutenant colonel, colonel and the headquarters staff of adjutant, quartermaster, chaplain, surgeon and surgeon's mate. At full strength the Regiment would number some 718 men and was organised into eight line companies plus two flank companies – the grenadiers and the light company. [31]

Perhaps the most exposed part of the British Isles were the Channel Islands, positioned just a few miles from the French coast. A strong force was needed to deter any French attempt to seize the islands and the Glengarry Fencibles took post there in the summer of 1795 and formed part of the garrison of Guernsey for the next three years.

Garrison duty was not, perhaps, entirely to the taste of Colonel Macdonell or of his men and even the exotic novelty of Guernsey must have worn off fairly swiftly. One advantage that the posting brought to the Colonel was that he could find excuses to go to the mainland on military business from time to time, and when in Southampton could take time out to visit London and attempt to further his career plans with Henry Dundas at the War Office.

A Colonel of Fencibles at twenty-one might have been a reasonably satisfactory career progression for many men but the appointment was only a wartime one and Glengarry was ambitious to construct a more permanent military career for himself. Commissions in the regular army were bought and sold like any other piece of property, although the consent of the Commander in Chief was required and a fixed price tariff was nominally in place. In April 1795 Glengarry had confided to Dundas that it was his intention to purchase a commission in the regular army. [32] There was a scheme whereby officers in Glengarry's situation who purchased a commission in the regulars were granted an additional promotion *gratis* by the Government. In the same letter he outlined his plans to raise a line battalion, that is a regular rather than a fencible regiment. There seems little doubt that he had in his mind that he would occupy the post of Lieutenant Colonel Commandant. In October 1795 he wrote to Henry Dundas from Guernsey, saying that he had to inform Dundas that:

> . . . it has invariably been my most sanguine wish (ever since your goodness procured me that privilege) to obtain the permanent rank of Lieutenant Colonel in the Army from the date of my Letters of Service. With this view I purchased an Ensigncy and Lieutenancy in the Line and lodged money for a Captain-Lieutenancy in the 32nd Regt. several months ago, all of which time the money for my Majority has been lying idle in hand. The stop to this promotion chagreen'd me much and made me resolve to take advantage of transacting a little Regtl. business at Southampton (tho' very circumscribed in point of time) by laying my situation before you, to whom alone I owe the advantage of the Government step, having every reason to trust that the same disinterested Friendship which at first procur'd me the above, will immediately remove the obstacles which now stand between me and the enjoyment of it. [33]

Glengarry, as we can learn from this letter, had purchased the first and second steps in the commissioned ranks, Ensign and Lieutenant. There was not, of course, any suggestion that Colonel Macdonell would actually perform the duties of the officers in the line regiments whose posts he had purchased. In addition to these completed purchases he had paid over his money for the next rank, that of Captain-Lieutenant. This now vanished rank, of which there was only one holder in any battalion, ranked above all the Lieutenants, commanded the Colonel's company and gave seniority in the army as a Captain from the date of appointment as Captain-Lieutenant. The rank was abolished in 1804. Glengarry had found an old officer, yet another Macdonell, who held the rank of Captain-Lieutenant in the 32nd Foot and had been given permission, on the grounds that his age made him unfit for service, to sell out to a suitable candidate.

As Macdonell says that he had the cash available to purchase the next step, a Major's commission, we may assume that the final step, the Lieutenant-Colonelcy, the most expensive purchase, was to be the 'Government step' and, as each promotion had to be bought in turn, the delay in approving his Captain-Lieutenancy would indeed have 'chagreen'd' him.

Matters dragged on over the winter and in February 1796, Glengarry, having obtained leave of absence from his command, was in London and wrote again to Dundas:

> Confident that your interference in my behalf had removed the obstacles that prevented so long my being gazetted Captain-Lieutenant I writ a note to Colonel Brownrigg requesting that my Gazetting might come out this week but from his answer which I take the liberty to enclose I find myself this day as far from the object of my pursuit as ever. [34]

We may assume that Dundas had done his best for Glengarry whose phrase 'your interference on my behalf' is not a criticism but an acknowledgement of help. The Colonel Brownrigg referred to was the Military Secretary to the Duke of York and a powerful figure in officers' appointments. Glengarry went on, after sketching the history of his proposed purchase of Captain-Lieutenant Macdonell's post, in a somewhat flowery paragraph which seems to have been intended to answer criticisms that he wished to hold a double commission, as Colonel of the Glengarries and as an officer in the regular army.

> Whoever thinks that I will give up my Regiment must be very ignorant indeed of the consequences derived from the inviolable attachment of a numerous tribe of faithful Highlanders – especially when their service may be rendered so very useful to Government as at the present critical juncture – no consideration on Earth will separate me from my men or make me forfeit the confidence they repose in me.

If this is to be taken at face value then Glengarry must have hoped that his Fencible Regiment might be reconstituted in another form, as he very clearly could not continue to command the Glengarry Fencibles and another unit. His plans for such a unit are indicated in the next paragraph, and it looks as though his plans for a line regiment have been modified in the interests of pragmatism:

> In consequence of what you mentioned to me at last interview I have been preparing to give in proposals for raising any number of men from one to six hundred to serve by Sea or Land as His Majesty's Ministers may judge most beneficial for Government.
> I have no view to hold a double commission only to go through the regular steps in order to establish my Rank so far – nor is my case singular – for I can produce many instances where even double commissions exist at this moment and why particularly me.

He concludes:

> But as all my hopes and dependance are entirely centred in your friendship and good offices I still trust my recommendation to the Capt. Lieutenancy will be laid before the King tomorrow and as to my further offers to serve my King and Country shall be directed by yourself.

Unfortunately the reply from Colonel Brownrigg, to which Glengarry refers in his opening paragraph, does not survive. A letter, presumably from Brownrigg and dated 20th September 1796 is attached to the previous letter in the Melville Papers. It is short and discouraging:

> From an anxious desire to oblige you if possible rather than from any hopes of success I have been induced again to apply to the Duke of York upon the subject of your repeated application, the enclosed is the answer which will shew you how unavailing it is to continue in the prosecution of the object you solicit. I am exceedingly sorry that any part of your conduct should have brought you into such a predicament. [35]

There is no enclosed answer from the Duke of York but its contents were clearly negative and final. Quite what is to be read into the last sentence is unclear. What can certainly be concluded is that the Duke of York was not prepared to have Alasdair Macdonell in the regular army at any price, at any rate in a rank above that of Lieutenant. Had Glengarry followed a normal military career he might well have learned enough of his profession to creditably occupy a Lieutenancy by the time he was in his early twenties. There are indications of irregularities in his command of the Glengarries in Guernsey, but these only seem to have come to light after he resigned his appointment so it may well be that the Duke of York was basing his judgement on Glengarry's earlier conduct and on the view that his Scottish commander, Lord Adam Gordon, had formed of him as 'a young chieftain composed of vanity and folly', who might do well enough commanding fencibles but was not to be trusted in a senior rank in the regular army.

By the time that the last mentioned letter had been written Glengarry had resigned his command of his Regiment. He had written, from London, to Colonel Brownrigg on 10th August 1796:

> I hereby resign the command of my Regt. in favour of Captain McDonell of the Scotch Brigade, whose character as an Officer I believe you are not unaccounted with, and possessing confidence of the officers and soldiers will I hope have due influence with Field Marshall His Royal Highness the Duke of York, before whom I request you to lay the contents of this letter and to obtain His Royal Highness's permission for its taking place . . . [36]

It is hard to judge what, exactly, Glengarry's motives were in resigning his command and parting from 'the inviolable attachment of a numerous tribe of faithful Highlanders' of which he had written so movingly just four months before. Possibly trouble in the Regiment, possibly the tedium of garrison life did not suit a hyperactive nature like his and possibly it was a last throw in the game of getting a commission in the regulars; if he simplified matters by resigning his fencible commission at least the accusation of double commissions would be answered. In all probability all three factors may have played a part, however the long-term aim of a regular commission would seem likely to have been the most influential.

His nominated successor Donald Macdonell, yet another of the seemingly endless and endlessly confusing tribe of Macdonells who populate the story and the British Army, was to command the Glengarry Fencibles in Guernsey, on active service in Ireland from 1798 and until their demobilisation in 1802. Every account of the Glengarry Fencibles suggests that Alasdair Ranaldson Macdonell commanded the Regiment when it was sent to Ireland. However the documentary records of Muster Rolls makes it very clear that Colonel Donald Macdonell was the commanding officer. Much of this confusion has been due in part to writers not consulting the archives and in part to an uncritical acceptance of the writings of the Regimental Chaplain, the Rev. Alexander Macdonell.

It is hard to suggest exactly why the Chaplain was so evasive or confusing. He speaks of Glengarry commanding the Regiment when raised, mentions their stay in Guernsey, and in describing the Regiment's involvement in putting down the Irish rebellion of 1798 writes:

> . . . the command of the town devolved on Col. McDonell [37]

and the only possible clue that a change of command has taken place is the different spelling of McDonell. However as he goes on to write, seemingly indiscriminately, of 'Col. McD.':

> Col. McD. who now commanded the Brigade . . .

and of 'Col. Macdonell':

> . . . the strict discipline enforced by Col. Macdonell

it is hard to draw any very positive conclusions from his spelling. Certainly the impression that seems to be intended to be given, and which has been taken by previous writers, is that Alasdair Ranaldson Macdonell commanded his Regiment throughout.

It is however impossible that Father Macdonell was unaware that the Colonel Macdonell, so prominent for his exertions in Ireland, was not the Colonel Macdonell who raised the Regiment, but it is also impossible not to conclude that he was trying to give exactly this impression. Quite apart from the evidence in the army records there are three very strong reasons why this is not the case. Firstly, as we shall see in the next chapter, Glengarry was in Scotland, fighting a duel and standing trial for murder in the summer of 1798 – when the Regiment was posted to Ireland. Secondly, as will be explored in Chapter 6, Glengarry spent much of 1799 and almost all of 1800 travelling on the Continent. Finally, if as the Rev. Alexander Macdonell says, the officer commanding the Glengarry Fencibles was promoted to Brigadier (even as a temporary or local appointment), it is utterly inconceivable, knowing what we do of Alasdair Ranaldson, that he would not thereafter have claimed this rank on all possible occasions!

The Guernsey Muster Rolls of the Regiment show Glengarry to have been absent, with leave, for much of 1795 and 1796 up to the date of his resignation. Some official returns were signed by Charles MacLean, the Lieutenant Colonel, who seems also to have left the scene, and a Major Dalrymple, Acting Lieutenant Colonel, writes a memo to the Commander in Chief in July 1796. Dalrymple seems to have been an outsider, possibly from his name a Lowland Scot, perhaps sent in to bring some order into the Regiment's affairs. A memo he wrote to Colonel Brownrigg in August 1796 seems to suggest that the confusing clannish nature of the Regiment was all too much for him:

> . . . I suppose it is not of much importance how these names are spelt, as even in the Regiment, the Officers seem not to know the exact name of each other . . . [38]

A month later Dalrymple writes again to Brownrigg with news of what seems to have been a piece of corrupt practice worked by, or at best allowed by, Glengarry:

> I take the liberty to enclose a List of men's names who
> received furloughs from Col. McDonell.

The timing and context of this letter makes it clear that Glengarry
is meant – Donald Macdonell had evidently not yet taken up his
commission:

> and of the number of those with whom he is supposed to
> have made a bargain for their discharge at a certain time
> and whose pay perhaps at present makes an annuity to
> some body or another . . . [39]

The implication is clear. Pay was being drawn for men who
were no longer serving with the Regiment and presumably the
Colonel, who was required to have the muster roll regularly made
up and, indeed, sworn before a local Justice of the Peace, should
have known what was going on.

We also learn of further trouble in the Regiment from a letter
the Chaplain wrote in 1803 which says:

> In 1797 Major MacDonell, the Adjutant of the Regiment
> and I prevented Glengarry from being brought to a
> General Court Martial by some of his officers but before
> we could succeed we were obliged to give them our
> obligations to see ample justice done to them in their
> charge against their Col. provided those charges were
> substantiated in a private manner by competent judges
> mutually chosen by both parties. [40]

This is one of those very annoying letters, the meaning of which is
quite clear to its author, but which is irritatingly unspecific when
read two hundred years later. There are also a number of problems:
is the 1797 date correct considering that Glengarry resigned his
commission in August 1796, and who is Major MacDonell? The
Glengarries' Major was Matthew McAlister who resigned at about
the same time as Glengarry and we already know of Major
Dalyrmple. Could the Chaplain have got Colonel Donald
Macdonell's rank wrong, or was it one of a number of Captain
Macdonells?

In any event this event had, years later, an unfortunate
consequence for Father Macdonell when, in 1802, he was arrested
for debt. In his attempt to avoid a potential Court Martial for his

chief the Chaplain had stood guarantor for a large sum of money and at the moment of crisis found that Glengarry withheld:

> . . . the aid or support which it was his interest as well as his duty to give.[41]

The unfortunate Chaplain spent three months in various gaols or debtors lock-up houses in London. Eventually the money was found and paid into the Court of Common Pleas. Father Macdonell returned to Scotland and started proceedings in the Court of Session for recovery of the money – an action which was eventually settled out of court at the insistence of Glengarry's man of business Coll Macdonald. This incident, perhaps understandably, resulted in a final breach between Glengarry and his former Chaplain. Glengarry wrote angrily to Bishop Chisholm seeking Father Macdonell's suspension and Bishop Chisholm had a report on the incident from the Rev. Mr. Macdonell which he felt 'artful' and which made:

> . . . very coolly and deliberately a most detestable character of Glengarry while it gives a little more importance to the writer than I would wish him to take in the circumstances.[42]

Although Glengarry would retain a proprietorial interest in the Regiment his active involvement ceased when he resigned his commission. For example he wrote to Sir James Grant, in Grant's capacity as Lord Lieutenant of Inverness-shire, on 5th May 1798 about a young man who had been balloted to serve in the militia but who wanted to serve elsewhere:

> The bearer hereof is a fine young fellow who tho' duly called can not be prevailed upon to do things smoothly and an open opposition from a Lad of his spirit might be attended with fatal consequences not only to his person but so far as his example might have influence. I have therefore been prevailed upon to suggest that you may be good enough to include him in the few supplementaries reserved for accidents and as a proof that it is not from any bad principle, only a decided prejudice to the Militia that had made him so positive I bind myself that he shall join my Regt. in Guernsey without the smallest delay where many of his relations and companions are. . . .[43]

Perhaps Glengarry recognised a fellow spirit in the 'fine young fellow' who could not 'be prevailed upon to do things smoothly.' Glengarry's letter was written two days after he had fought a duel at Inverness – a duel which would see him stand trial for murder in the High Court of Justiciary in Edinburgh later that summer.

I. KAY. 1799   140

Lord Eskgrove from John Kay's Original Portraits –
Eskgrove presided at the High Court trial of
Glengarry for murder

CHAPTER 5

The Duel and the Trial

'. . . did wickedly and feloniously discharge a pistol. . .'

Tuesday 1st May 1798 was a reasonably busy day in the life of the twenty four year old Glengarry. He was in Inverness to attend, as a Deputy Lord Lieutenant of the County, a meeting of the Lieutenancy of Inverness-shire, and in the evening he would go on to a social engagement at a subscription ball being given at Fort George, the great military base at Ardersier on the Moray Firth, just ten miles from the Highland capital.

The ball showed Glengarry at his most arrogant and overbearing and the subsequent events, which ended in a duel between Glengarry and a fellow officer, brought him to trial for his life at the High Court of Justiciary in Edinburgh on a charge of murder.

The ball had been going on for some time, and the supper break had been taken, when Glengarry came up to the beautiful Sarah Forbes of Culloden. He reminded her of what he claimed was her promise to give him the last dance. Miss Forbes protested that she did not recall giving such a promise and that anyway she was engaged to have the last dance with Ranald MacDonald. Glengarry went off, and returning some time later, said to Sarah Forbes that Ranald MacDonald had relinquished his right to dance with Sarah in favour of him.

Not unnaturally Miss Forbes responded to this démarche by declaring, in a properly spirited manner, that she would dance with neither Glengarry nor MacDonald. An onlooker, Lieutenant Norman MacLeod of the 42nd Foot (The Black Watch), intervened:

> Why do you teaze the lady? can't you allow her to chuse
> for herself; you are one of the stewards and may
> command as many dances as you please. [1]

This gallant, if meddlesome, bystander was the grandson of Flora MacDonald, the rescuer of Prince Charles Edward Stuart in 1746.

Miss Forbes, in her evidence in Court, stated that Glengarry had declared the matter to be no concern of MacLeod's and that he had insisted that MacLeod should not interfere. MacLeod, she said, replied that he only did so in a friendly manner and she further testified that while Glengarry 'seemed warm', MacLeod was 'perfectly calm'. She then danced a reel with MacLeod, which must have rubbed salt into Glengarry's wounded pride, after which she left the room.

Ranald MacDonald's evidence was that he had been promised the last country dance with Sarah Forbes but, to oblige Glengarry, had at the young chief's request given up his right to this dance. Reading between the lines of Ranald MacDonald's evidence one can fairly surmise that MacDonald, an advocate by profession, thought that the breach of etiquette, which could be considered as amounting almost to an insult, involved in breaking his commitment to dance with Miss Forbes was preferable to facing-up to the hot-tempered Glengarry. That MacDonald could have taken such a decision, in polite society and in the very formal atmosphere of an eighteenth century ball, speaks volumes about the abrasive and mercurial character of Glengarry, and suggests that the need to avoid provoking an unseemly incident was recognised by Glengarry's contemporaries. MacDonald, who must presumably be the Reginald MacDonald recorded in the roll of the Faculty of Advocates (there being no Ranald MacDonald therein listed), had only been admitted to the Faculty in March 1798 and was still ten days away from his 21st birthday. The altercation over the right to dance with Miss Forbes was a young man's quarrel, with all the potential for hot-headedness and posturing implied by such events.

When Ranald MacDonald returned to the Ball after escorting some ladies to their carriage he met Glengarry and Lieutenant MacLeod leaving the ballroom, still quarrelling. The argument continued as they went into the Officers' Mess of the 79th Regiment (later the Cameron Highlanders).†

In the Mess Lieutenant MacLeod accused Glengarry of being impertinent and Glengarry struck Lieutenant MacLeod on the head with his stick. They continued down the Mess, one either side of the long dining table, abusing one another, until reaching the bottom of the table Glengarry struck MacLeod a blow on the face and then kicked him twice on his backside. MacLeod drew his dirk, bystanders intervened to separate them and Ranald MacDonald went to report the incident to a Major MacCaskill, MacLeod's superior, and, in his evidence, declared that he thought that MacLeod was then placed under arrest.

Captain Neil Campbell of the 79th, who would be MacLeod's second at the duel, generally confirmed Ranald MacDonald's evidence, but said that when the Lieutenant drew his dirk he had not made to stab him but had said that:

> . . . if he was not more of a gentleman than Glengarry he would run it through his body. . .

Major Duncan MacDonald of the 15th Regiment, who was to act as Glengarry's second at the duel, gave evidence to the effect that MacLeod had said to Glengarry 'You are damned impertinent' and that Glengarry had struck him with a small stick on the bonnet and that 'a great deal of high words ensued'.

---

† Many of the accounts of this incident suggest that the ball took place in the town of Inverness, possibly on the mistaken assumption that it was one of the regular series of Northern Meeting Balls held there. However, as the evidence shows that Glengarry and MacLeod could continue their argument by walking from the dance-floor to the Officers' Mess of the 79th. it is clear that the ball took place in Fort George. There was not indeed accommodation for a unit of 600 or 700 men in Inverness since the old fort in the centre of the town had been destroyed by the Jacobites in 1746. After the duel the Regiment's assistant surgeon took MacLeod back to Fort George to attend to his wound, again confirming that the Regimental H.Q. and services were based there.

Matters had inevitably gone beyond 'high words'. MacLeod, contrary to Ranald MacDonald's statement in evidence, was seemingly not placed under arrest, because he was able to go off to another room and prepare a formal challenge to a duel which was duly delivered to Glengarry by his second, Neil Campbell.

On 2nd May MacLeod and Captain Campbell went to the designated spot, The Longman, near Fort George, but Glengarry, apparently mistaking the appointed rendezvous, failed to turn up and the challenger's party were obliged to quit the scene when a magistrate from Inverness turned up with the intention of preventing the duel from taking place. MacLeod and Campbell repaired to Sinclair's Inn, three miles from Inverness, where Campbell wrote a note to Glengarry's second suggesting the Inn as a suitably convenient site for the duel. No reply was received and Campbell went off to Inverness to find Glengarry's second, Major MacDonald, who advised him that Glengarry was staying at Culloden House, the home of the Forbes family, and promised an answer on the morning of the next day (Thursday 3rd May).

The following day all parties duly met at Campbeltown, near Fort George, and an attempt was made by Major MacDonald to arrange an amicable settlement of the dispute. MacLeod proposed that Glengarry should apologise in writing. Evidence is a little confused as to the nature of this apology. One witness, Campbell, said that the terms would be dictated by two senior officers of the 79th while Major MacDonald said that MacLeod himself would dictate the terms and it was to be written before the officers of the 79th. Glengarry, to his credit, agreed to an apology in one form or other. However the point of real difficulty was MacLeod's insistence that he should hand over the stick which he had used to assault MacLeod, 'to be used as he thought proper'. This proved unacceptable; Glengarry's second said in evidence that he had 'never heard of a British officer making such a concession'. The obvious implication of MacLeod's demand for the cane 'to be used as he thought proper' and Glengarry's resistance was that he proposed to thrash Glengarry with it – a point which Captain Campbell in his evidence at the trial conceded was a distinct possibility. As a result of MacLeod's stubborn insistence on this point and Glengarry's equally stubborn (if understandable) refusal to concede the point matters inevitably proceeded to the duel.

MacLeod hardly comes out of this episode covered in glory – his insistence on humiliating Glengarry by demanding the surrender of the cane and his probable intention to beat Glengarry, who was after all much his senior in military rank, was unwise and unworthy. Glengarry's courage in choosing to face MacLeod's bullet rather than surrender his cane cannot be questioned – but the inflexibility and intransigence he showed is very much part of the man's character, and confirms the personality feature he displayed when he persuaded Ranald MacDonald to give up his dance with Miss Forbes.

A certain degree of inexperience betrayed itself in the technical arrangements for the duel, probably reflecting the fact that duelling was by no means an everyday event in 1798. Campbell had brought along a pair of pistols, but the balls provided were too small for the weapons – hardly the most convincing display of military preparedness. Captain Campbell proposed that the balls should be wrapped in a piece of leather to ensure a better fit. However Glengarry's second would not agree to this.

The bullets being too small for the bore of the pistol meant that the accuracy of aim would be considerably impaired. An undersized bullet will move from side to side around the barrel when the charge is fired and, as a result, it becomes something of a matter of luck exactly the direction it takes when it leaves the gun.

The two principals lined up at eleven paces apart – a compromise between Campbell's proposal of ten paces and MacDonald's of twelve and a reflection of the limited range and accuracy of eighteenth century side arms.

On both the points of what might be called the technical debate, the wish to ensure accuracy by wrapping the balls and the wish for the duellists to stand closer, MacLeod's side seems to have gone for the more deadly option and the Glengarry side favoured the more risk reducing option. It does seem as if MacLeod and his second were more concerned with ensuring a sanguinary result and Glengarry and his second with going through the motions and ensuring that honour was satisfied.

On the signal being given the two men fired and Lieutenant MacLeod was wounded, apparently only slightly. There seemed for a moment to be the possibility of another exchange of shots but both sides accepted that honour had been satisfied, according to the accepted rules of the duel and the contemporary sense of propriety. MacLeod expressed his regret for the part he had played in the affair and Glengarry expressed his sorrow for his conduct, the two shook hands and parted. Major MacDonald, Glengarry's second, stated in his evidence that:

> . . . he was certain Glengarry did not entertain any malice
> against [MacLeod], and he was convinced he always
> wished for an accommodation.

Glengarry returned home to Glengarry House, where on the 5th of May, he busied himself with routine military affairs, writing to Sir James Grant of Grant, the Lord Lieutenant of the County, about a matter concerned with the recruitment ballot for the local Militia.

Lieutenant MacLeod returned to Fort George in a post chaise, under the care of Ebenezer Brown, Assistant Surgeon to the 79th Foot, who had been in attendance at the duel. Brown extracted a ball from below the left shoulder blade. The ball had evidently entered the body under the right arm pit and travelled across the back to the left shoulder blade. Such a wound was consistent with MacLeod standing side on to Glengarry, aiming his own pistol at him in his outstretched right hand.

Under Brown's care MacLeod seemed to do well and recovered for the first fourteen days, but on the fifteenth day he grew worse and died on 3rd June, exactly a month after the duel.

Duelling, even if it did not result in the death of a participant, was of course illegal. A Scots statute of 1600 provided for the death penalty for duelling, while a later Act of 1696 enacted that:

> . . . whosoever, principal or second, or other
> interposed person, gives a challenge to fight a duel, or
> single combat, or whosoever accepts the same, or

> whosoever, either principal or second, on either side,
> engages therein, albeit no fighting ensue, shall be
> punished by the pain of banishment and escheat of
> moveables, without prejudice to the act already made
> against the fighting of duels. [2]

However little Glengarry seems to have shown himself concerned by the event by returning to Glengarry House and carrying on with his normal business, he had, together with all the other participants in the affair at Cambeltown, put himself outside the criminal law. The abortive duel on 2nd May had become known to the civil authorities in Inverness and although the encounter of the 3rd May passed off without interruption by the arrival of a magistrate the event and its outcome could hardly have been kept secret from either the civil or the military authorities. Whatever action the authorities might have taken against the duellists and their accomplices had Norman MacLeod made a full recovery, the death of the unfortunate Lieutenant precipitated an investigation by the Lord Advocate, the chief Scottish law officer and public prosecutor, and brought in its wake the inevitable consequence of a trial for murder.

Trials of Scotland's most serious criminal cases were held in Edinburgh throughout most of the year, and in nine circuit towns in the Spring and Autumn of each year. Inverness was a High Court Circuit town and the Autumn diet fell due to be held there in September. As the alleged crime took place in the environs of Inverness and as Glengarry and all the witnesses came from or were based in and around Inverness there would seem to have been every reason to have disposed of the case before the two High Court Judges appointed to sit in Inverness. However it was decided to hear the case in Edinburgh and on Monday August 6th Glengarry appeared before the High Court of Justiciary. Absent, due to illness, was the redoubtable Robert McQueen, Lord Braxfield, Lord Justice-Clerk and head of the Scottish criminal judiciary. In Braxfield's absence David Rae, Lord Eskgrove, presided, accompanied by Lords Swinton and Dunsinnan.

It is, incidentally, curious that many references to this trial suggest that it took place in Inverness. Even the Dictionary of National Biography (which also manages to put the ball at Fort

William rather than Fort George) claims the trial was in Inverness. The fact that the trial was held in the High Court in Edinburgh, rather than in the seemingly obvious place, is not without significance. It seems unlikely that a concern for swift administration of justice was at the root of the authorities' decision to go for an Edinburgh trial – only another month would have elapsed before the circuit judges would sit in Inverness. It is much more probable that the high profile nature of the case and the local passions that it aroused made it expedient to try it in Edinburgh before a full Bench and a lowland jury. It was not, after all, an everyday occurrence for a clan chief, a major landowner, a Depute Lord Lieutenant, and a Colonel of Fencibles, all wrapped up in one twenty-four year-old body to be accused of murdering a brother officer after what could, not unfairly, be described as a dance-hall brawl. It would probably have been hard, in view of the restricted pool of jurors in late eighteenth century Scotland, to have empanelled fifteen Inverness-shire jurymen who were not personally acquainted with Glengarry and MacLeod.

Even in Edinburgh the trial attracted enormous interest. The *Edinburgh Evening Courant* noted that:

> The Court was crowded throughout the whole day.
> A great number of Ladies, and persons of rank and
> fashion, were present. [3]

The libel, or statement of charge, read:

> That on the 3rd day of May last, on the Muir or Links
> between Fort George and Arderseir, the said Alexander
> Macdonell did wickedly and feloniously discharge a
> pistol loaded with ball at the now deceased Lieutenant
> Norman McLeod of the 42nd regiment of foot; in
> consequence of which the said Lieutenant Norman
> McLeod was wounded on the right side immediately
> under the arm, the ball having penetrated through the
> right arm-pit into the back; and, not withstanding every
> medical assistance having been immediately procured,
> the said Norman McLeod did, in consequence of the
> wound given him, as aforesaid, by the said Alexander
> Macdonell, expire on the 3rd day of June thereafter. . . [4]

As befitted the gravity of the charge and the status of the accused the Crown was represented by the Lord Advocate, Robert

Dundas, supported by the Solicitor General, Robert Blair, and James Oswald. Glengarry was represented by Henry Erskine, one of the leading advocates of the day, and a former Dean of the Faculty of Advocates. Erskine was a leading Whig and had been ousted from his position as Dean and replaced by Robert Dundas, due to his political stance on parliamentary reform. Erskine was thus not likely to be personally sympathetic to the very pro-Government Macdonell who had attached himself to the Dundas cause and looked upon the Dundases as his political patrons. However the ethics of the Scottish bar demanded that even political opponents were entitled to the best defence. Erskine was assisted in his seemingly unpromising task by James Montgomery and William Rae. Rae was then in the early years of his bar career but later himself became Lord Advocate. In the somewhat enclosed and incestuous world of eighteenth century Scots law nobody, apparently, thought it remarkable that one of the counsel for Glengarry was the son of the presiding judge. Indeed so much of a family affair was the law in Scotland at that time that it would probably have been impossible to run the legal system if every family connection was held to disqualify advocates or judges from acting.

Fifteen highly respectable jurors, landowners and profession-al men from Edinburgh and the Lothians, were sworn and the case opened with legal argument. Rae attempted to argue that the actions of Glengarry, 'the pannel' in the terminology of Scots law, after the quarrel and before the duel,

> . . . had been such as would exculpate him from the
> heavy charge brought against him by the public
> prosecutor and craved that the pannel might be allowed
> a proof of all the facts and circumstances which might
> extenuate or exculpate.

The judges argued the matter and in the *Scots Magazine's* view their Lordships reached the conclusion:

> . . . that, by the law of Scotland, killing in a duel was
> murder, and that it could not be brought under the
> crime of culpable homicide: That a person tried for
> killing in a duel must be either found guilty of
> murder or acquitted.

However, the Court allowed the defence team to introduce proof relevant to the extenuating circumstances. Lord Swinton, one of the panel of three judges, read out a number of reported cases where the precedent suggested that self-defence or a desire for reconciliation had not proved sufficient to avoid a capital sentence.

One of the incidents of the trial was the entry of the star witness, the beautiful Miss Forbes whose favours on the dance-floor had been the occasion of the quarrel between Glengarry and MacLeod. Miss Forbes (who had since married and was now Mrs Duff) entered court veiled – a mode of dress which greatly upset Eskgrove, who rebuked her thus before administering the oath:

> Young woman! you will now consider yourself as in
> the presence of Almighty God and of this High Court.
> Lift up your veil, throw off all modesty, and look me
> in the face. [5]

After the evidence had been heard Lord Advocate Dundas summed-up for the Crown and Henry Erskine for the accused and the presiding judge, Lord Eskgrove:

> . . . charged the Jury in a pretty long speech, in which he
> recapitulated the evidence with great candour and clarity. [6]

Indeed it would be 'a pretty long speech'. Eskgrove was known for his prolixity and tedious manner and the whole trial had already consumed a long day. Erskine's summing up, for example, did not start until midnight and lasted for three hours. In it he emphasised the persistent attempts which had been made by Glengarry and his second to reconcile matters and to make every honourable apology.

Glengarry was sent back to the Canongate Tolbooth, although he was so confident of an acquittal that he protested at the necessity. His solicitor, Coll MacDonald, consulted Erskine on this but the shrewd advocate advised that it was important not to give an appearance of overconfidence and counselled a quiet return to prison. The long-suffering jury was told to report back next day with their verdict. They duly returned at noon on Tuesday 7th having considered their verdict, and, hopefully, having had a few hours rest. Improbably, in the teeth of the evidence, and seemingly against all the legal precedents cited, their foreman, or Chancellor, Charles Brown of Coalston, reported a Not Guilty verdict. Brown, after the verdict was recorded, said that he had been asked by the Jury to make a statement:

> . . . the sole ground on which the verdict proceeded, was the anxious desire latterly manifested by the pannel and his friend Major MacDonald, amicably to settle the matter, and prevent proceeding to extremities, by making an apology, as the Jury highly disapproved of the pannel's conduct at the beginning of the unhappy dispute; and it was fortunate for him that the duel did not take place so soon as intended, before any attempt was made to apologise, as in that case it was highly probable that they would have returned a very different verdict. At the same time it was proper to observe, that the Jury had no idea of finding, by their verdict, that what is called fairly killing a man in a duel, could afford by itself any defence against a charge of murder.

A statement from a Jury on the reasons for their decision was, and is, extremely rare. A statement of such gloriously muddled thought must be even rarer. The Jury's decision can only have been based on the view that MacLeod had brought his fate on himself by being unreasonable in demanding the surrender of Glengarry's cane – because this was the only sticking point between the two sides in the preliminary discussions before the duel. MacLeod may indeed have been unreasonable, but this hardly justifies the withdrawal of the sanctions of the law from his killer, especially when the Jury specifically reject the idea of 'fair killing' in a duel as a defence against a murder charge. In other words they rejected the idea that a duel was private engagement outwith the law in which the two parties were equally guilty (or equally innocent). So we are left with the conclusion that Glengarry was allowed to walk free because he and his second had made moves towards an apology and that if the duel had taken place before these exchanges and attempts at reconciliation he would have faced 'a very different verdict'.

Lord Eskgrove, presiding, 'declared his approbation of the sentiments expressed by the Jury' but went on to warn Glengarry and all others to avoid 'so illegal and dangerous a practice as that of duelling' and declared that it was:

> ... incumbent on both Judges and Juries to repress,
> by conviction of the surviving party, as guilty of the
> crime of murder, in all cases where the circumstances
> did justify so doing.

Which might, possibly, be seen as his Lordship having his cake and eating it.

Lord Swinton, noting the Not Guilty verdict, rather resignedly observed that there was nothing for the Court to do but acquit the prisoner and dismiss him from the bar. However as the Jury had thought fit to make a statement he would take the liberty of expressing his own sentiments upon the case, and others of the same kind. Swinton argued, with a better grasp of the law than Eskgrove or the jury, that it was not competent for the Court to admit a plea of self-defence in favour of the survivor of a duel, or to support a defence of the killing based on the special circumstances of the case.

> This was a Court of Law, and the Judges could not
> erect themselves into a Court of Honour; as little was
> it competent for the Jury to erect themselves into
> such a Court.

Swinton was in favour of allowing evidence to be given which might tend to exculpate or alleviate but this exculpation and alleviation was not a matter for the law, where nothing could exculpate or alleviate the crime. It was indeed, in his view, properly a matter for a Court of Honour, and such a Court, Swinton insisted, did exist:

> Where? In his Majesty's royal breast alone.

Swinton, was thus clearly arguing that a finding of guilty on the evidence should have been returned and the matter of any pardon or remission of punishment should rest with the Royal Prerogative of Mercy.

Swinton went on to hope that the Jury's comments, presumably those against the 'fair killing' doctrine, would:

> . . . have the effect to weigh against an unfavourable
> construction of their verdict being supposed an excuse
> of duelling. . .

and went on to comment on a recent trial in England where a person had been sentenced to twelve months imprisonment merely for sending a challenge. In that case the Lord Chief Justice had said that the public was much obliged to the Attorney-General for bringing the case and Lord Swinton reflected that:

> . . . he should be happy to give like thanks for such a trial
> in this part of the kingdom.

Swinton was clearly unhappy with the outcome. Others were, in equal measure, surprised. Coll MacDonald of Dalness, W.S., Glengarry's law agent wrote:

> The verdict returned does not meet with the general
> approbation of the public . . . the public voice was so
> much against Glengarry, that not a single one among his
> friends thought he would have been acquitted by a
> unanimous verdict. [7]

It should, however, be understood that MacDonald's opinion on public sentiment related to the time before the trial, there is evidence that the public mood swung in favour of Glengarry in the course of the trial – Henry Erskine's advocacy did not just influence the jury.

One legal comment from the Highlands is significant in the light that it sheds on Glengarry's difficult and unstable character – James Fraser of Gortuleg wrote of Glengarry's narrow escape:

> I sincerely wish he may make a good use of the
> hairbreadth escape. [8]

Fraser was presumably hoping that Glengarry would learn a lesson from his experience and take a more measured approach to life. Sadly, Fraser's pious wish was not to be fulfilled. Glengarry came close to fighting another duel, in 1808, and would face a number of charges of assault, one of which resulted in civil damages of £2000 being adjudged against him. He also became a regular litigant in the Court of Session.

Henry Erskine's reaction to the acquittal was interesting.

Glengarry's friends, with a certain lack of taste, arranged a grand dinner in an Edinburgh hotel to celebrate his acquittal. Erskine was invited but declined the invitation – apparently anxious to preserve a distinction between his duty to a client and approval of his client's actions and behaviour. In the words of Erskine's biographer:

> . . . his admiration of the part played by his client in the late tragedy was not sufficiently strong to admit of his being present. [9]

Acquittal, whether deserved or not, did not quite end the MacLeod affair for Glengarry. Years afterwards he went to Skye to visit Lord MacDonald and was in Portree on a busy market day to lunch in the Inn with a number of local gentlemen – inevitably including relatives of the late Lieutenant MacLeod. Glengarry, who for all his failings could never be accused of a lack of generosity or of lacking a taste for the grand gesture, had a cask of whisky provided for the enjoyment of those attending the market. In the Inn the meal went forward well enough, but outside the free drink had an unfortunate effect on the populace, particularly those of Clan MacLeod. A crowd gathered outside the Inn demanding Glengarry dead or alive as they were determined to avenge Lieutenant MacLeod's murder. Lachlan Mackinnon of Corry, who was presiding at the meal in the Inn went outside and addressed the crowd:

> . . . praying them not to forget the laws of hospitality, or so far forget themselves as to cause injury or to insult the guest of the great Chief of the Island [Lord MacDonald]. [10]

Mackinnon's oratory having no effect he decided that Glengarry must be removed from the scene and had him smuggled out of the back door of the Inn, on to a horse and off, post haste to the Kylrhea ferry and safety.

However Glengarry never travelled alone and on his Skye visit he was accompanied, as usual by gillies and some of his beloved stag-hounds. While Glengarry left by the back door the gillies and the dogs were left in the power of the Portree mob. The men were spared but the dogs had their ears and tails cropped and men and dogs were sent back to the mainland with the message that if Glengarry should ever return to Skye his head would come off. This, perhaps not surprisingly, is on record as Glengarry's last visit to Skye.

Macdonell of Glengarry painted by the artist Angelica
Kauffmann in Rome in 1800 during his ill-fated tour
Permission: Scottish National Portrait Gallery

CHAPTER 6

The Grand Tour

'. . .a gentleman of considerable landed estate, and of a very antient family. . .'

An eighteenth century young gentleman of good family might usually anticipate being sent abroad to do the Grand Tour as the culmination of his education. After two or three years at university a year or so spent travelling on the Continent would round him off and fit him for his future life. The Grand Tour was not, could not in the travelling conditions of the period be, merely a brief holiday excursion. It was a prolonged immersion in the culture and society of Europe and the young man would, it was hoped, learn about European politics and European manners, art and architecture, culture and gastronomy, make friends and useful contacts and become exposed to both classical learning and contemporary ideas. Although this was perhaps less overtly stated the Tour also afforded an opportunity to sow wild oats far from home.

The young Glengarry might have anticipated being able to make his Grand Tour around 1794, when he had attained his majority and come into unfettered possession of the family estate. At that time he would have completed three years at University College, acquired a degree of Oxford polish and a period on the Continent would have been seen as an appropriate pause before starting to manage the estate or taking up politics or a military career.

The itinerary of the Grand Tour varied, but almost all travellers included a prolonged stay in Italy – after all Dr. Johnson had declared that 'the grand object of travelling is to see the shores of the Mediterranean.' However for Glengarry and his generation there was a problem – the French Revolution and then a European war from 1792. The theatres of conflict ranged widely over the classic terrain of the Grand Tour and although shifting alliances and the fortunes of war made some areas accessible one year and others accessible another the constant state of war between Britain and France made one traditional route to the South, from the Channel to Paris, Lyons and thence down the Rhone to the Mediterranean, impossible.

In any case Glengarry had, as we have seen, other things on his mind than travelling for pleasure and education in Europe. From 1793 he was pursuing a military career, first in the Grant Fencibles and then with the Glengarries. After 1796 when he resigned his command in favour of Donald Macdonell he was still ambitious to have a career in the regular army and his unavailing correspondence on this subject stretches into 1798. This was the year of the duel and the murder trial and of an unpleasant incident at his birthday party in September when he was assaulted by one of the guests, a Dr. MacDonald of Fort Augustus.

After these episodes it might well have been thought by Glengarry or his advisers that a spell out of Scotland would be no bad thing. In any event on 29th March 1799 the Foreign Office issued a passport to Colonel Macdonell and servants for the purpose of 'Voyageant dans les pays etr. [etrangers]' [1] The only servant accompanying Glengarry on his travels, of whom there is a record, is yet another Alexander Macdonell. Fortunately he seems to have gone by the nickname of 'Saunders' – which does allow for a little less confusion.

Quite who 'Saunders' was is not clear – but he was literate and in 1800 Glengarry's Edinburgh law agent, Coll MacDonald, wrote to him in terms of some familiarity. Probably Saunders had grown up with Glengarry and would count himself as some sort of distant kin. Years later Glengarry's daughter writes of a Saunders Macdonell, the tenant of Kyles in Knoydart but it seems impossible to make a positive identification between the two. Indeed almost everyone in this chapter in Glengarry's story describes themselves as a relative – Colonel Donald Macdonell, his successor in the Glengarry Fencibles, the Rev. Alexander Macdonell, the Glengarries' Chaplain, Coll MacDonald, Angus MacDonald, the Regiment's Agent.

Highland cousinship took in many very distant degrees of relationship, not all of which would today be recognised by that name.

We next hear of Glengarry in August 1799. At this time he is in Berlin, intending to travel on by way of the Saxon capital, Dresden, to Vienna – and although information is not available it is reasonable to suppose that he had taken what was at that period the normal route to Berlin by sailing from an English port to Hamburg and thence travelling, by land, up the valleys of the Elbe and the Spree. He presented himself to the British Minister at the Prussian Court, Thomas Grenville, and sought documents to allow him to continue his travels. Grenville wrote to his opposite number at Vienna, the newly appointed Ambassador, Lord Minto, about Glengarry:

> . . . he is a gentleman of considerable landed estate, and of a very antient family, you will find him very desirous of obtaining your protection, and I am assured by those who have much longer knowledge of him than I have that he will do no discredit to any assistance or kindness which you may do him at Vienna. I assume that his name and family are not unknown to you and I understand that he will wait only for the necessary passport from you at Vienna to enable him to pay his respects to you there. [2]

Grenville makes the assumption that Glengarry's name and family would be known to Minto because Minto was also a Scot. The first Baron Minto of Minto, his title had been created in 1797, was originally Sir Gilbert Elliot, a Borderer from Roxburghshire, and it is fair to assume that, in the small world of eighteenth century Scotland, even if Minto had not met Macdonell he would know just where to place him in the social hierarchy and would receive him at the Vienna embassy.

After travelling through Prussia and Saxony Glengarry arrived in Vienna at some point in the autumn of 1799 and remained there through the autumn and winter of 1799/1800, enjoying the polite society of the capital of the Austro-Hungarian Empire.

Lord Minto later wrote:

> Col. Macdonell had resided at Vienna during the winter

> 1799-1800 and had been thought strange and particular
> in manner and conversation even at that time. But these
> particularities were ascribed to the effects of wine and he
> was not then suspected of insanity, at least such an
> opinion never reach'd me. . . He was remarkable
> however for good nature and an obliging disposition
> which procured him indulgence for the peculiarities
> which were remarked in him. [3]

Sadly the Ambassador, who was writing a private memorandum, does not say precisely what form Glengarry's strangeness
took, but Glengarry seems to have enjoyed his stay in Vienna. A
description of Austrian society at the period exists in letters Minto
wrote to his wife. Lady Minto had remained at home and was not
able, due to the changing fortunes of the war and winter travelling
problems, to come out to Vienna until the spring of 1800. In one of
these letters, written in September 1799, he reassures her that:

> There are certainly a sufficient number of well-bred,
> pleasant people here, especially of women, to afford you
> an agreeable private society, besides the world in which
> you must live a great deal. [4]

And a year later, Lady Minto, having become established in Vienna,
would write home to Lady Malmesbury:

> The society here is as easy as possible, and nothing is
> thought odd or strange. so that one may do as one likes.
> There is no gossip, but a great deal of good nature and a
> great desire of obliging. [5]

This does make Lord Minto's comment that Glengarry's
'strange and particular' manner had been noted in Viennese circles
suggest that this must have been something more than just mild
eccentricity or provincialism, or indeed an inability to hold his
liquor. Equally the tolerant nature of Viennese society is suggested
both by Lady Minto's reference to 'good nature and a great desire
of obliging' and Lord Minto's comment that it was Glengarry's
'good nature and an obliging disposition which procured him
indulgence for the peculiarities which were remarked in him.'

After his winter season in Vienna Glengarry and his servant
pressed on when the more clement weather made travelling easier.
He was in Venice on 2 March 1800 and wrote to Minto from there,

thanking him for his civility to him during his stay in Vienna and advising him of his future travel plans. [6] Glengarry planned to travel on from Venice through the Veneto to Verona and thence to Mantua and Bologna and down to Florence.

No papers appear to survive from this part of Glengarry's Grand Tour, although a fellow-Scot, Pryse Lockhart Gordon gives an account of Glengarry at a dinner party in Florence. Gordon, born in Inverness-shire in 1762, held a commission in the Gordon Fencibles, but was on extended leave travelling with Alexander Lord Montgomerie, the heir to the Earl of Eglintoun who was in Italy for his health. Gordon and Montgomerie, who Gordon describes as a relation of Glengarry (the relationship was an extremely distant one), were in Florence when Glengarry arrived and Montgomerie entertained him to dinner. Gordon's account of Glengarry in Florentine society is worth quoting at length.

> . . . we had another inmate of rather eccentric manner, a great chieftain of the north (who had made his debut in Italy on the opening of Lombardy) the Laird of Glengarry. Being related to Lord Montgomery, we invited him to dinner, which he returned by a grand entertainment that occasioned a very laughable incident. The chieftain had brought letters of introduction to several Florentine nobles, who with our minister formed the party; and as he wore on such solemn occasions the dress of a Highland chieftain, which being set off by a handsome and warlike person, was greatly admired. The bottle circulated *à l'Inglese,* and when the champagne and Tuscan grape began to mount into the chieftain's head, his eloquence increased. He had for some time been entertaining his guests with a description of mountain habits and customs, which was not understood by the Italians; but it was in vain that his English friends tried to change the conversation into French. He went *con strepito* to the climax, the mode of catching wild cattle in Lochaber, on which subject he seemed quite *au fait,* but in order to 'suit the action to the word' and to show the *modus operandi,* he laid hold of the Marchese (who sat at the post of honour on his right) with both hands, stretching out his vigorous arms at full length. 'In this way,' exclaimed our chief, seizing the unfortunate man by the collar, 'one takes the cow by the horns, while another lays hold of the tail, pulling the

beast to the ground.' Conceive the astonishment and dismay of the poor Florentine, thus grappled by a powerful man, 'armed to the teeth' with pistol, sword, and dagger, and bellowing in a barbarous and to him unintelligible language. He had the power and courage however to get on his legs, and with some difficulty extricated himself from the gripe of his friend, demanding in a French *patois,* which he imagined might probably be understood, the cause of such an outrage. In the mean time, another guest who sat near me took the alarm, and jumping up made a precipitate retreat, overturning various articles in his flight; and so quick were his motions that he was in the vestibule before I could overtake him and explain the affair as well as I could, with my slender knowledge of Italian, I persuaded him to return, when we found that his friend was pacified by the intercession of Mr. W____, and harmony was speedily restored. But it was not so easy to appease the chieftain, who naturally felt much hurt that he should be suspected of committing an unprovoked assault on a gentleman whom he had invited to partake of his hospitalities. It was also evident that the guests sat on thorns, for in half an hour they pleaded an engagement at the theatre, and made their bows.

When they had retired, Glengarry saw the folly of taking amiss the terrors of these poor Italians, which he had so unwittingly occasioned, and shortly joined in the general laugh, in which his other two Italian guests, who had seen more of the world and had better nerves, heartily participated. [7]

By some point in the spring or early summer of 1800 he had reached Rome, possibly travelling there with Montgomerie. The two young men (both were twenty-seven years old) would have had much in common – apart from any blood relationship. They were well-born Scots in a foreign land, and both had followed a military career, Montgomerie had held a commission in the 42nd Highlanders, the Black Watch before transferring to the Glasgow Regiment. Both men had their portraits painted in Rome in 1800 by Angelica Kauffmann. One of the accepted rituals of the Grand Tour was to commission a portrait for the ancestral home from a Continental artist. Angelica Kauffmann (1741-1807) was undoubtedly one of the more distinguished artists working in Rome at this period. Of Swiss nationality she had moved between Rome, Venice and London (where she became a founder-member of the Royal Academy in 1768) before returning to Rome in 1781. The portraits of Glengarry and Montgomerie are among the last of her recorded works. [8]

The logistical problems of the Grand Tour must have been formidable. The Glengarry portrait measures 220 cm by 146 cm – say 7 feet by 4 feet 9 inches – so would certainly not come back as hand luggage. Another dimension to the problems of the Tour is that both Glengarry and Montgomerie chose to be portrayed in Scottish national dress – Glengarry in what appears to be a civilian version of full Highland regalia and Lord Montgomerie in the dress uniform of the Black Watch – feather bonnet and all. Quite how comfortable these costumes would have been to wear while posing for Kauffmann in the summer heat of Rome hardly bears contemplation. Obviously these costumes were not in Angelica Kauffmann's property box and would have had to have been carried all the way from Scotland to Rome. Gordon's account of Glengarry's war-like appearance at the Florentine dinner-party: armed to the teeth with sword, dagger and pistols underlines the point. Gentlemen on the Grand Tour did not travel lightly and the role of Saunders in loading all Glengarry's boxes and cases in and out of coaches and carriages across Europe made his post no sinecure.

Glengarry found the Italian climate to be uncongenial, and the Italian people not to be to his taste. For all this he seems to have travelled fairly widely and taken in the full list of tourist attractions – he even claimed to have visited Sicily and climbed Mount Etna. On a visit to Florence he had a bout of illness and was treated by an English doctor resident there – a fortunate chance as he discovered that he had little faith in Italian medical men.

However worse was to come. He resolved to pay a visit to his countryman, Admiral Lord Keith, the Commander in Chief of the Mediterranean Fleet. The Scottish Admiral was engaged in the blockade of Genoa in the early summer of 1800 and Glengarry sailed out to meet him but fell in with a French privateer; that is a privately owned armed vessel commissioned by a belligerent nation to carry on naval warfare. The privateer, as a Viennese doctor later noted:

> . . . took from him a great number of precious things the loss of which seemed to have made a deep impression on him and which with the ready money he valued to near £3000 sterling.

There is undoubtedly an interesting and exciting story to be told of Glengarry's encounter with the privateer – but nothing else seems to be known of this incident. One wonders exactly where Glengarry got 'precious things' and cash to the value of £3000 and why he was carrying this enormous amount of money and valuables with him around Europe. To put the sum in context – the annual rental income from the entire Glengarry estate in 1802 was only £5090. [9] So in one stroke of ill-fortune he had lost around eight months gross income.

He was put ashore by the privateers and made his way across Italy to Trieste. By this time he was suffering from a fever and had also observed that he had a swollen testicle. Not wishing to place any further trust in Italian medical science he resolved to make for Vienna. Fortunately he fell in with Charles Duff in Trieste. This gentleman, yet another Scot, was a diplomatic messenger travelling from Lord Elgin, the British Minister to the Ottoman Empire, to Vienna. The two men posted in a light coach, night and day, in the height of the summer from Trieste to the Austrian capital. It is hardly surprising that Glengarry's condition worsened.

Arriving in Vienna about 10th August he, and Saunders, booked in to Wolff's Hotel, much favoured by foreign visitors, and sought the medical assistance of Dr. Decarro, a graduate of both Vienna and Edinburgh Universities. Decarro prescribed appropriate medicines both for the fever and for the testicular swelling.

Lord Minto, who seems also to have been a patient of Decarro, was at this time staying at his country house at St. Veit, a former monastery a few miles from the centre of Vienna, so did not immediately hear news of Glengarry's return or of his illness.

On 15th August Herr Wolff, the hotel proprietor, called on Minto to report that Glengarry was much indisposed, that he had refused admittance to Dr. Decarro and others and that Saunders had not been seen. Fears were entertained for the safety of the servant and for Glengarry; the police had been sent for but were holding back at present because Glengarry was a British subject.

Minto, in the middle of conducting Britain's delicate foreign policy towards its ally Austria, put aside the weighty affairs of state and accompanied Wolff to look after this distressed British subject.

The Glengarry affair and its aftermath was to occupy much of the Ambassador's valuable time for many months and although he must often have rued the day that Glengarry decided to take the Grand Tour it is due to the exhaustive file of correspondence that he kept on the case and the long memorandum he wrote for the record that we know anything of this episode in Glengarry's life. The file and memorandum exist largely because the circumstances of Glengarry's second stay in Vienna were so extraordinary and the difficulties occasioned, both by Macdonell and his family, to those who attempted to help Glengarry were so acute that Minto was obliged, in his own defence, to preserve as full a record of the episode as possible. Unless otherwise indicated all quotations in this chapter are from this source. [10]

When Minto arrived at Wolff's Hotel Decarro reported that he had been treating Glengarry for the swollen testicle, which he said was not venereal in its origins, but that he had now been dismissed from attendance and refused admission. Charles Duff, Glengarry's travelling companion from Trieste, who conveniently spoke Gaelic, was admitted but even with this linguistic advantage failed to persuade Glengarry to readmit the Doctor. Glengarry did, however, confide in Duff that he was now treating himself for the swelling in the testicle and to this end had 'tied a cord tight round the scrotum' and sought Duff's assistance in procuring a second cord for the same painful purpose.

At around this time another British resident in the hotel had managed to get into Glengarry's apartment by a back door and released the unfortunate Saunders who had been beaten violently on the head and face by Glengarry, put into an inner room and 'threatened with life if he stirr'd or cried out'.

Decarro advised Minto that if Glengarry's scrotum had indeed been tied tightly between the testicles and the body for several hours then he was in great danger. An entry was forced and Minto found Glengarry sitting wearing only a shirt (and the whipcord round his scrotum) and looking pale and ill. Glengarry ordered Minto out and even approached the Ambassador with clenched fists. Minto signalled to the waiting police to seize him and the Doctor, with some difficulty, used the point of a penknife to cut the cord which was sunk into the swollen tissue of the scrotum – Minto records that Glengarry's:

> . . . testicles were at that time swell'd to a very large
> size and had become a livid colour.

Arrangements were made for Glengarry's restraint and continuing medical care, and at the request of Herr Wolff, (who clearly thought little of half-naked Highland chiefs who beat their servants and tied up their genitals with whipcord as suitable patrons for his hotel), a search was started for alternative accommodation in a quiet quarter of the city.

As a ligature around the scrotum was clearly not the best medical advice available to Glengarry in his distressing situation, the question arises as to why he decided to engage in this clearly excruciating form of self-treatment. Fortunately, a couple of weeks later, Glengarry was able to tell Lord Minto exactly why he had acted so bizarrely. The answer was equally bizarre – witchcraft.

Glengarry considered himself afflicted with witches and sorcerers. It must be concluded that there was a strongly superstitious streak in his nature and that this belief in malign supernatural forces was not simply a product of his illness. He carried everywhere, Minto records, a charm in the form of several balls or bullets, obtained from one of his tenants in the Highlands. When Minto was visiting him Glengarry actually had one of these balls in his mouth, for more effective protection against the powers of darkness.

Minto's memorandum recounts Glengarry's explanation for the ligature:

> He then described his contest with the witches on the

occasion of his confinement. He told us that a witch
had insinuated herself into his scrotum. That after she
had tormented him some time he determined to
destroy her. That for this purpose he had fastened
some whipcord round his scrotum and had by that
means secured the enchantress bodily and prevented
her escape. That her head was still at liberty – that she
had bit the vessels which convey the seed to the left
testicle, that he had been under the necessity of
fastening a second cord with which he dextrously got
hold of her neck and strangled her, which was
fortunately accomplished before Dr. Decarro cut the
cord.

On the same occasion Glengarry confided to Minto that his
new apartment, in what was then the suburbs of Vienna, at 122
Alstergasse, was bewitched. Minto noted:

His room was hung round with a great many prints
framed, many of them glazed. He told us that these
were witches and sorcerers of different descriptions
but he had taken his precautions against them.

Minto's conclusion was that Glengarry:

. . . did not utter one sentence that was not insane
during the whole visit & he spoke incessantly with
little or no answer from myself . . . above an hour.

His Lordship also notes, as additional proof of Glengarry's mental
state, that in the course of explaining about his charm, 'he was led
into a digression on the genealogy of Glengarry.' However lengthy
digressions on the genealogy of his family were always to be a
feature of Glengarry's conversation and writing, whether sane or
mad, so too much need not be read into this piece of evidence.

Obviously some arrangement had to be made for the care, and
eventual repatriation, of Glengarry. Soon after the incident at
Wolff's Hotel Minto wrote to Angus MacDonald, an Army Agent
in Pall Mall, London, who was the regimental agent for the
Glengarry Fencibles and dealt with Glengarry's London business,
to acquaint him with the situation. Passing delicately over the
inflammation in the testicles as 'another complaint of a painful
nature' he reported that Glengarry had been:

> . . . seized with the most violent frenzy which led him to
> put his servant's life as well as his own in danger. [11]

He explained that he had authorised the use of force to save
Macdonell's life and had made appropriate medical arrangements.
The Ambassador's conclusion was that:

> I see no reason as yet to conclude that his alienation of
> mind is more than the frenzy that has been occasioned
> by his fever & the great pain he had endured – his bodily
> complaint is considerably diminished.

He ended his letter with the request that Glengarry's nearer
relations should be advised and that:

> It would be very desirable that some friend should come
> to Vienna to take charge of him.

One of Minto's first acts had been to seal up all Glengarry's
personal effects and papers. It seems unlikely that he had much
ready money on him, if the story of the French privateer is to be
taken at face value. Clearly Glengarry's care would involve
considerable expenses and these could not properly fall on the
Embassy's account. Minto advised Angus MacDonald that while
he would exercise all due prudence he would eventually have to
draw a bill on him for the costs incurred and assumed that, as
Glengarry's agent, he would honour this.

Minto also arranged for a British physician who chanced to be
in Vienna, a Doctor Hallifax, to examine Glengarry and Hallifax
concurred in Decarro's view that his condition required restraint.
Unfortunately Glengarry's friends in Vienna seemed less
convinced of his continuing mental derangement and kept
requesting greater freedom for him. Duff, who had witnessed the
incident at Wolff's Hotel, nevertheless wrote to Minto early in
September asking that Glengarry be allowed out without
attendants. This request was politely but firmly turned down:

> Although I am very desirous of affording every comfort
> & gratification to Col. Macdonell which his unhappy
> situation admits of, yet acting on this occasion in some
> degree as a magistrate and merely by virtue of my office
> which makes me responsible for his safety and for that of
> other people, I do not think I should be justified if I were

to take any material step without, or especially contrary
to the opinion of the medical men who attend him. [12]

Minto's letter to Captain Duff ends with an invitation, which
is also a reminder that the Ambassador had quite a full agenda
without a deranged Highland chief on his hands:

I hope you will dine here today exactly at three – you
will meet Lord Nelson and Dr. Hallifax.

Admiral Nelson, Lord Hamilton, lately Ambassador to the
Neapolitan Court, and Emma, Lady Hamilton, Nelson's mistress,
were passing through Vienna on their way back to England. Minto,
an enthusiastic admirer of Nelson, had earlier in the year written
to his wife about Nelson's infatuation with Emma Hamilton:

But it is hard to condemn and use ill a hero, as he is in
his own element, for being foolish about a woman
who has art enough to make fools of many wiser than
an admiral. [13]

With the problematical Austrian Empire to keep on the allied
side, with a heroic admiral, a fellow ambassador and the famously
beautiful mistress of one and wife of the other visiting, Lord Minto
could have been forgiven for taking only a passing interest in
Glengarry's condition. Austria had been defeated in June at the
Battle of Marengo in Northern Italy and pressure was mounting
for a separate peace with France – pressure which would become
irresistible after the Austrian catastrophe at Hohenlinden in
Germany in December 1800. It is to his credit that he continued to
find the time to exercise what Angus MacDonald later described
as 'a fatherly charge' over Glengarry.

For most of September matters progressed steadily – Minto
noted in his record of events:

He appears to get gradually better and he was indulged
with a good deal of liberty. He went out when he
pleased, visited his friends, dined with them and was
even a good deal in Society. [14]

However he went on to note that he thought that Glengarry's
condition was still such as to require care but:

. . . having no time to attend to it myself and all his

> attendants being either bribed, or overawed or
> intimidated by him I found it impossible to keep any
> restraint over him.

Towards the end of September Glengarry and Duff called on Minto and the Ambassador asked Glengarry to give instructions to settle the bills that had been incurred. Glengarry refused to do this unless Minto stated that he was at liberty and perfectly capable of managing his own affairs. Minto felt unable to make such a statement (a judgment which subsequent events proved wise) and they parted with Glengarry agreeing to return and discuss the matter further on the next day. Despite their failure to agree Minto noted:

> Nothing insolent or angry passed in this conversation on
> either side.

On leaving the Ambassador Glengarry went for a stroll on a public walk on the outskirts of the town. As he passed the magnificent baroque Karlskirche he was unaccountably seized by a frenzy, mounted up on a statue of an angel holding a crucifix which stands in the porch of the Karslkirche and, drawing a razor from his pocket, hacked at the crucifix. Unsurprisingly, an angry crowd gathered, at which Glengarry cut the buttons off his clothes and threw them at the crowd:

> whom he called the French – and in fine exhibited to
> an immense concourse of people a scene of the
> utmost mania.

The police were called, ten cavalry soldiers were summoned to assist the police, and four men were employed to bring him down from:

> . . . the statue on which he was mounted and where he
> defended himself with a razor.

Glengarry was duly escorted from the Karlskirche to the Narrenturm, the Madmen's Tower, an annexe to the Allgemeines Krankenhaus, the General Hospital of Vienna. This remarkable, purpose-built, cylindrically shaped building of 1784 (now used as the Federal Museum of Pathology and Anatomy) had on its five floors more than 140 individual cells for the incarceration of lunatics.

However, the intervention of his friends resulted in his being released back to his lodgings in the Alstergasse. Minto ordered Dr. Decarro to resume attendance on Glengarry and, if necessary, to use force to restrain him.

What happened next is recounted by Minto in his memorandum:

> The people who attended him were however so much under his influence that this order was not attended to. He was left alone in the room where he slept, the attendants remaining in the adjoining antechamber. In the middle of the night he rose, fastened and barricaded his door. He then fell with a fury on every thing in the room. The prints with their frames were soon destroyed – there was not one article of furnishing of any sort that was not broke and not merely broke but smashed in a thousand pieces.

The Viennese police applied to Minto for authority to remove him from the Alstergasse apartment and confine him in the interests of public safety:

> Having myself experienced the infidelity of those who were charged with the custody of Col. M and whom he had persuaded to think he was a prince descended from the Kings of Scotland and possessing a vast fortune I complied with the desire of the magistrate and consented to his being removed to the Lunatic Hospital.

This time thirteen cavalrymen had to be called to escort Glengarry to the Hospital and also to prevent the mob entering into his house. Clearly the presence of Macdonell at large in the streets of Vienna was becoming a serious threat to public order.

Once again Lord Minto had to contact Angus MacDonald. In a letter dated 29 September 1800 and sent by diplomatic courier he wrote:

> . . . although Col. Macdonell has made so much progress in the recovery from his unhappy malady as to be allowed a good deal of liberty and to have attained hopes of his returning to England without restraint he has unfortunately had so violent a relapse within this last few days and committed acts of such fury, that the police has interfered and I have been obliged to deposit him in the hospital of lunaticks.

> Shocking as such a situation is, it is become absolutely
> necessary, as there are no private establishments of
> that kind at Vienna as in England, and I have found it
> impossible to secure him from danger to himself and
> violence to others, by any mode of superintendance
> that can be procured here . . .

> He did inconceivable damage in his apartments in this
> last fit of violence. I am afraid it will amount to a
> considerable sum. Not an article of furniture nor a
> print, of which there were a great many, framed and
> glazed, has escaped. The expence already incurred
> and for which I shall have to draw will probably be
> about 250£ The expence at present is next to nothing; a
> few shillings a day. He has every indulgence
> respecting food and other comforts that his situation
> admits of but the physician will not hear of his being
> lodged otherwise than the other patients, that is to say
> in one small room, as he cannot otherwise depend on
> securing him. His health in all other points is now
> perfectly good, but his insanity, I am afraid, must be
> considered as confirmed. His family may depend on
> my paying as much attention to him as the duties of
> my office admit of, but I should wish to know whether
> one of his relations proposes to come and take charge
> of him. I concur that some regular and legal
> proceedings would be advisable in order to put his
> affairs at home in a state of proper administration. [15]

After some time Glengarry recovered sufficiently to be moved
from the Narrenturm to the General Hospital. Around this time
he made the acquaintance of an Italian silk manufacturer, a
gentleman blessed with an 'extremely handsome' daughter, and
also of two doctors associated with the General Hospital. Dr. Nord
and another unnamed doctor – 'a native of one of the Venetian
islands' – took a surprising and somewhat different view of
Glengarry's condition. They felt that the Karslkirche incident and
the wrecking of the Alstergasse apartment were insufficient
evidence that Macdonell was in a state of mental derangement
when he was admitted to the Lunatic Asylum. They attributed his
actions to 'Zorn' or rage at suffering loss of liberty and detention
of his papers. Minto suspected that the Italian doctor was in league
with the silk merchant who planned to marry off his 'extremely
handsome' daughter to this supposedly rich scion of the Kings of

Scotland – for such was the story that had circulated about Glengarry's status. Minto rather bitterly wrote:

> To Dr. Nord I impute only extreme dullness and an
> extraordinary degree of weakness which made him
> the dupe of the other. This was the more easy as he
> did not understand a word of any language that
> Col. M. spoke and had no means of judging the state
> of his mind. [16]

The weight of medical opinion certainly was on Minto's side – Decarro, Hallifax and the Director of the General Hospital Dr. Frank all concluded that Glengarry had been a danger to himself and others.

Despite Minto's requests that some member of the Macdonell family should come to Vienna and take charge of their ailing kinsman nothing very positive happened. The unfortunate Angus MacDonald, caught between Minto and Glengarry's nearer family, wrote to the Ambassador on 22 October acknowledging Minto's letter of 29 September (quoted above):

> . . . a copy of which I have sent to Colonel Macdonell's
> uncle and likewise to his man of business in Edinburgh
> who seem to give themselves but little concern
> respecting his unfortunate situation, and are desirous of
> heaping both the trouble and expences upon me. . .

However steps were being taken in both Vienna and the United Kingdom to find a solution to the problem. A Scottish doctor, travelling through Vienna on his way to Italy, a Dr. Charles MacLean, was prevailed upon by Minto to agree to change his travel plans and escort Glengarry back to England. At home there had been some stirring on the part of Coll MacDonald – he wrote to Glengarry on 24 October a tactful letter which put the best possible construction on the affair and regretted that he was:

> . . . indisposed in consequence of the fatigue suffered on
> your journey from Trieste. I hope this will find you much
> recovered and as a proof of your recovery that you will
> write me with your own hand two or three lines
> acknowledging receipt of this letter.
>
> I have been lately at Glengarry where everything goes
> on finely. The Chaplain of the Glengarry Regiment

> will I hope visit you soon at Vienna and accompany
> you to this country.

Coll MacDonald's request for two or three lines in Glengarry's own hand was presumably an attempt to establish exactly how mentally incompetent the chief was and whether steps should be taken to arrange for legal guardianship of his affairs. His letter was sent under cover to Minto and gave the Ambassador permission to withhold it if he considered it would be prejudicial to Glengarry's health, so he clearly knew that there was more amiss than a simple indisposition due to fatigue. In the event his letter reached Vienna after Glengarry's departure. At the same time Coll wrote to Saunders, Glengarry's servant:

> I will never forgive you for not writing to me regarding
> the health of Glengarry. The only way you can make up
> for it is to write on receipt the particulars of the present
> situation – the cause of the complaint so far as you know
> – and particularly say if he had been taking Mercury or
> any other medicine.

Saunders had in fact been sent home earlier, because Glengarry had developed an irrational dislike for him. Coll's enquiry about the cause of the complaint and whether Macdonell had been taking mercury suggests that he assumed the cause of the disease and insanity was venereal – mercury was the standard treatment for syphillis until the introduction of the potassium iodine treatment in the 1830s.

Donald Macdonell, commanding the Glengarry Fencibles at Galway, wrote to Minto on November 4, thanking him, as a relative of the Colonel, for his care of Glengarry and confirming that the regimental chaplain, the Rev. Alexander Macdonell, a near relative of Glengarry's and one who 'enjoys his entire confidence', was on his way out to Vienna. The chaplain himself wrote to Minto on November 26 from London – which was as far as he had got on his way to Austria – to say that he now understood Glengarry had started on his way back home. A similar letter, dated November 27, came from Glengarry's youngest brother, Somerled, who had obtained Admiralty leave to quit his ship and travel to Vienna to care for his brother. It would seem that the family had started to take matters seriously only after the Karlskirche incident – but too late to be of any assistance to Glengarry who left Vienna in early November, travelling by Prague and Berlin, and had reached Hamburg by 29 November.

However the work of clearing up after Glengarry would continue for many months and the paperwork, carefully preserved by Minto, gives much detail of the turmoil Glengarry caused during his stay in Vienna. Some of the accounts are for trivial amounts – although few gentlemen on the Grand Tour can have incurred a bill for 6 florins 40 kreutzer for :

> 10 cavalry soldiers called to escort him from the St.
> Charles Church to the madhouse and from the
> madhouse to his lodgings.

Fewer still can have occasioned the production of a document such as the 'Inventaire des effets brisés dans un accés de delire par Monsieur le Colonel de Macdonell dans son quartiers aux faubourg nommé Alstergasse No. 122' – that is an Inventory of goods broken during a fit of delirium by Colonel Macdonell of Glengarry in his apartments at the suburb named 122 Alstergasse. This bill included 300 florins for the repairs to 134 framed prints (those haunts of witches and sorcerers) smashed by Macdonell and for repair or replacement of a long list of furnishings and fittings.

Minto wrote in his account of the episode that he had made such a full record because of the financial problems arising from the case and because he felt there was a:

> . . . design also to cast on me some very black and
> diabolical imputations . . . But I own I have been
> surprised to learn that any member of his family would
> forget the honour of their relation so far as to support
> him in this attempt to defraud the friends who have
> served him at their own risk and at the same time to
> blacken the character of one who has certainly been his
> benefactor.

Macdonell's expenses, Minto reported to Angus MacDonald, would hopefully not exceed £400 – in fact once everything was added up they came to £510. In addition, Dr. MacLean, who escorted Glengarry back to England, was to receive £100 for his services and as compensation for his inconvenience.

On December 3 Angus MacDonald wrote to Glengarry seeking settlement of outstanding accounts – £835.10.2 owed to his firm on Glengarry's personal and clothing accounts. Due to this sum being outstanding he had felt that he could not put Minto's bills through the firm and had dealt with them on his own personal account and now asked Glengarry for settlement of the £510. He advised Glengarry, who was evidently repudiating his debts and obligations, to pay MacLean:

> . . . in a handsome manner and agreeable to the tenor of Lord Minto's letter to me . . . For my own part I shall write to his Lordship specifying that you directed me not paying Dr. MacLean but if his Lordship should draw Bills on me on that or any other Account in which I consider my honor engaged I shall certainly pay them.

Angus MacDonald was clearly at the end of his patience with Glengarry and went on to write:

> I have repeatedly drawn on myself the censure of my relations and friends for having taken concern in your affairs and as it has in many instances been very prejudicial to my Interest you will readily excuse me if I decline acting for you hereafter. . .

On December 16 Glengarry wrote to Angus MacDonald:

> I have never empowered you to answer any drafts upon me either to Lord Minto or any other without written order to that effect but as you well know have verbally and by letter uniformly directed a different line of conduct to be observed . . .

The 'assistance or kindness' Thomas Grenville anticipated that Minto might do Glengarry at Vienna had turned out to be considerably greater, and considerably less appreciated, than either Ambassador might have expected. The great adventure of the Grand Tour had ended in illness, insanity and a morass of recriminations and bitterness. Were it not for the survival of the letters and documents in the Minto Papers there would be little or no evidence for this period of fifteen or sixteen months in Glengarry's life. There does not appear to be any reference to his travels in his later correspondence and it may well be concluded that he sought to draw a veil over this period. For a man with a great pride in his physical strength and prowess, the memory of a debilitating illness, confinement and the loss of reason would surely have been a bitter one.

Glengarry was back in England by early December 1800. Around October/November 1801 he ordered a survey of his estate. No documents have been found covering the period between December 1800 and October 1801 – whether this period included any further medical treatment or whether he lived quietly on his estate is not known.

CHAPTER 7

The Volunteers

*. . .the Corps is composed of a body of real
Highlanders, unmixed in every respect. . .*

In March 1802, Britain and France concluded the Treaty of
Amiens, bringing to an end a war that had lasted for over nine
years. Most of Britain's territorial gains from the conflict in Europe
and round the world were to be handed back to France or her
allies and the nation's defences were swiftly reduced to a peacetime
footing.

The regiment Glengarry had raised and, for a time, commanded was a victim of this peacetime retrenchment. Despite their
excellent record in Ireland the Glengarry Fencibles were brought
back to Scotland and demobilised at Ayr on 1st July. Forty four
Scottish regiments met a similar fate in 1802. Whatever difficulties
there might have been in the past, the history of the unit under the
command of Lieutenant-Colonel Donald Macdonell was a good
one and a good atmosphere evidently prevailed within the
regiment. As the *Glasgow Courier* reported:

> In acknowledgement of their high regard for their
> Officers, the privates, after they were disembodied,
> procured carriages in which they drew their Officers
> through the streets of the town to their quarters. Officers
> and men expressed equal satisfaction in the connection
> which has subsisted between them and perfect readiness
> to renew that connection at any future period should the
> service of their country require it. [1]

All the officers and men were discharged, with Lieutenant Colonel
Macdonell being placed on half-pay.

There were few opportunities for several hundred men of
military age to resettle in the Highlands. Glengarry's earlier pledge,

reported by the Rev. Alexander Macdonell, to find land for all who joined his regiment seemed unlikely to be fulfilled. Indeed, Glengarry's mind was probably turning more to reducing the numbers of his tenantry than increasing it. The economy would take time to recover from the disruption of war and create renewed opportunities for factory work in Glasgow and the industrial lowlands, the area where many of the Glengarries had been recruited. The men of the Glengarry Fencibles were just one small part of a major social problem – around 30,000 men would have been released onto the labour market by the disbandment of the Scottish fencible and regular regiments.

Alexander Macdonell, the Regimental Chaplain, planned a mass emigration of members of the Regiment, their families and dependants to Upper Canada and travelled to London to negotiate a grant of land with the Prime Minister, Henry Addington. After some false starts in which land in Trinidad (captured from the Spanish in the late war and retained by Britain under the Treaty of Amiens) was offered, in March 1803 an order, granting each emigrant family two hundred acres of land, was signed.

The plan was met with opposition by landed interests in the Highlands, concerned about the loss of manpower in that area. Glengarry had earlier expressed serious concerns about the dangers of Highland depopulation in a letter to the Home Secretary, Lord Pelham:

> . . . it is my opinion, from the disposition to emigrate that now prevails in this quarter, if the Government or the Legislature do not speedily & decisively interpose, the Highlands will be depopulated. [2]

The problem of the redundant Glengarries could probably have been solved, at least in the short term, by a return to the colours. In May 1803 the Peace of Amiens broke down and Britain and France were again at war. Britain, faced with Napoleon's refusal to honour the Amiens treaty obligations, plunged into rearmament, enlistment and another round of colonial wars designed to recapture the bases and territories which had been surrendered just a year earlier.

At home measures were taken for the defence of Britain and

in June 1803 the 4th Inverness Volunteer Battalion was formed with Glengarry as Colonel. This battalion drew its strength from the Glengarry, Morar and Letterfindlay areas of Western Inverness-shire. In September 1803 in a General Return of Volunteer Infantry for Inverness-shire the Lord Lieutenant of the county, Sir James Grant of Grant, reported that the battalion would have a total authorised strength of 369 private soldiers, 427 all ranks. Four of the six companies would be raised from the Glengarry area. The Lord Lieutenant noted:

> The four companies which were allocated to Glengarry of the Glengarry, Morar & Letterfindlay Battalion have not yet been reported owing first to Mr. Macdonell of Glengarry having been at Edinburgh and then to his being ill but I expect to hear in a few days time that he has completed the inrollment & have sent him the form of Return. [3]

The terms of service of the Volunteers were that they:

> . . . enrolled to serve within the Northern Military District and in case of invasion to march to any part of Great Britain.

Most of Glengarry's company commanders in the Glengarry, Morar and Letterfindlay battalion were veterans of the old Glengarry Fencibles. The regimental adjutant was Alexander Macdonell at Kinloch, also late of the Glengarry Fencibles.

Battalion strength Volunteer units were to be commanded by a Lieutenant Colonel, a ruling which posed difficulties of status for the ever sensitive Glengarry. On 6th October 1803 the Lord Lieutenant was obliged to write to Charles Yorke, the newly appointed Home Secretary that:

> Alex. Macdonell Esq. of Glengarry . . . declined taking command of the Glengarry, Morar & Letterfindlay Volunteer Battalion unless he got the rank of Colonel, having enjoyed that rank in His Majesty's service.

Grant was in something of a difficulty. He felt unable to authorise a full Colonel's commission for what was a small battalion, considerably below the strength of a normal line unit. He was also conscious that if Glengarry's ambition to retain his Colonel's rank was to be granted then others, in similar positions, would wish equal treatment – Donald Cameron of Lochiel, another of the

Volunteer Battalion commanders, was specifically named in Grant's letter to Yorke. Sir James Grant had, of course, been the Colonel of the Grant Fencibles, in which Glengarry had briefly, if controversially, served in the earlier war, and had also been one of the trustees or curators on Glengarry's estate during his minority. Sir James thus knew Glengarry's strengths and weaknesses as few others could. It is noticeable that more correspondence survives in the Home Office Militia Correspondence files relating to Glengarry's battalion than to any of the other Inverness-shire units; Glengarry was not the easiest subordinate for Sir James to have.

The Home Office granted permission for both Lochiel and Glengarry to retain their Colonel's rank and in November the establishment of the battalion was reported with Alexander MacDonald of Glencoe as Lieutenant Colonel and Coll Macdonell of Barrisdale as Major and officer commanding the 3rd Company. He replaced, in this latter role, Ronald Macdonell who had failed to raise his quota of men. By the year end the Glengarry, Morar and Letterfindlay Volunteers were at full strength and ready to face foreign foe or civil commotion. Some minor irritations inevitably existed; the *London Gazette* had gazetted Glengarry as Alexander Macdonald not Macdonell and the Lord Lieutenant had to write to London to ensure that this error was not repeated in the commission documents.

The problems of part-time Highland soldiering were touched upon in a letter from Glengarry to the Lord Lieutenant in March 1804 when he indicated that no offer of service on permanent pay and duty could be looked for from his men until the various crops were safely planted. This statement evokes memories of older Highland armies, who were unavailable for service at seed time and harvest. Despite the problems of combining agricultural work with a military career and however unwilling the Glengarry, Morar and Letterfindlay men might be to sign up for permanent service and thus leave their wives and families to do the heavy work of the land on their own, Glengarry had no fears of their enthusiasm and patriotism. He asserted that they would prove:

> . . . equally eager in regaining Discipline, as Gallant in assault on an invading Foe, should he dare to touch our sacred Shores. [4]

Some indication of quite how effective the battalion might be in dealing with 'an invading Foe' is given in an inspection report in 1805. The state of their clothes was described as good but it was noted that there were only thirty seven sets of cross belts in the Corps. The more important issue of the state of discipline and effectiveness was the subject of a mixed report. The Inspecting Officer noted 'great progress since last inspection' but concluded that they were 'not yet fit to act with the line' – that is to take their place alongside full-time troops of the regiments of the line.

This report was in fact the least satisfactory one out of all of the mainland units of the Inverness-shire Volunteers. Most of the others were either declared fit to act with troops of the line or 'serviceable.' [5] The scattered recruitment area of the 4th Battalion may perhaps have played a part in this disappointing report. The other two battalion-sized detachments – the Culloden and Fort William units – drew their strength from more densely settled areas of Inverness-shire.

The system of inspection of the Volunteer units by Field Officers of the regular army was an important means of bringing these units up to an acceptable level of efficiency. In addition it was undoubtedly a valuable aid to unit morale, confirming as it did the value and seriousness of their service and the importance of the Volunteer Movement in the eyes of the military establishment.

In 1805 Glengarry was obliged to write to the Inspecting Officer with a complaint about two of his company commanders who were refusing to bring their companies forward for the period of Permanent Duty. He complained that:

> . . . the grounds upon which they refuse appear to me so
> frivolous that I suspect their plans have been concerted
> together, the other officers and men of the Battalion
> having come forward with their usual alacrity. [6]

In 1806 new regulations were introduced for Volunteer Infantry and in September of that year Glengarry was able to report to the Lord Lieutenant that his battalion had unanimously agreed to serve under the new regulations. The Government continued to have concerns about the value of Volunteers and in particular their use, by many, as a way of avoiding the ballot for the Militia and the regular army. In 1808 Viscount Castlereagh, as Secretary for War, introduced an Act establishing a Local Militia. This new force, with limited service obligations, sought to incorporate the Volunteers. The Government's intention was that the efficient Volunteer units would transfer to the Local Militia while inefficient units would be disbanded and their redundant personnel made available for balloting to fill the original militia and the regular army. A bounty of two guineas would be paid to all Volunteers transferring to the Local Militia.

In January 1809 Grant wrote to the Home Office recommending that the 2nd Battalion Inverness-shire Local Militia be formed out of the former Glengarry, Morar & Letterfindlay and Fort William Volunteer Battalions and that Glengarry be appointed Colonel with the former commander of the Fort William battalion, John Cameron, as Lieutenant Colonel. Grant obviously felt confident in confirming Glengarry as a full Colonel for he wrote to Lord Liverpool, the Home Secretary:

> Although the Establishment of this Regiment as transmitted by your Lordship does not specify an officer with the rank of Colonel yet as Col. Macdonell held that rank last War and likewise during the present War since he commanded the Glengarry etc. Volunteer Battalion; and as the Local Militia Act in such cases admits of the rank of Colonel being given I flatter myself His Majesty will graciously allow it Col. Macdonell. [7]

As soon as he was confirmed in his command, with Colonel's rank, Glengarry raised a question that was always close to his heart – that of Highland dress. Grant forwarded a letter to the Home Secretary from Glengarry seeking the King's approval for outfitting his battalion in Highland dress:

> I am anxious previous to a final arrangement with the clothiers to obtain permission to give the Battalion their National Garb, for which the predilection of real Highlanders (of which this Corps is entirely composed) is well known – I make this application which I beg of you to forward with your recommendation from a knowledge that it is their ardent wish and will contribute substantially to that National Spirit which distinguishes the Highlander *under his Native Garb* in the Battles of his Country.

PS I am led to think these sentiments congenial to the other three L[ocal] M[ilitia] Regts. in the County having learned as much *indirectly* from all of them.

Later that year, and before an answer had been received regarding the Highland dress question, his concern grew more acute over the consequences of the threatened imposition of standard military uniform on the Highland Local Militia. Glengarry wrote to the Home Secretary, enclosing a memorial on behalf of himself and his battalion. He assured Lord Liverpool that:

> The men comprising this fine Regiment are native Highlanders and tho' as Loyal subjects as any in Great Britain and as ready to stand forward in the cause of their King and Country, they are unquestionably chagrined at the idea of being deprived of their National Garb (the Highland Uniform) . . . the Corps is composed of a Body of real Highlanders, unmixed in every aspect; that the greater part of them have worn no other than the Highland Dress since their infancy, and that tho' a Loyal Spirit and Inclination is congenial to them, yet it must be allowed that the Dress had some attraction in bringing them into the Volunteer Establishment, where the Highland Garb was their Uniform, and from which Establishment they transferred their services into the new Local Militia, with an expectation that they should be indulged in their Native Dress. That being *obliged* to put on Breeches is very unwelcome, and *to them* a much regretted inconvenience.

The Home Office capitulated in the face of Glengarry's assault and within a month Colonel Fraser of Lovat, commanding the 1st Battalion of Inverness-shire Local Militia, was seeking the same privilege:

> . . . as the 2nd Regiment of Local Militia of this Shire have with great propriety been favoured with leave to wear the native dress of their country.

1809 also saw the start of a long-running dispute between Glengarry and some of the permanent staff officers of his battalion. This first manifested itself in a conflict with one of the two adjutants. Adjutant Cameron (late of the Fort William Volunteers) attracted Glengarry's displeasure in May 1809. The Colonel had engaged, at his own expense, a drill sergeant from a line regiment, who had learned his trade under the famous General Sir John Moore. Moore's camp at Shornecliffe had revolutionised the training and tactics of light infantry. Moore himself had been killed at the retreat to Corunna in January 1809 – the incident immortalised in Charles Wolfe's poem *The Burial of Sir John Moore after Corunna:*

> Not a drum was heard, not a funeral note,
> As his corse to the rampart we hurried . . .

– but his reputation as an innovative trainer of troops, and indeed as a national hero, was still riding high. Glengarry clearly felt that he had achieved something of a coup by acquiring the services of an experienced, non-commissioned officer who had worked at Shornecliffe Camp under the great Moore's supervision. The appointment of this sergeant, at his own expense, does indicate Glengarry's military enthusiasm and his undoubted commitment to his unit's efficiency.

Glengarry had instructed all his officers to attend the drills to be conducted by this expert NCO and he:

> . . . personally set them the example sticking to it for
> four weeks (without missing one drill).

Despite the Colonel's orders and fine example Adjutant Cameron refused to practise drill and seemed unwilling to take orders from anyone but a commissioned officer.

In 1811 Glengarry commenced a sustained campaign to rid himself of his two troublesome adjutants. A letter of 23 September from Glengarry House, to an unidentified recipient (possibly the Military Secretary to the Commander in Chief):

> Sir
> In cases of peculiar mischief and emergency strong
> and summary measures are resorted to and justified.
> And upon this data I have now the honour to
> address you – soliciting, most earnestly, soliciting the
> removal of two Staff Officers, both adjutants, from
> the 2nd Batt. of Inverness-shire Militia under my
> immediate command. Granting me permission either
> to recommend (through the proper channels) an
> officer qualified to fill that situation with advantage

to the service, or otherwise appoint one, so qualified, from any Regiment of the Line in their room.

The ground upon which I advance this claim is briefly laid in a letter from me to His Majesty's Lieutenant for Inverness-shire of date 8th curt. and I this day write Col. Grant to request he may communicate it for the consideration of HM's Secretary of State. And finding two of the Permanent Sergeants are already subborned (*sic*) by them I beg permission to add that unless this representation meets with a ready ear I can not consider myself longer answerable for the consequences of delay. [8]

Colonel Grant, the new Lord Lieutenant, the son of Sir James Grant (who had resigned the Lieutenancy in 1809), forwarded to Richard Ryder, the Home Secretary, a bundle of correspondence on the case. Counter charges had been laid by the Adjutants outlining their grievances against Glengarry – these included the transfer of the battalion depot from Fort William to Fort Augustus, the distance involved in travelling to musters, the employment of the drill sergeant, and various financial irregularities regarding accounts and shoes.

Glengarry's correspondence with the Lord Lieutenant was forwarded to London. This included his comment (dated 7th September 1811) that the case was:

... nothing less than that both Adjutants have conspired together to form a combination among the Permanents egging them up to groundless discontents and complaints by giving them universally to believe that they are oppressed by being obliged to store up (or clean when dirty) the arms, accoutrements and clothing of their companies. . .

The 'Permanents' being the full time Sergeants who formed the administrative staff of the battalion.

A fortnight later he wrote again in an even more colourful manner:

They have suborned to their Diabolical Measures two of the permanent Sergeants – figure then my situation without an effective staff or any aid beyond eight

sergeants and perhaps even those not all to be relied
upon against mutinous and turbulent hands.

Even accepting that the Adjutants were guilty of disloyalty
and insubordination, 'Diabolical Measures' seems a rather extreme
turn of phrase. Quite what the evidence might be for the unit being
riddled with 'mutinous and turbulent hands' is unclear but in
October Glengarry wrote to the Lord Lieutenant:

> . . . you will see with what duplicity and how undutifully
> both as an officer and a man Adjutant Cameron has acted
> by me. Adjutant Macdonell, I may venture to affirm, will
> be fully implicated in every step and part taken by
> Adjutant Cameron. . .

Despite some reluctance on the Lord Lieutenant's part to see
matters pushed to a trial, probably due to a desire to avoid a
distasteful episode which would reflect adversely on the Inverness-
shire Militia as a whole, Court Martial papers were prepared
against Adjutants Cameron and Macdonell. They appeared for
Court Martial at Edinburgh Castle on 16th April 1812 each charged
'with various irregularities in the discharge of his duties' and were
found guilty. Cameron was sentenced to be cashiered (that is
dismissed the service) while Macdonell was sentenced to a lesser
penalty 'to be dismissed from the 2nd Inverness Local Militia' [9] –
which theoretically meant that he could take up another army
appointment, if anyone could be found to take on an officer with
such a blemish on his record.

The case of Adjutant Macdonell was the more embarrassing
as he was related by marriage to Glengarry and there would seem
to have been some family disputes mixed in with the service issues.
In 1814 ex-Adjutant Macdonell wrote to the Prince Regent asking
the Prince to secure him a military appointment, and pointing out
that the Court Martial had only dismissed him from the Inverness-
shire Militia, not cashiered him. In this letter he referred to 'some
private family difference' and to his having 'used all the
conciliating means in his power which proved fruitless.' [10]

Glengarry, for all his undoubted enthusiasm and commitment,
seems, chiefly, to have considered his own convenience in making
arrangements for the regiment. In 1810 he had proposed to the

Lord Lieutenant that the unit's headquarters be moved from Fort William to Fort Augustus – conveniently close to his home at Invergarry House. He made the case to Grant that:

> As a home for the Arms and Clothing it is more convenient and being so immediately in the vicinity of my own residence, I can give that attention to their care, which otherwise they would not have the benefit of. You are aware Sir, that I have applied for permission to do the portion of Permanent Duty allotted to us in Nairn this season; but at some future period Fort Augustus may answer every purpose, as it has the advantage of a good drill ground, which cannot be found at Fort William. [11]

There was undoubtedly truth in what Glengarry wrote, but the transfer of headquarters from the larger community and commercial centre of Fort William to the much smaller rural backwater of Fort Augustus, some thirty miles away, undoubtedly inconvenienced many members of the regiment. Robert Smith, a Fort William surgeon who also served as surgeon to the 2nd Battalion, submitted his resignation in 1811 due to this removal of the headquarters from Fort William and to the location of the summer camp at Inverness. The travelling involved took him too far away from his civilian practice. In a revealing section of his letter of resignation he casts some light on Glengarry's high-handed approach:

> Upwards of two years ago I had the honour of being appointed to be Surgeon to the 2nd Inverness-shire Local Militia in consequence of your recommendation for which I felt exceedingly grateful. You procured my appointment to that office without consulting my inclinations . . . [12]

He went on to say that as no one else was available he had felt it his duty to accept the post.

Once rid of his two troublesome adjutants Glengarry sought the appointment of Lieutenant Charles Morgan of the 13th Foot as Captain & Adjutant. Morgan came highly recommended by Glengarry's brother, James, now a Lieutenant Colonel in the Coldstream Guards.

Adjutants Cameron and Macdonell were not the only staff

officers who crossed Glengarry's path. In 1813 he had occasion to write to the Home Secretary about Quartermaster MacPherson's 'culpable apathy and neglect' and was successful in obtaining his dismissal. This measure provoked MacPherson to write to the Home Office:

> . . . I am totally unacquainted with the nature of the
> complaint exhibited against me by the Colonel, nor am I
> conscious of having incurred his displeasure by any part
> of my conduct. [13]

Which hardly squared with Glengarry's letter to the Home Secretary, Lord Sidmouth, in May 1813 claiming that it would be impossible for MacPherson to account satisfactorily for his conduct and noting:

> . . . shortcomings of arms and accoutrements, the
> unfinished state of his accounts and intromissions . . . the
> most culpable apathy and neglect in every branch of his
> duty. [14]

Sidmouth replied in June, advising that it was the Prince Regent's pleasure that Mr. MacPherson be 'displaced from his situation in that Regiment.'

In the winter of 1813/14 Local Militia units were asked to volunteer for service outwith their normal area. In January 1814 Glengarry wrote offering his battalion's services:

> to garrison Edinburgh Castle; or to do garrison duty in
> any other fortification northwards, within this island,
> should occasion be found for accepting our services
> during the current year in consequence of zeal
> manifested by any regular militia regiment serving in
> Scotland or any change that may take place in the
> employment of His Majesty's Regular Forces now
> serving in North Britain. [15]

North Britain was at this time the usual official term for Scotland – the army commander in Scotland, for example being described as commanding His Majesty's Forces in North Britain. There is less evidence for the term South Britain being widely used to describe England.

The annual commitment for the rank and file members of the

2nd Inverness-shire Local Militia was for twenty eight days training each year. This was chiefly made up of an annual summer camp when the unit came together for a period of approximately three weeks 'permanent duty' – usually at Inverness.

In 1810 the annual service arrangements were typical: the permanent NCOs and drummers would assemble at Invergarry on 18th June, being joined by the balance of the battalion on Monday 25th June. They would then march the thirty eight miles to Inverness in two days and remain there for training and exercise for a fortnight. The *Inverness Journal* reported the corps to consist of between 700 and 800 men, and told its readers that there was:

> . . . not a man in it who did not understand and speak
> the Gaelic language, and indeed prefer it to any other. [16]

A fortnight later the *Journal* was able to tell of 'a handsome stand of colours, given by Glengarry' being presented to the Regiment by Mrs Chisholm of Chisholm (Glengarry's sister Elizabeth.)

The Local Militia could be called into active service not only to deal with foreign invasion but to cope with civil unrest. The Act establishing the Local Militia authorised the Lieutenancy of the County:

> . . . to call out and assemble the Local Militia, or any part
> of the Local Militia, of any County or Stewartry, for the
> Suppression of any Riots or Tumults in such County or
> Stewartry. . . [17]

for a period of not more than fourteen days in a year.

Glengarry's men do not appear ever to have been used in this way – but the idea was certainly one which had an attraction for Macdonell. In 1819, long after the Local Militia had been stood down, there were concerns over reform agitation. The Peterloo Massacre of August 1819, when an 80,000 strong pro-reform demonstration in Manchester was brutally charged down by Yeomanry Cavalry with the loss of eleven lives and four hundred injuries, was a controversial example of the use of volunteer forces in the support to the civil power role. Rumours of conspiracy and insurrection abounded with Glasgow and central Scotland being seen as particularly likely centres for trouble. A series of strikes and demonstrations culminating in a small and ineffective armed rising, the so-called Radical War, ended with a skirmish between the insurrectionists and troops at Bonnymuir, Stirlingshire in April 1820. In January 1820 Glengarry wrote, enthusiastically if not entirely coherently, to Viscount Melville. Melville was at this time First Lord of the Admiralty, Lord Privy Seal for Scotland, and, more significantly for Glengarry, the current representative of the Dundas dynasty in its role as Government manager in Scotland. Glengarry had always claimed client status with Melville's father, the first Viscount, the former Henry Dundas, and re-asserts his links with the Dundases in this letter. Glengarry's political conservatism may be deduced from his enthusiasm to take up arms against the reformers.

> My dear Lord
> I was duly honoured by receipt of your letter of the 7th Ultimo. and am happy to find my communication of the 22nd November approved of by your Lordship, tho' the services thereby tendered were not required. The fact is, that matters at that time were said to be in a much more alarming state in Glasgow and its neighbourhood than now appears to have been the case: And on that account I was ready had my offer been accepted to have step'd that far out of my way, to meet the Local Danger which you and your colleagues had put easier down than was then imagined to be practicable, by the means of ordinary measures.
> I have since then, as senior officer of Local Militia in Inverness-shire been expecting orders, but, as reasons of State Policy may induce His Majesty's Government to prefer the Tenders of Individuals, to giving a general call upon any description of Force, I beg leave to add that I and my People are at all times as ready as Ever! when their service may be deemed useful, and in any manner of way – which feeling I think it my duty to signify to Viscount Sidmouth, as Secretary of State for the Home Department by letter of this date – And as my services always received the unqualified approbation of the late Lord Melville so far back even as 1794-5, so we trust we shall continue to merit and enjoy that of the present Viscount's; should anything be found for us to do. [18]

Glengarry's feud with his adjutants, his unhappiness over the performance of Quartermaster MacPherson, the dispute with

Surgeon Smith perhaps suggest an unhappy unit at loggerheads with its Commanding Officer. There is undoubtedly some truth in this, but it is probably not the whole truth.

Glengarry was without question a difficult man. Sir Walter Scott summed him up in his Journal when he wrote, in 1826:

> This gentleman is a kind of Quixote in our age, having retained, in their full extent, the whole feelings of clanship and chieftainship, elsewhere so long abandoned. He seems to have lived a century too late, and to exist, in a state of complete law and order, like a Glengarry of old, whose will was law to his sept. Warm-hearted, generous, friendly, he is beloved by those who know him, and his efforts are unceasing to show kindness to those of his clan who are disposed fully to admit his pretensions. To dispute them is to incur his resentment, which has sometimes broken out in acts of violence which have brought him in collision with the law. [19]

Glengarry treated his Regiment as an extension of his household and clan, and if the members of the Regiment would, in Scott's phrase, 'admit his pretensions', then all was well – if not, trouble loomed. Of course, matters were perhaps simplified by so many of the officers being members of cadet branches of the house of Macdonell. Or, perhaps, the knowledge that they would have a continuing relationship with Glengarry after their militia service was over might have induced many of his officers to acquiesce in Glengarry's actions and policies, whatever private reservations there might have been.

In fairness it should also be said that army regiments in that period were very much the private property of their Colonels and Glengarry's possessive approach and unwillingness to be crossed in any way would have been much less remarkable in the early nineteenth century than in the modern world. Highland regiments in particular, with their local loyalties and local recruitment, their clan affiliations and traditions, were in some senses like an extended family. Glengarry would seem to have been at ease in the paternalistic, if autocratic, role that this ethos implied rather than in any more modern managerial or professional command role.

There are certainly instances of good feeling between the officers and their Colonel, to set against the feuding and bickering. In 1804, for example, the officers of the 4th Inverness-shire Volunteers presented Glengarry with a broadsword, dating from the period of the 1745 Jacobite Rising, a gesture which would surely not have been made to an entirely unpopular or unworthy commander.

Service in the ranks of the local militia attracted many and Glengarry evidently had little trouble filling his ranks, as a sad episode, recorded in the *Inverness Journal*, indicates.

> A number of young men attended the Glengarry
> regiment of Local Militia to this place as volunteers in
> the expectation of being brought on the strength of the
> battalion but it unfortunately happened that many were
> rejected, there being no vacancies to fill, one of these,
> who it is conjectured, had exhausted his little means
> during his stay in hope of being received, and whose
> pride would not allow him to beg, was found dead on
> the road on his return homeward. [20]

Glengarry's prickly nature was well displayed in a controversy over emigration in 1813. The 5th Earl of Selkirk, who had started a programme of large-scale emigration from the Highlands to Canada in 1803 was organising another and set his sights on men in Glengarry's regiment. Selkirk's migration scheme was a military one – he proposed to raise a regiment for the defence of the Canadian colonies against the threat of the United States of America. Britain and the United States were at this time at war with each other and concerns were felt about the security of the vast, if under-populated, British territories in Canada. Selkirk's attempted poaching of his men would have been sure to enrage Glengarry but matters were made worse by his former Adjutant, Alexander Macdonell, turning up like a bad penny. Glengarry, writing from his summer home, Inverie in Knoydart, wrote to Lord Sidmouth, the Home Secretary:

> Just as I was leaving Glengarry for this, I heard it
> whispered that Lord Selkirk had received permission or
> was (on what grounds I know not) raising a Regiment
> for America, and that Alexr. Macdonell, lately
> discharged, by Court Martial as Adjutant in the 2nd

Regt. of Inverness-shire Local Militia was appointed
Quarter Master in the Earl of Selkirk's levy. . . That many
of the Local Militia men now in my Regiment were led
into the snare and that the reduced Adjutant was
singularly active in those underhand manoeuvres not
intended for my ears. . . [21]

Glengarry goes on to say that, in the absence of Adjutant
Morgan, he ordered the Sergeant Major and the permanent
sergeants to attend the meeting and to:

. . . signify my objections to any interference with the
attested men of the 2nd Regt. of Inverness-shire Local
Militia as I conceived them to be bound for four years
longer or to enter His Majesty's Service in less
objectionable shape. This however was disregarded on
the part of Lord Selkirk whose agents said they would
take their risk of all consequences and advanced money
notwithstanding the protests . . . even openly told the
Sergeant Major, who is uncle to the reduced Adjutant,
that they believed they could take him, or any one of the
Permanents, if he or they chose to incline so. Many, I am
credibly informed, of the Local Militia under my
immediate command were accordingly engaged but
from the clandestine manner in which it was arranged I
cannot ascertain the numbers. . .

The problems of Highland soldiering become more evident
when family relationships cut across the military chain of
command. The position of the Sergeant Major is hardly an enviable
one. His nephew, a commissioned officer, having been dismissed
the regiment, he has to attend the meeting to convey the Colonel's
objections to Selkirk's scheme.

Glengarry was not prepared to accept this situation and
advised the Home Secretary:

Many of the names given me are the Flower of the Youth
and it is said that a second Migration is already projected
by them for the Married Men next season. Under these
circumstances My Lord, and in the absence of His
Majesty's Lieutenant, I shall by this express order
Captain & Adjutant Charles Morgan, in whose zeal and
activity I have every confidence, to consult the Vice
Lieutenant of Inverness-shire on how to proceed and I
will authorise him to obstruct the measure they are

> carrying on *viz.* applying to the Commanding Officer at
> Fort George for a party sufficient to arrest them at the
> place of embarkation till your Lordship's pleasure shall
> be known regarding them.

Although the answer to Glengarry's letter does not appear in
the Home Office files the nature of it can easily be judged from a
letter Glengarry wrote in September to Lord Sidmouth.

> When I had the honor of addressing your Lordship some
> time ago on the subject of Lord Selkirk's raising men in
> the Highlands, I could perceive by the reply from your
> Lordship's office that His Majesty's Ministers were (at
> least) not averse to the Colonising system.

It might well be felt that if the Government had agreed to
Selkirk raising a regiment for service in Canada the Government
would resent Glengarry's obstruction and would hardly approve
of his calling out the regular army to arrest Selkirk's agents and
their recruits.

However, quick to see which way the wind was blowing,
Glengarry continued:

> Under that impression I therefore address your Lordship
> with proposals of a similar nature: *viz.* to Colonize a
> Regiment of Highlanders from the Mountains and Isles
> of Scotland for the protection of His Majesty's
> possessions in North America.

> The general principals (*sic*) of which I understand are
> already submitted by Lt. Col. Stewart of the Royal W.
> India Rangers and have been favourably received by His
> Royal Highness the Commander in Chief and by the Rt.
> Honble. the Secretary of State.

> Should this tender be approved of by your Lordship I
> shall look for as liberal terms (in every particular) as may
> be granted to any other, and that my Provincial Rank
> will be nothing less than it is in Inverness-shire.

> I consider my zeal and powers to serve my King and
> Country (particularly in this instance) as inferior to none
> and I shall therefore trust to your Lordship's good
> offices, as far as it may be compatible to be allowed to
> retain my present situation at the same time that I fulfil
> my proposed engagements. [22]

In other words Glengarry was now offering to raise a regiment of soldier/settlers for Canada if he was allowed Colonel's rank and could keep on his present appointment while making arrangements for the migration scheme. Glengarry's offer was not taken up.

When, with the defeat of Napoleon in 1814, the Volunteers were stood down Glengarry, who, whatever his faults, always did things handsomely, inserted an advertisement in the *Inverness Journal*, printing the text of the vote of thanks of the Houses of Parliament and prefaced it with his own comments:

> Gentlemen and brother soldiers
> Having received through the directions of His Majesty's
> Lieutenant of the County, the vote of thanks of both
> Houses of Parliament to the Local Militia and Volunteer
> Corps, I embrace (with the greatest pleasure) this mode
> of communicating to you the very high and gratifying
> honour thereby conferred on us, being the most
> flattering testimony of the estimation held of our wishes
> and exertions to serve our King and Country when
> called upon. [23]

The 'Hundred Days', Napoleon's return from Elba in March 1815 culminating in the battle of Waterloo in June, was too short-lived a crisis to bring about a comprehensive remobilisation of the Volunteers. However there is correspondence between Glengarry and the Home Office in April 1815 about plans for erecting a depot in the case of emergency. Glengarry had provided ground for this but his colleagues in the Lieutenancy of Inverness-shire had proved unsympathetic to his plans.

With the coming of peace to Europe and the demobilisation of the Local Militia Glengarry had lost an important part of his life and, perhaps in compensation, threw himself into other activities – such as the Society of True Highlanders.

CHAPTER 8

Glengarry at Home

'. . . intense love of, and pride in, all Highland things . . .'

On the 20th January 1802, in Edinburgh, Colonel Alasdair Ranaldson Macdonell of Glengarry married Rebecca Forbes. Rebecca was the second daughter of Sir William Forbes of Pitsligo. Forbes, a baronet, an Edinburgh banker of great wealth, a man of high social standing and literary tastes was a friend of Dr. Johnson and James Boswell, who noted of him in his *Journal of a Tour to the Hebrides*, that he was:

> . . . a man of whom too much good cannot be said; who, with distinguished abilities and application in his profession of a banker, is at once a good companion and a good Christian – which I think is saying enough. [1]

Forbes was a noted benefactor of many charities in Edinburgh, an advisor to the Government on financial law and practice, and a generous supporter of the Episcopal Church in Edinburgh. He was descended from an old, but decayed, land-owning family in Aberdeenshire and had restored the family fortunes by his success in the business world. He was senior partner in the firm of Sir William Forbes & Sir J H Blair & Company, who operated from premises in Parliament Close.

Rebecca Forbes was twenty two when she married Glengarry and had moved all her life in fashionable Edinburgh society and with her father's considerable wealth and family connections behind her would certainly not have been constrained in her choice of marriage partner. Glengarry, handsome, high spirited, of ancient and distinguished family was an eligible, if not a brilliant, match. The scandal of his duel with MacLeod and trial for murder was now almost four years in the past and the disturbing incident of his bout of insanity in Vienna was now well behind him and had presumably never become public knowledge.

The daughter of a wealthy and well-connected banker was, of course, likely to bring to the marriage a satisfactory dowry.

Rebecca, by marrying Glengarry, was entering into a very different environment from that of her domestic Edinburgh circle and also by marrying Glengarry was taking on a difficult, eccentric and intensely opinionated man with as many enemies as friends. Sir Walter Scott, writing in his journal in 1826 reflected on Glengarry that:

> He was fortunate in marrying a daughter of Sir William Forbes, who, by yielding to his peculiar ideas in general, possesses much deserved influence with him. [2]

This perceptive comment comes from one who had ample opportunity to know the two people involved – and Scott was, in addition, a long-standing friend of the Forbes family.

One of Rebecca's daughters, Louise Christian, left a series of reminiscences of her early life which were published in *Blackwood's Magazine* in 1893 and 1895. These give a vivid impression of life in the Glengarry household as it was experienced by a small child. Louise was born in 1815 and was thus only 13 when her father died and her family's life at Invergarry came to an end.

Allowing for the considerable passage of time between the events and the publication of these memoirs, and with due caution as to those events and personalities that fell outwith her experience, Louise's memoirs give a lively and often charming account of her childhood and provide valuable insights. These glimpses into the character of her parents are perhaps more reliable and accurate than the precise detail of family connections and dates.

In the first extract from her memoirs Louise writes of her mother's culture shock at being translated from urban life in Sir William Forbes house at 39 George Street in Edinburgh's New Town to become chatelaine of an isolated Highland mansion. The isolation of Glengarry House is indicated by the fact that, until the Caledonian Canal was opened up in 1822, coal was unknown in the house and only peat and wood were burned for heating and cooking. The following two tales of Rebecca's early experiences, illustrating the differences between Edinburgh and Inverness-shire life, have something of the air of favourite and oft-repeated family anecdotes:

> On coming to the Highlands she was somewhat
> bewildered by the sort of life she had to lead. Instead of
> going to shops for butcher-meat, whole animals were
> brought into the larder at once; and, that she might really
> understand how to arrange the pieces for use at table,
> she got a sheep cut up exactly as if it had been a bullock.
> The smallness of the sirloins and rounds that this
> produced may be imagined, but she learned her lesson.
> Soon after she went north the housekeeper said she was
> short of needles. To my mother's amazement she heard
> that none could be got nearer than Inverness, forty-two
> miles distant. The needles being an absolute necessity, a
> man with a cart and horse had to be sent for them. [3]

Rebecca's new home was the relatively modern mansion of Glengarry or Invergarry House by Loch Oich, the principal seat of the family and a replacement for the historic Invergarry half a mile away down the loch on Creagan an Fhithich – the Raven's Rock that had given the clan its traditional slogan or war cry. The old castle had been burned and looted by the Duke of Cumberland's troops in 1746.

The domestic problems of the new mistress of Glengarry House were compounded by the summertime move to Inverie in Knoydart at the other end of the Glengarry estate. This annual journey into the 'Rough Bounds of Knoydart,' then, as now, unconnected to the outside world by roads, had something of the quality of an epic. Louise's account gives a flavour of the scale of the expedition:

> We started from Glengarry in our own carriage; twenty-
> seven miles to Loch Hourn head – stopping half-way at
> Tomdown to feed the horses and get something for
> ourselves at the little inn . . . When we reached Loch
> Hourn we got into a large boat rowed by four men,
> generally singing Gaelic songs to keep time. My elder
> sister and I, who had splendid voices, used to sing the
> whole way, each placed on a bench beside one of the
> rowers. After about eight miles of rowing, we arrived at

> Barrisdale, one of our tacksmen's houses where we
> generally spent a night.

The Macdonells of Barrisdale were one of the leading cadet branches of the clan and a Coll Macdonell of Barrisdale had commanded one of the battalions of the Glengarry regiment in the '45.

After a night at Barrisdale on the north coast of the Knoydart peninsula the Glengarry *hegira* continued:

> Immediately after breakfast we all got into the boat again
> to row round to Inverie by Loch Ness.

Which sounds a pleasant enough trip until one realises that this was a thirty mile long voyage in an open boat in potentially dangerous waters. More than just potentially dangerous perhaps: Louise recollected one more than usually difficult passage:

> But on the occasion of my early remembrance there was
> a terrific storm. The maids were groaning and screaming
> with fear, and the men declared that we children must all
> sit in the bottom of the boat. When about half-way, it was
> resolved that we should leave the boat and go across
> country to Inverie . . . I was packed up in a plaid on a
> Highlander's back, and the sister a year younger than I
> was carried by the nurse.

Louise relates that the return journey from the summer home and the sea-bathing at Inverie was often made by land, over the Mam Barrisdale pass (1476 feet), when she and her sister were put in a creel and carried one on each side of a pony the twelve miles across Knoydart. Inverie had been added to by Glengarry and Louise describes this part:

> . . . the dining room, drawing room, and four bedrooms
> were built by my father on the old-fashioned wattled
> system. Magnificent beams of Scotch fir sprang from the
> clay floor to a roof with similar beams. Between the
> beams was regular basket-work of hazel-wood. The
> outside of the walls and the roof were slated. The front
> door opened into this part of the house, and opposite it
> was another door entering into the stone-and-lime part.

In her other *Blackwood's* article Louise describes this as a 'creel-house' and the phrase, with its image of a wicker-work basket used for carrying peats, gives a vivid picture of the nature of the family's summer dwelling. The 'creel house' was, after the Knoydart estate passed out of the Glengarry family's possession, taken down and replaced with a more conventional set of rooms.

Alexander Beith, Minister of Glenelg, writing the account of his parish for the New Statistical Account in 1836, describes Inverie in similar terms, noting that it had been built by the late Colonel Macdonell:

> . . . who has been described as the last of that class of Highland Chiefs, of whom he formed so perfect a specimen in all his feelings and habits. [4]

The minister went on to comment on the artistic effect of Inverie, which still reflected Glengarry's tastes and enthusiasms:

> . . . the whole finishing being truly Celtic, and in excellent keeping with the tartans which grace its hospitable and accomplished inmates.

The Glengarrys' move to Inverie in the summer was a somewhat more grandiose version of the traditional Highland practice of transhumance, moving with the flocks to high level summer pasture and living in sheilings in the hills.

The domestic arrangements of the family were further complicated when, around 1814, Glengarry built a third house, a villa standing in three acres of ground, on a newly feued development on the Barnhill Estate on the outskirts of Perth. This house, rather modestly called Garry Cottage, provided a winter home for the family in the genteel and cultured environment of Perth and a taste, perhaps not entirely welcome, of a more ordered life for the children. Louise wrote:

> At Garry Cottage we were more civilised and better dressed than at home; but our hair was cut quite close all over except a little on the top of our heads, which was tossed up like a boy's, as papa thought much hair only caused headaches. [5]

To judge from the evidence of letters dated from Perth, Glengarry was most often at Garry Cottage between November and March. However, the Perth house was used at other times – often as a convenient staging post on the way back north from

England or Edinburgh. Garry Cottage still stands, and has more recently been in use as part of Hillside Hospital.

Rebecca Macdonell gave birth to fourteen children but, as was all too frequently the case in the period, saw many of her children die in infancy and childhood. The boys seem to have been particularly sickly and six of the seven died under the age of three. A plaque to the memory of his six deceased infant sons, erected by Glengarry in the little church he built at South Laggan, is a touching reminder of the repeated grief that the parents must have borne over the fifteen years of births and early deaths. Of the seven girls, however, six lived to adulthood.

The first child, Elizabeth, was born in November 1802, eleven months after the wedding and, as the birth took place in Edinburgh, Rebecca had presumably followed the common practice of returning to her parents' home for her first childbirth. An unnamed son was born in October 1803 and died immediately. The next birth, that of the first Æneas, was in July 1806. This child lived for less than a year and another son, the eventual heir, also named Æneas, a traditional family name reminiscent of the 1st Lord Macdonell and Aros of the seventeenth century, was born in July 1808. Alastair was born in January 1811 but died in May of the same year. Thereafter children were produced at regular intervals: Marsali in 1812, Duncan Alastair in 1813 only to die aged two years three months, Jemima 1814, Louise 1815, Forbes Reginald in December 1816, who only lived three weeks, James George (who died aged thirteen months) in February 1818 and so on to 1825. With such a regular pattern of childbearing it would seem very possible that there was room for pregnancies, which did not go to full term, to have occurred between the births of the stillborn son of 1803 and Æneas (I) and again between the birth of Æneas (II) and Alasdair. Rebecca Macdonell had her last child at the rather late age of forty-six. This remorseless cycle of pregnancies did not seem to have greatly affected Rebecca who survived until the age of sixty one.

Most of the children were born at Glengarry House, although Forbes Reginald and James George were born at Garry Cottage and Alasdair was born at Cheltenham. Cheltenham seems to have been a favoured English resort of the Macdonells – in April 1810

Glengarry wrote a couple of letters on Militia business from there and in 1824, when writing to Robert Peel, he noted that he was about to depart for Cheltenham with the ladies of his family.

The children of the family who survived infancy seem to have had a simple but enjoyable life at Glengarry House. Louise wrote of the happy reminiscences of their healthy childhood. Their education under a governess started at five and practical skills were not neglected – Louise reported that by six or seven she and her sisters were competent needlewomen. Saturday mornings were given over to the darning of stockings and the mending of clothes but these chores were lightened by the girls singing songs under the guidance of their Edinburgh-born governess Miss Patterson. This lady perhaps had some difficulties adjusting to the ethos of the Glengarry household. Louise noted that:

> She must have found it difficult to understand the value
> set upon birth, old family being considered
> independently of wealth or poverty. [6]

There were, in addition, some difficulties over Sabbath observance, a point on which the more liberal views and practices of the Episcopalian household at Glengarry House differed from the beliefs of the Merchant Maiden Hospital educated, Presbyterian daughter of a respectable Edinburgh tradesman.

However one quality of Miss Patterson's which commended her both to Glengarry and to the children was her love of music. Not only did she teach the girls Scots songs, particularly the Jacobite ones of which their father was so fond, but she also managed:

> . . . at enormous trouble to herself to teach us to sing
> Gaelic ones, though she knew nothing of that
> language. Sometimes our father wished us to learn a
> good old Gaelic song he had once heard one of our
> maidservants, or perhaps a shepherd's daughter sing:
> the servant or country girl was sent into the
> schoolroom on various occasions till Miss P. and one
> or more of us mastered the air by the ear, and then she
> wrote down the words, also by the ear, till we had it fit
> to sing after dinner, when our father corrected any
> wrong pronunciation.

The children were of course growing up in a Gaelic-speaking environment at Glengarry and even more so at Inverie, where the Minister wrote in the Statistical Account:

> Glenelg being a purely Highland district, the language spoken is almost exclusively Gaelic. A few individuals understand a little English, and are able to speak it; but Gaelic is the language in which all business is transacted, and will probably long continue to be so. [7]

Oddly enough, this process of learning Gaelic, in part at least, from song seems to have echoed the process that Glengarry himself had gone through. Louise notes that Glengarry and his brothers, growing up at Invergarry in the 1770s and 1780s, must have been accustomed to hear and speak Gaelic in the home. However when he came of age and raised the Glengarry Fencibles he made a more formal study of Gaelic:

> . . . with the assistance of some one he studied reading and writing in Gaelic, which I have heard him say he did chiefly through the oldest Gaelic songs [8]

It is perhaps reasonable to assume that Glengarry's tutor in Gaelic in the regiment was the Chaplain, Alexander Macdonell. In 1810 Glengarry was able to claim that his Militia regiment did not contain a single man who did not speak and understand the Gaelic language and prefer it to any other.

Despite the need for Gaelic in the kitchen, on the hill and in the army camp the social pressure to adopt English was irresistible. The Minister of Glenelg wrote in his Account:

> Here, as throughout the whole Highlands, there exists the greatest ambition for the acquirement of English. Without it, it is well known there is little probability of advancing in the world. [9]

Although Louise does not refer to instruction in Gaelic in her articles, Charles Fraser-Mackintosh in his *Antiquarian Notes* states that the children were taught Gaelic by Alexander Campbell, later Minister of Croy. Louise's education, other than in Gaelic, commenced with reading and sewing, moved on to arithmetic and writing at seven, the piano at nine, French at eleven, dancing, singing and Italian at sixteen, by which time she was at school in London.

Her brother's education followed a not dissimilar path, with a series of tutors (one of whom, John MacIntyre, was a Church of Scotland divinity student who was later presented to the local parish of Kilmonivaig by Glengarry), attendance at Perth Academy and then south to Eton in January 1824 before entering Edinburgh University in the autumn of 1825, where he was a student when his father died and he inherited the estates and chiefship.

Æneas's future career was naturally a matter of some concern to Glengarry and a fascinating letter written to his son on the eve of his sixteenth birthday (28th July 1824) reveals something of his ambitions. After telling Æneas that he planned to celebrate his birthday on the 29th by a day's deer stalking he goes on to say that he had derived much satisfaction from his son's last letter:

> . . . as it shews me that you have reflected seriously on your choice of Profession and that the alteration in your mind proceeds not from thoughtless indecision but from matured and well grounded reflection after ample deliberation: And it may be satisfactory for you to learn, that I see nothing inconsistent nor derogatory to the character of 'a steady Man', which comprehends much in your having turned your thoughts at one time to the Field and at another to the Bar . . . [10]

Æneas had evidently expressed a wish to be both a soldier and a barrister. Glengarry saw nothing wrong in this indecision, the more so because he was able to cite the historical precedent of the 1st Lord Macdonell and Aros who, as he reminded his son, had been a General under Montrose and helped defeat Argyll at the Battle of Kilsyth, and also went on to be Chancellor of the Scottish Parliament and took a seat in the Court of Session. Young Æneas could thus be seen as simply following in the family tradition. Whether this was an appropriate procedure in the nineteenth century was a point which Glengarry proposed to slide round. He went on to outline the arrangements in somewhat disjointed prose. Confident in Æneas's steadiness he proposed to have him:

> . . . Gazetted a subaltern, so as to be gaining Rank if your own wish, it being understood between us, that the so doing is not so interrupting your study of the Law; my

> plan is, soon after your Gazettment and rather than have
> your studies broken in upon, you retire on half pay, soe
> (*sic*) keeping our own ulterior views to ourselves, and
> indeed I see nothing insurmountable in keeping Terms at
> an Inn of Court, and acquiring considerable Military
> Rank during peace at the same time. Though most
> military men and most civilians too will say No, but the
> answer is simply '*Videamus!*' [Let us see.]

Glengarry enclosed a Bank Bill which Æneas could have negotiated by his Eton tutor, Mr. James, and gave his son a word of advice about the desirability of improving his handwriting.

As may be seen from the reference to an Inn of Court, Æneas's inclination was to a career as an English barrister rather than a Scots advocate. There is no evidence that any part of this ingenious master plan was put into action. Æneas proceeded from Eton to Edinburgh University where he was studying when his father's death and the acute financial crisis in the estate made other career options impracticable.

While Æneas had to consider a career, his sisters, of course, had no such opportunities and required simply to gain sufficient accomplishments to fit them for polite society and married life. Louise writes of a new governess coming (whether this was Miss Patterson or not is unclear) and having heard from Rebecca Macdonell's youngest sister that her charges were 'wild as goats'. When the new governess arrived her worst fears about her Highland charges and her new Highland home were perhaps fulfilled:

> . . . one of the large deer-hounds seized her fur muff
> and carried it off . . . her eldest pupil appeared on the
> scene and presented it to her again, having taken it
> from the dog, and no doubt scolded him in Gaelic. [11]

This anecdote does suggest that the Macdonell children had certainly learned Gaelic enough at least to speak to the deer-hounds!

The children's lifestyle was simple – a regular round of rising at 7, Bible lesson from 8 to 9, breakfast of porridge and milk at 9, lessons from 10 to 12, lunch of oatcake or broth, from 1 to 3 a walk round the home park (that is, the fields near the house), dinner at

3, supper of porridge or oatcake and milk at 6. After 6 the children were dressed in their fine clothes and came down to join the grown-ups in the dining room when the fruit course was being eaten. Afterwards they sang for the company. Dinner was accompanied by a piper who played three times during dinner and three times after the ladies had withdrawn.

The diet, strong on porridge and oatcakes, might have seemed dull enough as it was but Louise tells how when the children learned that the family of a lock-keeper on the Caledonian Canal had only cold water to take to their porridge they resolved to eat their porridge with cold water as a gesture of sympathy. The bowl of milk was, however, drunk afterwards. Whether the children or the adults of the house were behind another change in dietary policy is not clear. Louise relates:

> Some years after we resolved (as much as possible) to eat nothing except what grew in Scotland. This made us refuse sugar with our stewed apples, and take plain milk and warm water instead of sugar. We could not, of course, help taking any sugar used in cooking puddings etc. [12]

It would certainly seem to be in keeping with Glengarry's character that he should try to keep to the old manner of living off his own estates and eschewing foreign imports. The children showed the influence of their father and their Highland lifestyle in an intense consciousness of their innate superiority as Highlanders. Louise remembered an incident in which she was scalded with boiling water and commented:

> We rarely, I might say we never, cried for pain. We held that Lowlanders, not Highlanders, would do that. [13]

Glengarry saw to it that his children were brought up with a good knowledge of the traditions and legends of their family. Apart from this clan lore he also shared with the children his belief in dreams and prophecies. It will be recalled that in Vienna Lord Minto had found him to have a deeply superstitious nature (even when not in the grip of insanity), carrying amulets to ward off the forces of darkness and Louise tells of him recounting dreams and visions which he and his father had experienced.

Louise relates how the children were given pocket-money once a year on Handsel-Monday, the first Monday of the New Year. This ranged from 6d for the youngest children up to 8 shillings for the older ones. There was, as she says, little to spend money on at Glengarry other than the occasional visit of a travelling packman – a source of great excitement for the children, provided that they had been prudent enough to conserve sufficient money to afford his delights.

Glengarry, as one could perhaps predict, had very firm, if occasionally eccentric, ideas about child-rearing. His belief that much hair encouraged headaches has already been noted. He encouraged the children to have as much exercise as possible in the open air and also worked out a curious programme of exercises indoors.

> My father encouraged us in all sorts of exercise. He used to throw his stick, a very stout heavy one, on the ground, and tell Caroline [5 years younger than Louise] to pick it up between us and try which of us would take it from the other, he standing by to see fair play. My eldest sister [Elizabeth] told me she remembered when she and her sister [Marsali] had done the same; afterwards she had to take it against both her sister and her brother [Æneas], and ultimately from her brother alone, who was about seven years younger than herself. We did all sorts of exercises. We lay down flat on our backs on the floor, and had to rise straight up on our feet without turning to either side or putting our elbows on the floor. We did manage to sit up clasping our hands, and as it were pulling ourselves forward, after which we drew in our feet, and with another strong effort pulled our bodies forward till we stood upright. Another exercise could only be done in our nightgowns. Our thumbs were tied together behind our backs, and we had to pass our bodies, feet and all, between our arms, so that we stood with our thumbs tied in front of our waists. [14]

It is perhaps unsurprising that Glengarry placed such emphasis on his children's physical development. He gloried in his own strength and endurance, telling tales of how he had pursued deer through the hills for more than 24 hours at a time. The Highland

Games which were held at Glengarry to celebrate the Chief's birthday on the 15th September, placed great emphasis on feats of strength – throwing heavy stones and hammers, tossing the caber, leaping over a pony's back.

The children's moral and spiritual education was well catered for, in a remarkably ecumenical spirit. Louise relates how her father announced his determination to join the Episcopal Church and the somewhat confused story of his religious affiliations has been discussed earlier. We have it on Louise's authority that Æneas (II) was baptised by a Presbyterian, Church of Scotland clergyman and her sister Jemima by an Episcopalian.

However the registration of the children's baptisms seems to have been quite uniformly neglected. Elizabeth, the first born child, was baptised in Kilmonivaig parish but there are no extant baptismal records traceable for the later children – perhaps an indication of Glengarry's adoption of the Episcopalian ordinances. Registration of births, marriages and deaths was, at this time, a matter for the Established Church. If a family, like the Macdonells, followed another denomination then a special effort had to be made to register the event with a perhaps distant clergyman who was not in any way involved with the event. Some members of dissenting sects also had an ethically based reluctance to pay a registration fee to a Church they did not believe in. To compound the problem John MacIntyre, the Minister of Kilmonivaig, writing in the Second Statistical Account noted that the parochial register of births and marriages, which commenced in 1780 was kept very irregularly until 1820. The unreliability of these registers for non-members of the Established Church is underlined by his comment that:

> The Roman Catholic population seldom use this
> record for baptisms, but most of their marriages are
> entered in it. [15]

At the time MacIntyre wrote (1841) half the population of Kilmonivaig were members of the Church of Scotland and half were Roman Catholics. There were two families of Episcopalians.

Glengarry was, as a landowner in the parish, a heritor. He was thus, whatever his own religious affiliations, or lack of them, responsible for the maintenance of the church, manse and parish school, and for the stipend of the parish minister. In Kilmonivaig there was, most unusually, neither a manse nor a glebe – an area of farmland on which the minister could grow crops and keep cattle. Instead a cash allowance was made to the incumbent, this stood at £20 sterling in the 1780s and had risen to £70 by 1841. Glengarry also shared, with the Duke of Gordon, the right of presentation, that is the right to appoint, when a vacancy occurred, a Minister to the parish.

Æneas's tutor, John MacIntyre, benefited from this right. When Thomas Ross, who had been Minister of Kilmonivaig since 1776, died in 1822 Glengarry nominated MacIntyre to the vacancy. There was however a competing claim from the Commissioners for the Duke of Gordon and MacIntyre was not ordained and admitted to the charge until 1828. As a temporary measure, there being no function for him at Glengarry House as a tutor once Æneas had gone off to Eton and to Edinburgh University, he found employment as missionary at Fort Augustus, in the neighbouring parish of Boleskine and Abertarff.

This right of landowners to impose the clergyman of their choice on a parish was, of course, one of the great issues behind the Disruption in the Church of Scotland in 1843. There were particular anomalies in a landowner who, like Glengarry, was not even a member of the Church of Scotland determining who should minister to the people. His responsibility as a heritor in maintaining a church of another denomination seems to have been accepted as a natural part of land ownership however anomalous it may seem to us today.

Glengarry, however, seems to have been quite at ease with these relationships with the Established Church and it is noteworthy that John MacIntyre evidently thought highly of his employer and patron. MacIntyre's first child (born in 1827) was named Rebecca Ranaldson Macdonell, and after naming his first son Duncan (born in 1831), after his own father, named his second son (born in 1832) Alexander Æneas Ranaldson Macdonell. Certainly by the time of the 1832 birth the financial plight of the Macdonells would have been common knowledge and Glengarry was four years dead so it can scarcely have been mercenary motives that inspired MacIntyre to name his children after Glengarry and his wife. In the face of all the accounts of Glengarry's abrasiveness, irrationality and unpleasantness it is proper, and pleasant, to note this evidence of a friendly relationship across the divides of class and denomination.

Despite his embracing Episcopalianism, at whatever date, and his wife Rebecca's lifetime membership of that Church, the Glengarrys were happy to employ a 'stickit minister' of the Kirk as his son's tutor, a Presbyterian as his daughters' governess, and for the children's Sunday scripture recitals to be based on the Psalms of David and the Scottish Paraphrases and not on the collects from the Prayer-book used by the Scottish Episcopal Church. An Episcopal chapel was built two or three miles from Glengarry House at South Laggan but there were, in 1824, only eight Episcopalians in the entire parish – doubtless all accounted for by the family at the big house. There was an Episcopal clergyman whose responsibilities included Glengarry, although there would hardly have been regular Episcopal services there. It was unlikely, in any event, that a regular attendance at the Parish Church would have been looked for – Glengarry House was inconveniently far from the seat of Kilmonivaig Parish, some twenty miles away at Spean Bridge. The family seems in consequence to have been extremely flexible in its religious observances. Louise Macdonell remembers the summer visits to Knoydart:

> Most of the people were Roman Catholics, a parish missionary sometimes coming from Glenelg to hold a Presbyterian service. If we happened to be there in June or July it was held in the open air, when we children found it very difficult to keep good and look at the minister when, perhaps, a grasshopper or a lovely blue butterfly moved about near us, or the shepherd-dogs began to quarrel, and a stone well directed sent the offender yelping away. When our Episcopal minister came from Glengarry, the dining-room was quite large enough to hold the small congregation. [16]

The house at Glengarry played host to a wide range of visitors – among them Glengarry's brother Sir James, the hero of Maida and Waterloo. Louise gives a delightful account of the relationship between James and his former nurse. She and her husband still stayed in Glengarry House, retired on light duties. Louise writes that when her uncle came to Glengarry he always bought his old nurse material for a dress which she made up but never wore until Sir James came again.

> Of a night when there was to be regular dancing he sent one of us to tell her he wished to have a dance, and would come for her soon. Shortly after that they might be seen coming arm in arm along the back passage, the little old woman so proud of the 6 feet 3 inch Colonel of the Coldstream Guards, and such a dance can be rarely seen now! – the little woman dancing so smoothly, with her hands never as high as her shoulders, snapping her fingers in answer to his wild whooping, with his arms right over her head, while he too snapped his fingers all the while. At the end of the dance they went as they came along the back passage, till he left her safely in her own kitchen. One day she was seated on a high bank of the River Garry while he was angling for salmon, his favourite sport. When asked why she was sitting there, she said she was watching for fear the 'coronel' would fall in the river! [17]

Among the other visitors to Glengarry House were the Hay Allen brothers – who later became known as the Sobieski Stuarts and improbably claimed legitimate descent from Prince Charles Edward Stuart. The brothers wrote the *Vestiarium Scoticum* – a work of more than dubious scholarship on clan tartans. Louise was an early doubter of the merits of this book – considering that the Royal Stuart and Hunting Stuart tartans that they had woven were their own inventions.

The Hay Allen brothers did not commend themselves to Rebecca Macdonell on their first visit (around 1822) by failing to turn up for breakfast at 9 a.m. and she seems to have consented to Louise teaching them a lesson about the benefits of early rising:

> Our brother and Jemima said there was a nice ploy for me. I was to take a jug of cold water to the door and very quietly open it. I went in, holding the jug behind my back. Charles was seated in front of the looking-glass in his shirt and kilt, and Ian was in bed. They both seemed pleased to see me, and Ian held out his hands to

welcome me, when I poured the jug of water over his
head, and ran off as fast as I could
. . . Both gentlemen were down for one o'clock lunch,
when we could hear our mother laughing with them
over the children's trick; but no doubt our mother had
much to do with it herself, for nothing of the kind could
have been done without her sanction. [18]

This particular interpretation of Highland hospitality was, it
may be assumed, not a typical part of life at Glengarry House,
where, it seems fair to conclude that Alasdair Macdonell was to be
seen at his best surrounded by his family, friends and loyal retainers
and where what Louise described as his '. . . intense love of, and
pride in, all Highland things' [19] could be given free rein.

Well of the Seven Heads Monument, Loch Oich
(Erected by Alasdair Ranaldson Macdonell in 1812,
it carries an inspription in four languages, English,
French, Gaelic and Latin commemorating his
ancestor's supposed actions in avenging murders
of his clansmen.)

CHAPTER 9

Creagan an Fhithich
– the Raven's Rock

'. . .there is not nowadays a chieftain
of a more truly Highland spirit.
Indeed it may almost be said of him . . .
that he is one of the last of the Chieftains . . .'

The Macdonells of Glengarry were major players in war, politics and land ownership in the Central Highlands for generations. A clan which could produce several hundred fighting men for the Jacobite cause was always a force to be reckoned with. Even after the post-Culloden pacification of the Highlands – which had seen the Glengarry's ancient castle on the Raven's Rock sacked and looted by Cumberland's forces – had broken the military power of the clans, the affairs and estate management policies of the chiefs of Glengarry were still matters of public notice and public controversy.

The traditional pattern of agriculture and land tenure in the Highlands had been based on the desire of the clan chiefs to have as many fighting men at their disposal as possible. The structure of land holding, descending from the chief, his principal tenants or tacksmen, and so on down through smaller tenants to cottars reflected the military structure of clan regiments, with the tacksmen and the kinsmen of the chief forming the officer class. The demilitarisation of the Highlands called into question the need for, or indeed the sustainability of, such a large population. An economy which had been based on subsistence agriculture, with the breeding of black cattle for export forming the major cash crop, no longer seemed to be relevant to contemporary conditions. Chiefs, particularly those who had found more congenial lifestyles outside the Highlands, came to value cash income more than long tenant rolls of potential fighting men.

While there had always been some rasing of the small indigenous breeds of sheep in the Highlands, the new element in the later eighteenth century was the discovery that larger and more productive breeds, such as the Blackface and Cheviot, could be successfully reared on Highland pastures. This new sheepfarming required extensive tracts of land which could be found by removing small tenants from the land and using their arable land and common grazing for sheep. This type of agriculture required far fewer workers but the skills required for the management of these large flocks were not traditional Highland ones and experienced shepherds were imported into the Highlands from the Lowlands and Borders along with the flocks of Blackface and Cheviot sheep. There was thus a two-pronged attack on the traditional Highland lifestyle – the ending or reduction of traditional tenancies and the importation of an alien work force. Alan MacDougall, Glengarry's bard, was just one of the Gaelic poets who reflected bitterly on the coming of the sheep and, in equal measure, on the coming of the lowland shepherds in his 1798 poem 'A Song on the Lowland Shepherds'.

The very substantial depopulation of the Glengarry estates over which Alasdair Ranaldson presided had commenced under his father Duncan, or, perhaps more truly, under the aggressive management of his mother Marjory. An emigration of many of the tacksmen of the clan and their followers to New England took place in 1773. These gentlemen settlers were largely those whose traditional place in Highland society was being eroded by the ending of traditional social structures and the move to a cash economy. By 1782 the introduction of large scale sheep farming had been seen in Glen Quoich. Evictions of small tenants in various parts of the estate took place in 1785 and 1786 and again in 1788.

Alasdair Ranaldson's father had even in 1786 managed to attract the critical notice of Robert Burns over the emigration of five hundred tenants from his Knoydart estate. *The Address of Beelzebub* was inspired by a meeting of the Highland Society which wished in Burns' words:

... to concert ways and means to frustrate the designs of
FIVE HUNDRED HIGHLANDERS who ... were so
audacious as to attempt an escape from theire lawful lords
and masters whose property they are by emigrating from
the lands of Mr. McDonald of Glengary to the wilds of
CANADA, in search of that fantastic thing – LIBERTY.

Burns' satirical attack is on the Earl of Breadalbane, the
President of the Society and MacKenzie of Applecross, who had
raised the matter of the Knoydart emigration, and above all on
Duncan Macdonell, the 14th Chief of Glengarry. He holds up the
prospect of the emigrants winning freedom from the control of
landlords and being able to 'mak what rules an' laws they please'
– a truly dangerous precedent:

> ...what right hae they
> To Meat or Sleep, or light o' day
> Far less to riches, pow'r, or freedom,
> But what your lordships PLEASE TO GIE THEM?
>
> But, hear me, my lord! Glengary hear!
> Your HAND'S OWRE LIGHT ON THEM, I fear:
> Your FACTORS, GRIEVES, TRUSTEES an' BAILIES,
> I canna say but they do gailies;
> They lay aside a' tender mercies
> An' tirl the HALLIONS to the BIRSIES;
> Yet, while they're only poin'd and herriet,
> They'll keep their stubborn Hielan spirit.
> But smash them! crush them a' to spails!
> An' rot the DYVORS i' the JAILS!
> The young dogs, swinge them to the labour,
> Let WARK an' HUNGER make them sober! ...

As we have seen, Alasdair Ranaldson, when he came into his
inheritance, did not hesitate to threaten the eviction of those tenants
and cottars who did not produce volunteers for his Fencible
Regiment.

Shortly before his marriage in January 1802 Glengarry had
carried out a survey of his estate and resolved to offer sitting
tenants new tenancies at ten per cent below the price at which he
would offer the tenancies to incomers. On returning to Invergarry
after his marriage he found that despite such inducements many
of his tenants were planning to go to Canada. This should not be
confused with the mass emigration later planned by Father

Macdonell, the Chaplain, for the former members of the Glengarry
Fencibles – the Regiment was still embodied at this time. Glengarry
wrote a letter to the Secretary of State for the Home Department
about this matter, on the grounds that he feared for the
depopulation of the Highlands. This letter seems to reveal a
fundamental inconsistency in Glengarry's approach to his tenantry.
Although he presided over the substantial depopulation of his
estate he was reluctant to see people leave on their own terms and
at their own time. It will be recalled that in 1813 he complained
bitterly about the Earl of Selkirk's emigration scheme and weeks
later proposed a similar scheme himself.

March 21 1802
Glengarry House, by Fort Augustus

To Rt. Honble. Lord Pelham
Secretary of State
Whitehall
My Lord
About four or five months ago I made a Survey of
my estate with the view of ascertaining the real value
of it, and thus from known data to be enabled to fix
the reduced price at which it would be reasonable I
should let it to my numerous tenants and
Dependants. Upon mature reflection and advice, it
appeared to me that Ten per Cent was a sacrifice as
great as I could afford, and accordingly I made offer
to my old tenants of remaining upon their lands at
said Ten per Cent below the amount of offers from
Strangers, with which the tenants appeared content,
and which the County regarded as a handsome
sacrifice on my part, and beyond what it was
supposed other proprietors would make. Upon my
return here about a month ago, I was very much
surprised to learn that the Tenants, for whose
comfort and encouragement I had proposed to make
the above sacrifices, in general wished to surrender
their leases, and that they had all (with very few
exceptions) signed engagements to go to America
(Canada I believe). That they might have no room or
excuse for charging me with embarrassing them I
accepted their surrender; but, as I said, that no blame
or suspicion of oppression should be attributed to
me, I have this day made new offers to them of the
most encouraging nature, namely, Life Rent Tenures

of their old holdings; and indemnities for all
improvements agreeable to Covenant. What the
effect of this last measure will be I know not; but it
seems to me that both my own interest & my public
duty require & direct that I should give your
Lordship this information, & to state further, that it is
my opinion, from the disposition to emigrate that
now prevails in this quarter, if the Government or
the Legislature do not speedily & decisively
interpose, the Highlands will be depopulated. . . [1]

Many Highland landowners shared Glengarry's desire to keep control of the population in their own hands and when Father Macdonell organised the Fencible's emigration in 1803 he found himself faced with opposition from Lord Moira, the Commander in Chief in Scotland, Charles Grant, the Member of Parliament for Inverness and other prominent figures. [2] There was undoubtedly a concern about the loss of military manpower (Glengarry pointed out to Lord Pelham that besides regular units there were ten fencible regiments recruited from the Highlands) but presumably there was also a desire to manage the conversion from traditional crofting tenancies to sheep farming at the pace and at the time the landlord thought fit. It was not to a landlord's advantage to have the land fall idle by the emigration of his tenants if he could not immediately afford to stock it with sheep or find a sheepfarming tenant.

Allan MacDougall had, in his 1798 poem, praised Glengarry for detesting sheep and those who forced up the price of land, and Glengarry's followers in the Grant Fencibles, when they petitioned to transfer to his new regiment, had offered to pay as high rents as the lowland incomers. MacDougall was perhaps being tactful to his new patron because there was every indication that, whatever romantic notions Glengarry may have had about tradition or whatever guarantees he made to his men, the reality was that the sheep were on the march in Glengarry's land. The prospects of his soldiers on their small farms being able to match the income levels that intensive sheep farming could produce were remote, and the reality of the situation was underlined by the mass emigration of the demobilised Glengarry Fencibles.

The extent of the conversion of the Glengarry estate to sheep by the 1820s is indicated by the comment of David Stuart of Garth that:

> The Glengarry farms contained 1500 souls. Those farms
> have now 35 persons.[3]

Indeed advertisements had appeared in the *Inverness Journal* of 3rd March 1815 offering to let eight separate sheepwalks on various parts of the Glengarry estate – among these were Kinlochnevis (10,735 acres) and Inverie (660 acres) in Knoydart, Kilfinnan (10,887 acres) beside Loch Lochy and the Royal Forest of Glenquoich.

The progressive clearance of tenants from the estate is shown in a list compiled by Charles Fraser-Mackintosh in his *Antiquarian Notes*. He notes eleven families evicted in Knoydart in 1804, nineteen from across the Glengarry estates who were evicted in 1806 and twenty-four families evicted in 1808. If one assumes a very modest average of five or six persons per family it is easy to see how quickly the total of persons evicted could rise to the figure implied by Stewart of Garth's letter and to justify his comment: 'Is not this extirpation?'

In the 1840s John McIntyre, the minister of Kilmonivaig Parish, which embraced most of Glengarry's Great Glen properties, wrote:

> It is supposed that there are upwards of 100,000 sheep
> reared in this parish every year. Some of the sheep farms
> are upwards of 100 square miles in extent.

It is worth noting that McIntyre's predecessor, Thomas Ross, writing in the 1790s, reported a figure of 60,000 sheep in the parish. McIntyre continued:

> Perhaps there is no part of the Highlands where nature
> has done more, and landlords so little, for the benefit of
> the inhabitants, as some parts of the parish of
> Kilmonivaig. In Glenspean alone, there are upwards of
> 40,000 acres of excellent soil, which, by the application of
> skill and capital, could be brought into cultivation. Thus,
> in the course of thirty years, the value of land might be
> increased tenfold. The character might be improved, and
> so might the habits, comforts, and morals of the
> inhabitants. Under a proper system of management, the
> people would have strong inducements to active
> exertion; and the present practice of spending a great
> part of their time in idleness, or in balls, raffles, shinty-

matches, and whisky shops, would disappear. An
improved system of husbandry, introduced into
Lochaber, would be of signal benefit to a great portion of
the Highlands. It would render meal and potatoes
plentiful, and keep in the country the money sent out of
it every year to procure these necessities of life. Great
quantities of butcher-meat could be reared, and easily
sent to the Glasgow and Liverpool markets by means of
the steam-boats. Ireland is not the only country that
suffers from the system of middlemen and absenteeism. [4]

In fairness, Glengarry could not be accused of absenteeism,
but the rest of the indictment could certainly be laid at his door, as
at that of the other proprietors. It is a significant indication of the
changing pattern of land use in the Highlands that McIntyre lists
eight principal landowners in his parish, including Lord Ward,
proprietor of Glengarry, and Edward Ellice, proprietor of Glenquoich, (together the successors to Macdonell) but notes that the
only resident proprietor by that date was Lieutenant-Colonel H J
Cameron of Letterfinlay 'who resides in a cottage.' The remaining
proprietors merely visited their estates during the shooting season.

The population of the area, in an era of general population
growth – Scotland's total population grew by 47 per cent over these
years, showed a very slow growth indeed.

| Glenelg | *1801* 2834 | *1831* 2874 | 1.4% increase |
| Kilmonivaig | *1801* 2541 | *1831* 2869 | 12.9% increase |

Glenelg was approximately twenty miles in length and about the
same in breadth, while Kilmonivaig was sixty miles from north to
south and at its broadest twenty miles. These are thus very small
populations, even allowing for much mountainous ground and
substantial lochs.

The primary purpose of many Highland estates had gone from
being producers of men for clan armies or King George, to being
producers of sheep, to being breeding grounds for stag and grouse.
Around the time McIntyre was writing his *Statistical Account* a list
was published in the *Inverness Courier* showing the activities of a
Mr. Bainbridge, who had leased the Glengarry lands from the
Marquess of Huntly, prior to its purchase by Lord Ward. Bainbridge
had actively preserved game on the estate – which meant that he

instructed his keepers to kill anything with a hooked beak. The total of raptors killed from 1837-1840 included:

27 sea eagles
15 golden eagles
18 ospreys
98 peregrines
275 kites
63 goshawks
285 buzzards
371 roughlegged buzzards
462 kestrels

Quite apart from the conversion of his property to sheep farms, Glengarry was an active and improving landlord, even if at times his enthusiasm for his projects of improvement may have been somewhat unrealistic. In the *Inverness Journal* for February 1813 he advertised a long list of sheep farms to let, including the presently tenanted property of Easter & Middle Aberchalder & Cullachy of 5,268 acres, South Laggan – in Glengarry's own hands – a property of 1,836 acres. In addition he announced the feuing of a village at Balalastair, beside Loch Lochy. Balalastair, of course, means the township of Alastair – Glengarry was following the common practice of naming a planned settlement after the founder or a member of the founder's family – Fraserburgh, Helensburgh, Jemimaville, Gordonstoun, and Grantown-on-Spey being other examples of this custom.

The new village was to be set off in building leases with 'preference given to mechanics, tradesmen, builders and settlers of all descriptions.' This was probably a reasonably sensible location for a new village – being well placed to service the Caledonian Canal, work on which was well-advanced at this period. His other planned village does however seem to have been a rather more doubtful speculation.

This advertisement offers land in the:

Village of Bally Bhey Ac in Airar of Knoydart. (To be set in feus for building & every encouragement will be afforded to mercantile speculations and enterprising settlers of capital, mechanics, tradesmen. etc.) [5]

and goes on to enthuse that there was not 'a situation of more flattering prospects' and of Bally Bhey Ac's 'centrical position for the western fisheries.' This is perhaps rather overstating the attractions of Airar (or Airor as it now appears on the Ordnance Survey maps). Airor is a small settlement on the west coast of Knoydart at the end of a nine mile single-track road from Inverie. However as Inverie is not connected by road to any part of the world outside Knoydart this does not exactly suggest that even the most enterprising settlers and their 'mercantile speculations' would have found it a particularly suitable location. While Airor does enjoy a small bay, sheltered from the westerly winds by Airor Island, this would seem to be the only advantage that it had as a 'centrical position for the western fisheries.' Whatever interest might have been shown, Bally Bhey Ac never developed into a Tobermory, a Mallaig or an Ullapool.

The same advertisement also intimated the availability to let of two iron ore mines, with Glengarry holding out the certainty of black lead (graphite or plumbago) and the possibility of cobalt deposits in the same mines. Birch timber and bark was also advertised at the same time.

In 1827 Glengarry advertised the lease of what he described as 'a most gentlemanlike tenement' – tenement in its original sense of a property or piece of land rather than in the sense of a flatted dwelling – of Inverguiseran in Knoydart. The estate of Scotos in Knoydart, presently occupied by Major Macdonell, late of the 17th Dragoons, was also available and could be combined with Inverguiseran for lease 'to a man of sufficient capital.'

A substantial portion of the estate was managed and farmed directly by Glengarry rather than by tenants, and he seems to have been a keen, intelligent and energetic farmer. The *General View of the Agriculture in the County of Inverness* noted that, although generally little wheat was grown in the western part of the County, Glengarry grew a little for the use of his family and ground it to flour with a steel mill. The coming of the Caledonian Canal and the purchase of ground for its construction had an impact on Glengarry's farming. In September 1814 he advertised in the *Inverness Journal:*

The land required for the purposes of the Caledonian

> Canal having deprived Glengarry of an extensive stretch
> of his most valuable Low Grounds, Arable and
> productive Natural Meadows, his Horse and Cattle
> Stocks must be diminished accordingly. . .[6]

In the following year he advertised the sale of bulls at the Balalastair Market on 13 June and also announced a competition for a 100 guinea stake open to any breeder of Highland black cattle who would match his beast against a black stirk bull of Glengarry's 'to prove . . . the superiority of this home-bred stock.'

In June 1818 Glengarry was able to report to his friends in the Society of True Highlanders a proposal by William Grant, from Manchester, to start a woollen manufactory on the farm of Shian near the Caledonian Canal, on his estate. £100 shares (or £50 half shares) were available and had to be subscribed by 20 July. Such a scheme was a useful contribution to the economy of the area, enabling the wool from the sheep to be processed in the Highlands rather than shipped to Lowland mills. A woollen mill had been suggested by the Rev. Thomas Ross in his *First Statistical Account* entry in the 1790s – the minister had pointed out that the lower ranks of tenants and cottars were very poor and likely to remain so unless they emigrated or:

> . . . some such thing as an woollen manufactory be
> established at Fort William; for which it is admirably
> adapted, surrounded as it is, by sheep farms in every
> direction for 40 miles, and from which little less than
> 20,000 stone of wool is exported annually to be
> manufactured in different parts of the kingdom. [7]

The location of the proposed manufactory, adjacent to the Caledonian Canal, emphasised Glengarry's essential pragmatism. He had many disputes with the Canal Commissioners, objected to the invasion of his privacy which Canal traffic brought, but did not decline to profit from the Canal or to make use of it for his own purposes.

All the natural resources of the estate were exploited, even those which many landlords would have kept in their own hands. We learn from his daughter Louise that Glengarry, though a passionate deerstalker, had no interest in grouse-shooting or salmon fishing. This perhaps explains his contract for letting the salmon-fisheries to the Dundee-based fish merchants Richardson & Company. In November 1804 they wrote to Glengarry:

> In consequence of the conversations which our Mr.
> Young had the honour of with you concerning your
> fishings. We shall make a trial of it for the ensuing season
> in order to ascertain as near as we can the value of it and
> we instructed our overseer Ed. Norman to provide hands
> and materials for it. We beg leave to offer you our best
> acknowledgement for the very handsome manner in
> which you are pleased to express yourself toward us. [8]

In February 1805 they again wrote to Glengarry:

> We were honored with your letter of 26th November.
> We perfectly approve of your proposal for having the
> produce of your fishing and the expences of managing
> it ascertained to you by the declaration upon oath of
> our servants employed there, and we some time ago
> wrote to Norman that this was required.
> It gives us pleasure to mention that your fishing has
> produced 46 salmon this season. Whenever we see by
> a season's trial what we can afford we trust that we
> shall not disagree as to terms. We are flattered by the
> handsome manner in which you are pleased to
> express yourself to us. [9]

The only trace of the sums actually produced by this agreement comes in November 1809 when a letter enclosing a draught for £20 being the fishing rent for season 1809 was sent. How long this arrangement subsisted is not clear, but perhaps it terminated when Glengarry's brother, Colonel James Macdonell, found himself less occupied with military duties after Waterloo brought a final peace to Europe and he was able to spend more time visiting his family home at Invergarry. James, unlike Alasdair, was an enthusiastic angler, and Louise Macdonell's charming description of him fishing on the Garry, watched over anxiously by his former nurse, was quoted in the previous chapter.

The general economic development of his area was also of interest to Glengarry. For example he invested significantly in a project to establish a coach service between Inverness and Fort William, with a connection onward by coach to Skye. Such a project, while doubtless to some degree a personal convenience to him and the many visitors to Invergarry House, was essentially a benefit to the wider community and Glengarry's involvement can fairly be seen in that light. The *Inverness Courier,* a paper which did not always see eye to eye with Glengarry, reported in September 1819:

> A meeting was held at the Kings Inn, Fort Augustus. . . which was attended by Colonel Macdonnell of Glengarry, Colonel Macdonnell of the Guards, Mr. Grant of Glenmoriston, and many other respectable gentlemen. The meeting were unanimous in their resolution to carry this most beneficial project into effect and £500 were subscribed for the purpose on the spot, of which Glengarry gave £100. It is expected that in the course of two or three months, the necessary arrangements for the establishment of the coach to Fort William will be completed. There is some difference of opinion about the route most proper for the Skye Coach, which it is intended to meet the Fort William one, either at Fort Augustus or at Invermoriston, as may be afterwards settled. Glengarry who possesses at all times the warm feelings of a true Highland Chief for the honour and interests of his country, has, on this occasion added to the obligations the Highlands owe him, by zealously extending his powerful aid and influence to promote this important object. [10]

This type of expenditure, which Glengarry clearly thought was an essential part of his role as a major local landowner, all contributed to the drain on the family finances. Some signs of the crash which took place after Glengarry's death can be seen as early as 1810 when Invergarry House and the associated shootings were let for the season to Lord O'Neill. It is hard to see any reason for this, other than economic necessity. There are numerous references over the years to money borrowed on the security of part of the estate and loans from a variety of sources. For example in 1811 he took out a bond with Æneas MacKintosh of MacKintosh to borrow £1150. [11]

Much of Glengarry's expenditure was designed to enhance his own position and to glorify the great name of Macdonell. For example, in 1812, he erected a memorial beside Loch Oich at the Well of the Seven Heads. This commemorated the action of his ancestor, Lord Macdonell and Aros, in avenging the murder of members of the Keppoch family in the seventeenth century. The monument, the work of the sculptor J Marshall, is an obelisk capped with a carving of the seven heads of the murderers, and carries an inscription in English, French, Gaelic and Latin:

> As a memorial of the ample and summary vengeance which in the swift course of feudal justice, inflicted by the orders of the Lord McDonnell and Aross, overtook the perpetrators of the foul murder of the Keppoch family, a branch of the powerful and illustrious clan, of which His Lordship was the chief. This monument is erected by Colonel McDonell of Glengarry XVII Mac Mhic Alastair his successor and representative in the year of our Lord 1812. The heads of the seven murderers were presented at the feet of the noble chief in Glengarry Castle, after having been washed in this spring; and ever since that event, which took place in the sixteenth century, it has been known by the name of 'Tobar-nan-Ceann', or the Well of the Seven Heads.

This inscription, is to say the least, confusing. Alasdair Ranaldson was the 15th, not the 17th of his line; the Keppoch murders took place in 1663, not in the sixteenth century, and the murderers were dealt with not by the Glengarry of the day but on the orders of MacDonald of Sleat. The presentation of the severed heads to Lord Macdonell may thus have been a coded attack on his inaction rather than a tribute to his 'ample and summary justice.' The traditional report has it that the attack on the murderers and the presentation of their heads to Glengarry was led by Iain Lom, the Bard of Keppoch. From what is known of this poet's nature and taste for the bloodthirsty, as evidenced in his great poem on the Battle of Inverlochy, this gruesome event and pointed rebuke seems quite in context. None of this, however, appears in Alasdair Ranaldson's text which simply glorifies his noble ancestor and, by implication, denigrates other sections of Clan Donald.

Perhaps for these reasons the monument was the subject of a vandal's attack in 1815. The authorities declined to prosecute, to Glengarry's anger, and left the matter up to Glengarry to take any private civil action he saw fit. The incident was the occasion for an angry exchange of letters between Glengarry and the Sheriff of Inverness-shire.

Some of his expenditure was, however, more sensibly geared to the economic realities of Highland life. His feuing of ground in 1813 to create a village at Balalastair has already been noted. He wrote in 1825, as part of his long-running feud with the Caledonian Canal Commissioners, a long letter which in part states:

> As to Balalastair, at that place there are various local advantages not always to be found in the central highlands for the formation of a village, and being anxious to carry on the improvement of the Country, I projected and commenced a village in that place. The village lies between Laggan and Shian on the south east side of the Canal, which has separated the inhabitants from their grazing ground and peat moss, which lies on the other side of the Canal; a considerable amount of houses have been erected, and I have also been at the sole expence of building and endowing a Chapel, for the accommodation of the people and convenience of the neighbourhood. [12]

The Caledonian Canal was a continuing source of trouble and irritation to Glengarry. He might well have expressed pious good wishes about the:

> . . . terms of cordiality on which I should wish to live hereafter with those who are to continue in the Superintendence of this Great National Work. . .

but the reality of the situation was rather different. Inevitably such a major building project, cutting through his land, was going to bring difficulties and tensions. The land that was compulsorily purchased from his estate was valued at £10,000 and he received this between 1814 and 1816 [13] but he still had general objections to the project and in particular its impact on Loch Oich, on the shores of which Invergarry House stood. The engineer of the Canal, Thomas Telford, had originally proposed to run the canal down the southern shore of Loch Oich and separate the canal from the loch by an embankment. This, in the event, proved impracticable, and further negotiations with Glengarry took place, without success, and the Commissioners eventually decided that the navigation would run on the obvious course down the centre of the loch and dredging was carried out to secure the requisite depth for traffic. This decision caused Glengarry two concerns – the damage to the fisheries of Loch Oich and the invasion of his privacy by boats sailing in front of the windows of Glengarry House and he demanded compensation for:

> . . . the loss of amenity occasioned by such a fine sheet of water in my pleasure-grounds being laid open to the public. [14]

There were other, more practical, problems caused by the canal, the separation of communities from their traditional grazing grounds by the waterway being one. This was, as we have seen, a particular problem at Balalastair. The obvious solution was the provision of bridges over the canal and the number and location of these was a fruitful source of argument between Glengarry and the Commissioners.

Glengarry's claim for compensation dragged on for years, and eventually was inherited by his son Æneas. The claim had sought, apart from payment for damages to the banks and to the fisheries of the loch, compensation for the occupation of part of the loch for the purposes of navigation, and specified that an area of four miles length and thirty-six yards breadth had been so appropriated. The Court of Session ruled that:

> . . . the loch of Oich, and the solum of that lake, are the exclusive property of the pursuer; and to this effect, decern and declare in terms of the first conclusion of his libel; but find the claims for damages alleged to arise from the use of that lake for the purpose of navigating the Caledonian Canal, and for the alleged injury done to the privacy, amenity, comfort, and security of the pursuer's mansion-grounds and garden, by or through the use of the said lake, for the purposes aforesaid, are incompetent under the provisions of the statutes libelled upon, and to that extent assoilizie the defenders, and decern and declare accordingly. [15]

The matter was remitted back to the Sheriff in Inverness to apply the provisions of the Statutes which laid down that he and a jury should consider any claims for damage to banks or to fisheries.

Had all Glengarry's controversies with the Canal Commiss-ioners and their employees been argued out in court matters might have been better. However in 1816 he took direct and unlawful action against the canal operations.

On 3rd September that year he and his estate workers attacked the Canal workmen engaged on operations at Loch Oich. The story is succinctly told in the court documents:

> That a breach of the public peace, as also obstructing a public national work and carrying away the boats and vessels used for carrying on that work to a distant part of the country, are crimes severely punishable. Yet Colonel Alexander Macdonell of Glengarry, was guilty actor or art and part, in so far as on the morning of 3rd September, 1816, he accompanied by several persons all armed with fire-arms, saws, hatchets, or axes, proceeded to the East End of Loch Oich, where the Canal workmen were preparing to begin work for the day, and he, the said Alexander Macdonell, aided and assisted as aforesaid, seized upon and violently and forcibly carried away a boat employed upon the said loch up to Invergarry House, and from thence placed her (sic) in a cart and carried her up to Lochgarry. Further, the said Colonel Alexander Macdonell, aided as aforesaid, threatened the workmen that their lives would be taken away if they did not desist from carrying the said Canal through Loch Oich, and the workmen were so intimidated that they did desist, and the Canal operations were stopped by the lawless behaviour of the said Colonel Alexander Macdonell. [16]

The Sheriff Depute of Inverness, William Fraser Tytler, took precognitions in early November from a wide range of participants in this event. [17] In these it emerges that not only was Glengarry involved in the assault but his brother, Colonel James, and Captain Morgan, the adjutant of the 2nd Inverness-shire Local Militia, were also present. John Hood, Glengarry's factor, stated that Glengarry had written to the nearest Justice of the Peace and Constable seeking their advice and to protect his property from the activities of the workmen. However matters were so far advanced that the punts were likely to be on the Loch in half an hour and there was no sign of the Justice of the Peace – hence his resort to direct action.

The papers in the case were sent to the Lord Advocate who, however, declined to prosecute the case. The possibility obviously existed of the Canal Commissioners mounting a civil prosecution for damages, but they, probably looking towards the desirable goal of good long-term relations with a major landowner along the line of the Canal, and having recovered their boat, let the matter drop.

One of the complexities of Glengarry's character was that he could describe the Canal as a 'great national work' and assault its workmen, sell land and timber to it and object to the navigation of Loch Oich and still participate fully in the celebrations of the opening of the Canal. Among the many fine qualities Glengarry undoubtedly possessed, the ability to detect internal inconsistencies in his own behaviour was certainly not one.

The *Inverness Courier* reported on the celebrations for the opening of the Canal from sea to sea in October 1823. The Commissioners and their guests set sail from Inverness in the steamship *Stirling* on 23rd October, reaching Fort Augustus that evening. The next day was the highlight of the celebrations:

> But the grand scene of festivity and congratulation was reserved for the ultimate point of the voyage, Fort William, for which place the party embarked at six o'clock on Thursday morning. After sailing about five miles and a half in the Canal, and passing through seven locks, the steam yacht entered at Loch-Oich. On approaching the mansion of GLENGARRY, which is finely situated on the north bank of this lake, the band struck up 'My name it is Donald Macdonald,' etc. and a salute was fired in honour of the Chief, which was returned from the old castle, the now tenantless residence of GLENGARRY'S Ancestors. The Ladies of the family stood in front of the modern mansion waving their handkerchiefs. GLENGARRY had set out by land to Fort Augustus, in order to accompany the party from thence, but met the yacht by the way, as it had started at a much earlier hour than he had calculated upon. He, however, joined the party on Loch-Oich, with his brother, Col. Macdonell of the Guards, and another friend, and proceeded with them to Fort William. Glengarry had, in honour of the occasion, requested his tenants to assemble at

> 11 o'clock, and give the voyagers a *feu de joie*, but the
> early passage of the vessel through Loch Oich
> frustrated this polite intention. [18]

That evening, at 7.30, sixty-seven gentlemen sat down to dinner and Glengarry was prominent among those who, after the meal, proposed toasts. After Charles Grant, former Member of Parliament for the County and one of the Canal Commissioners, had proposed a quite substantial list of toasts Glengarry rose and:

> . . . in a very appropriate speech proposed the health
> of their worthy *Chairman*, for his services to the
> County in general, and particularly as the colleague of
> these Commissioners, in forwarding all the measures
> connected with the Caledonian Canal – This Toast was
> received with the most unbounded applause, which
> showed that the company fully entered into the
> feelings of the Chief.

Glengarry went on to propose the health of the other Commissioners. The newspaper then notes that it cannot pretend to detail all the other proceedings and the many private and public toasts which were given, but gives a select list of the 'most worthy of notice.' This select list has thirty-two toasts in which Glengarry played a full and active part. He seems to have retired from the gathering before a formal close was called at midnight, although the newspaper report notes that:

> . . . some of the gentlemen still remained, and, with
> genuine Highland spirit, prolonged the festivities of this
> memorable evening.

It is perhaps worth considering the fact that, despite his frequently outrageous behaviour, Glengarry was still accepted as a perfectly respectable and worthy member of the community. Whether quite so much tolerance would have been extended to someone lower down the social hierarchy is, of course, rather doubtful. A certain allowance seems to have been made for the chief of Clan Macdonell which would not have been made for one of his more humble clansmen. However, even with this degree of toleration, Glengarry managed on quite a number of occasions to fall foul of the law in variously dramatic ways.

Having famously fought one duel, with Lieutenant MacLeod,

and escaped with his life from the subsequent court case, many people would have taken great care to avoid any similar circumstances in the future. Glengarry however seems to have been prepared to fight a duel with Grant of Rothiemurchus in 1808 – this affair was settled by the interposition of friends of the two men who managed to get their principals to agree that they never had any intention of insulting the other. [19]

If the Rothiemurchus duel was avoided by the intervention of friends another feud had expensive and damaging consequences. This was the incident in 1805 when Glengarry and his followers assaulted Dr. Donald MacDonald of Fort Augustus at the market in that town. There had been bad blood between the two men since Glengarry's birthday party in 1798 when MacDonald assaulted, or at least seized and threatened, the chief. Despite attempts by various parties, including the Rev. Thomas Ross, minister of Kilmonivaig, to get MacDonald to apologise and to reconcile matters the ill-feeling persisted. Unfortunately the two men were more or less bound to come in contact with each other, MacDonald having the tenancy of the sheep-farm of Scotos on Glengarry's Knoydart estate. On 30th September 1805 MacDonald was attacked and severely beaten by Glengarry and his followers and in due course a civil action for damages was heard at the Court of Session in Edinburgh with Glengarry, his factor Alexander Macdonell at Kinloch, his piper John Macdonell Jnr., and three others cited as defendants. The court found that the defendants:

> . . . were guilty of a violent and atrocious assault on the person of the pursuer, Mr. Donald Macdonald, to the effusion of his blood and danger of his life. Find that the said assault did not originate in a sudden quarrel, but was the result of long premeditated resentment and a deliberate purpose of revenge, and was attended with many circumstance of great barbarity and peculiar aggravation, especially on the part of the defender Alexander Macdonell of Glengarry. [20]

The court found the defenders liable jointly and severally for damages which were assessed at the very substantial sum of £2000 and the costs of the case. The court also took into consideration Glengarry's position in the County – observing that he was at the time:

> . . . a Justice of the Peace, and Deputy-Lieutenant for the
> County of Inverness, and was not only the aggressor in
> the above assault, and did not interfere to preserve the
> peace, but did by imprecations and outrageous threats of
> personal violence, deter and prevent John Mackay, head
> constable of the County of Inverness, from interfering to
> assist, and rescue the pursuer when officially called on
> by him so to do, thereby openly aiding and abetting the
> other defenders in their attack on the pursuer, and did
> likewise endeavour to prevent the Military Guard when
> called for, when coming to the pursuer's relief . . .

The court, properly, took a very stern view of this abuse of his
legal and administrative offices as an aggravating factor in the
assault and referred the matter to the Lord Advocate, the chief
law officer of the Crown in Scotland to:

> . . . consider how far it is proper that the said Alexander
> Macdonell of Glengarry, should any longer be continued
> in the Commission of the Peace and Lieutenancy for the
> County of Inverness, and in respect of the ungovernable
> resentment and violence manifested by the said
> defenders, also to consider whether it would not be
> proper that they should all of them be laid under proper
> security to keep the peace.

The implication of the latter point was that criminal, as well as
civil, charges might have been appropriate. The recommendations
of the court were not, it would seem, taken up by the Lord
Advocate, because there are later records of Glengarry's attendance
at meetings of the Lieutenancy. The verdict, though not unexpected
by Glengarry's lawyer, did surprise him by the extent of the
damages imposed.

Glengarry seemed to have an unfortunate propensity for
getting into legal trouble. Perhaps the most absurd example of this
was the case of Glengarry's hat and Fraser of Lovat's apartment.
Both Glengarry and Archibald Fraser of Lovat had attended the
Northern Meeting Ball in Inverness in the autumn of 1810 and at
the conclusion of the ball had by accident exchanged hats. When
Fraser returned to his hotel he discovered the mistake and returned
Alasadair Ranaldson's hat to Ettles Hotel (later the Caledonian)
where Glengarry was staying. However the hotel management
clearly failed to return the hat to Glengarry and the next day,

Sunday, Fraser was called out of the High Kirk in the middle of the service to see Glengarry on pressing business. Fraser continues the story in a letter written some months later to Sheriff Simon Fraser of Farraline:

> Upon going to Fraser's Hotel, not two hundred yards distant, I found Glengarry gone out of town, after beating open my locked door, in which there was a good deal of money and papers in a law contest I have with him for taking a grant of feu-duties due the Crown on my estate of Abertarff but granted to me 15 years ago – my apartment being ransacked, and his hat not found. The door was left open by Glengarry, who in a supercilious, dictatorial tone of voice hallooed to the landlord to have the lock mended at his, Glengarry's expense. The manners of the gentleman I overlook, but as a public man I demand Glengarry and all the world to be made sensible that any man's apartment is his sacred castle, and that it is criminal to break it open under any pretence without legal warrant. [21]

There is evidence that Fraser was just as fiery and haughty in temperament as Glengarry but he did display a certain delicacy in not pursuing his case until he was sure that Glengarry's wife, pregnant with their fourth son Alasdair, was 'out of all danger of a miscarriage.' The Crown refused to prosecute but indicated that they would concur in a private criminal process initiated by Fraser. In the event, mutual friends managed to secure a satisfactory settlement of the matter.

Glengarry, as a major landowner in the County was inevitably substantially involved in local politics. While his own ambitions to stand for Parliament were never realised he was active in the limited circle which made up the pre-Reform Act electorate of Inverness-shire. In 1818, Charles Grant Senior stood down from the representation of the County, to be replaced by his son Charles Grant Junior, who had previously been the member for the less prestigious, and perhaps more politically volatile, Inverness Burghs constituency. The *Inverness Courier* reported the delightfully simple electoral process:

> Colonel Macdonell of Glengarry, then proposed in a short but very animated speech, that Mr. Charles

> Grant, junior, should be elected representative in
> Parliament for this County, which proposal was
> received with acclamation. Glengarry's motion was
> seconded by Colonel MacLeod of Rasay.
> Glengarry addressed himself to the audience, and
> requested that they would remain for a few minutes. He
> remarked, that elections were here conducted on a plan
> different from that in England. Here the right of voting did
> not descend so low as it did there. It was not uncommon,
> however, to confer marks of popular approbation on a
> favourite candidate. The spirited Chief, therefore
> recommended to the audience to give three cheers to the
> new member; and this honour was immediately conferred,
> Glengarry, himself, giving the time. [22]

Glengarry was correct in observing that in Scotland the right of
voting did not descend so low as in England. Prior to the 1832
Reform Act Scotland had less than 5000 parliamentary electors and
in county seats like Inverness-shire the franchise was in effect
restricted to major landowners. In 1829 there were just seventy-
seven freeholders in the County with the right to vote. The Reform
Act did not introduce a very much wider franchise – the post-1832
electorate was only 546 in a county with a population of 95,000.

In 1820, when another General Election was necessitated by
the death of George III and the accession of George IV, Glengarry
was again charged with the duty of proposing the election of
Charles Grant.

Elections were not the only matters of County business which
required Glengarry's participation – as a Deputy Lord Lieutenant
he was involved in many matters of civic business and electoral
politics. For example in January 1819 he presided, presumably due
to the absence of the Lord Lieutenant, at a meeting of freeholders,
commissioners of supply, heritors and justices of the peace which
sent a message of condolence to the Prince Regent on the death of
his mother, Queen Charlotte. However Glengarry was not always
in agreement with the sentiments of his fellow Inverness-shire
landowners. In January 1821, when the entire country was greatly
exercised over the messy divorce of George IV and Queen Caroline,
a County Meeting was called to send a loyal address – the text of
which included a variety of references to sedition, blasphemous

press and the country being reduced to a state of disorder and anarchy. Glengarry did not attend this meeting; he was staying at Garry Cottage in Perth and considered that insufficient notice had been given. However he objected to the contents of the address and also to the Government's treatment of the Queen.

> A letter was also read from Colonel Macdonnell of Glengarry, dated at Perth, stating in substance, that being unable to be present at this meeting, he thought it right to state his opinion of the object, for which the County had been called together. That he saw no necessity for Addressing his Majesty at present: that the loyal and religious character of Highlanders had never been called in question. That sedition and blasphemy have not been known in this Country for a great length of time, and that it appeared to him that the use of such an Address would be to support the present administration in their conduct towards the Queen, but for his part he looked upon the whole proceedings against the Queen with pity. [23]

This was a rather unusual view of the Royal divorce proceedings for Glengarry to adopt – the Queen's supporters were more generally to be found among political radicals, not a category with which one would normally have associated Macdonell.

Glengarry enthusiastically involved himself in seemingly quite minor and insignificant matters such as the appointment of a new classical master to Inverness Royal Academy following the appointment of the former master to be Minister of Dores. This seemingly routine appointment occupied many of the leading citizens of Inverness and Inverness-shire in the winter and spring of 1819/20. The obvious candidate was perhaps the serving assistant classical master, John Clerk, but Glengarry promoted the candidature of Ewan MacLachlan, formerly the librarian of King's College, Aberdeen, currently master of the parish school in Old Machar, Aberdeen, and, perhaps more relevantly for Glengarry, Gaelic Secretary of the Society of True Highlanders.

On MacLachlan entering the field Clerk withdrew his application but another strong candidate emerged, A N Carmichael of Crieff. Glengarry's factor, representing his principal at a meeting of the Academy Directors, moved that both candidates should be sent down to Glasgow to be examined by the Professors of Latin and Greek in the university there. This they duly did but the Professors refused to act claiming that a brief examination was no way to judge the merits of two such well-qualified candidates. Upon receiving news of this Glengarry instructed his factor to order the two candidates to proceed to St Andrews to be examined by the classicists there. MacLachlan, who was a long-standing friend and protégé of Glengarry did so, but Carmichael properly ignored this high-handed usurpation of the rights of the Directors.

A remarkable feature of the election was the creation of new Directors – while the school was normally run by Directors made up of the Provost, Baillies and Dean of Guild of the Burgh of Inverness, the Moderator of Inverness Presbytery and five nominees of the Commissioners of Supply for Inverness-shire, anyone else who subscribed £50 could become a Director. Naturally enough most of the work and most of the decisions devolved on those Directors living in and around the town of Inverness. In the course of the election controversy forty-two new Directors so qualified, many of them, it was alleged, created by Glengarry to further his cause, although a proportion of the new Directors were opponents of the Glengarry camp and both factions seem to have been spending actively in the creation of new Directors. There appears to have been a strong element of rivalry between the Burgh and the County in this, as in many other matters, with country-dwellers, like Glengarry, feeling that the merchants and lawyers of Inverness had too large a share in the direction of the affairs of Inverness-shire.

At the meeting of Directors called to make a decision on the appointment a motion was proposed by Fraser of Relig, seconded by Glengarry's old adversary, Sheriff William Fraser Tytler, that:

> . . . it is irregular, and unjustifiable, and highly
> disrespectful to this meeting that an individual
> Director should assume a power (as has been in this
> case) of giving a mandate to the candidates to repair
> to St Andrews for examination without any authority
> from a General Meeting of the Directors. [24]

Glengarry, explaining that he was not a man of business or lawyer, claimed that he had acted on the wishes of a majority of the

Directors but had no intention of giving offence. With this soothing gesture the motion was withdrawn. In the end Carmichael was appointed although MacLachlan was given £100 from Academy funds as compensation for his travelling expenses around Scotland in pursuance of the Directors' and Glengarry's instructions. The assistant master, John Clerk, was also rewarded – he received an increase of £20 on his annual salary. The Academy could well afford such generosity – the new Directors' subscriptions had brought in over £2000 to the Academy funds. In appointing Carmichael the Directors rejected one of the most distinguished scholars that the Highlands had produced, although Carmichael was a more than well-qualified candidate. It is hard to avoid the conclusion that the Directors were not voting so much against MacLachlan as against Glengarry's attempt to impose him on them.

His energetic promotion of MacLachlan's claims does reflect the lengths to which he would go to help a friend. If Glengarry could be a bad enemy he was equally a kind, active and thoughtful friend, although perhaps his friendship could at times prove embarrassingly counterproductive. His kinsman, Coll Macdonell of Barrisdale wrote of his chief in 1814:

> With all his faults he is a sincere and most strenuous advocate for his friends, and, had he been independent, had the heart of a prince. [25]

With such a combative personality it is not perhaps surprising that Glengarry was a regular litigant in both Inverness Sheriff Court and the Court of Session in Edinburgh. Some of these cases were probably unavoidable. He was, after all, owner of a huge tract of land and many of the problems that this would always throw up were more or less bound to end up in court. However the volume of cases and their character does tend to suggest a reluctance to compromise matters and a taste for litigation. One case, involving William Cameron, tenant of the sheep farm of Torrery, even went from the Court of Session to the House of Lords. Another case, expensively argued before the Court of Session and determined a month after his death, was a dispute with the Duke of Gordon's trustees over the right of presentation to the Parish of Kilmonivaig. This case, which was over a right or a privilege with no financial advantage to the winner, the point at issue being the right to appoint the parish minister, was settled by a majority of seven to five in favour of Glengarry.

A less public and less serious matter perhaps, but one which quite vividly indicates the considerable perils of crossing Glengarry, was his action against Donald MacDonald, the toll-keeper of the Stone Bridge of Inverness, and the sub-tenant Margaret MacDonald. Glengarry was travelling back to Glengarry House in a coach with his wife in the morning of 26th November 1819 and found that the gates on the bridge were shut and no tollman was on hand to collect the fee and open the gates. Glengarry and his coachman knocked in vain for half an hour before finding the tollman:

> . . . in a neighbouring whisky house or retail house of spirituous liquors drinking at spirituous liquors from whence he or she was brought and the said gates opened. That in this detention the pursuer and his wife and family were upon the bridge for a period of about 30 minutes on a cold frosty morning, and their horses having in the meantime got restive, they ran off on the gates being opened, and the lives of the occupants of the said carriage were thereby in danger. [26]

Suitable apologies and compensation were extracted from the errant toll-keeper.

Glengarry's long and close relationship with Walter Scott has already been touched on. Glengarry supplied Scott with much historical material and Scott reciprocated, sharing documents he came across in the course of his historical and antiquarian researches. Glengarry also endeared himself to Scott by presenting him with the deer hound Maida, seen in many portraits of the novelist. Glengarry offered Scott this dog in 1816, explaining:

> . . . I have a Cross very much admired which generally attend my carriage, they can travel without inconvenience with any horse and make famous watch dogs. Their sire was the sheep dog called 'the Blue Dog' of Spain, that kills the wolf and preserves their valuable flocks from Bears etc., their Dam the genuine Highland Deer Hound, which race I have maintained likewise in perfect purity. . . [27]

and offering to send one to Abbotsford:

> . . . he shall be in your possession on Thursday first. His
> name is Maida, out of respect for that action in which my
> Brother had the honour to lead the 78th Highlanders to
> victory. This dog is now in his prime and has been bled
> to the Deer and Roe and should you wish for more of the
> Deer blood for yourself command me freely.

Two years later Glengarry was sending a bitch down to Abbotsford
to be mated to Maida:

> True Lass, whom I send per Bearer, tho' inferior in
> appearance etc. is own sister to Maida whose embraces
> she goes to receive as I am anxious to keep on that Breed
> as pure as possible [28]

Scott described Maida as 'the noblest dog ever seen on the Border
since Johnnie Armstrong's time – he is between the wolf and deer
greyhound, about six feet long from tip of the nose to the tail, and
high and strong in proportion, he is quite gentle, and a great
favourite.' [29] When Maida died in 1824, Glengarry was again swift
to come to the aid of his friend with the offer of a replacement:

> Dear Sir Walter
> I read yesterday in the Caledonian Mercury of 20th
> September the death (and interment) of my old friend
> Maida and seeing you have honoured him with an effigy
> and epitaph I beg permission to keep another spring pup
> for you, possessing a portion of his Blood. The animal I
> look forward to the production of, will I trust be found
> worthy of a place within your Portcullis, or, as guard to
> your carriage; if I may anticipate from Sire and Dam
> (now in my possession) what he is likely to prove. [30]

He was as good as his word. In June 1825 he wrote to advise that:

> The pup I have reared for you equals my expectations
> and gives a promise of rivalling old Maida in your
> family; I call him Nimrod and if properly bled to High
> Game I feel confident that he will support the character
> of his race. But even with the best deerhounds attention
> must be paid in entering and training them. He will
> make a handsome carriage dog in another year. [31]

Breeding his own line of deerhounds was just part of what
Glengarry saw as the proper role of a Highland gentleman. Just as

he travelled on all possible occasions with 'Glengarry's Tail' – the full retinue of gillies and henchman, bard and piper that would have been familiar to his fifteenth and sixteenth century ancestors, so the preservation of everything that spoke of the old Highlands was his passion. To aid this process, and to surround himself with like-minded sympathisers he founded the Society of True Highlanders. An advertisement in the *Inverness Journal* in June 1815 explains the motivation in characteristically Glengarryesque language:

> To preserve pure and uncontaminated the genuine characteristics and national distinctions of the SONS OF THE GAEL must be one of the dearest wishes of every patriotic Highlander. To him the nervous, energetic and harmonious LANGUAGE of his ancestors of unrivalled antiquity – the simplicity and sublimity of Gaelic POETRY – the martial, exhilarating, and melodious Music which charmed his youth – the graceful GARB in which the Roman Legions overcame all but the Sons of Caledonia – the fraternal affection of KINDRED, and reverence for patriarchal CHIEFS and hereditary Leaders – and the venerable, ancient, and becoming CUSTOMS and MANNERS of his forefathers, are subjects of veneration – stimuli to exertion – his boast in prosperity – his solace in adversity, and at all times the object of his solicitude and regard. By attention to these peculiarities, the Sons of our mountains have ever maintained a character, as a people, which rendered them the terror of their foes, the safeguard of their country, the prop of the throne, the guardians of the altar, and conspicuous for noble, generous, and heroic sentiments. By these characteristics, they have everywhere, and in every situation, attained a respectability of character to which there are few parallels; and desirous to maintain pure and uncontaminated their NATIONAL DISTINCTIONS, a Society was instituted at Inverlochy on the 15th June, 1815, under the title and designation of the SOCIETY OF TRUE HIGHLANDERS, when the following general Rules and Regulations were suggested, at a numerous and respectable Meeting of Highland Gentlemen assembled on the occasion, but subject to alteration at the first general Meeting.

1. The Society shall be governed by a President and an indefinite number of Vice Presidents, assisted by 36 Stewards, a Secretary, Under Secretary and Treasurer.

2. All real Chiefs shall be Hereditary Vice Presidents from whom the President shall be annually chosen by a majority of votes (be he in or out of the Peerage) so as his fortune enables him to support the consequent expense.

3. Peeresses in their own right, and maintaining their family following, whether Heiresses or Co-Heiresses, to be Female Vice Presidents for life.

4. The Heirs of Chiefs, after the age of 21, the Peers of the Clans, and other heads of Families of great standing and following, (having suitable fortune) to be Vice Presidents for life, so likewise are the *tanistears* of each clan . . . [32]

The Society flourished and many of the leading Highland figures joined, including such clan chiefs as the Marquess of Huntly, the Dukes of Argyll and Atholl, Chisholm of Chisholm, MacDonald of Sleat, MacKenzie of Seaforth, Mackintosh of Mackintosh, MacLeod of MacLeod. A resident secretary and treasurer, Duncan Stewart of Achnacone, was appointed and Macdonell's protégé, the Aberdeen-based Gaelic and classical scholar Ewan MacLachlan, appointed as Gaelic Secretary. Much of its activity was perfectly worthy and culturally inclined. Glengarry's bard composed a song in honour of the Society which was performed in October 1815 and '. . .which, as a modern composition, was considered a masterpiece.' [32] The Society also took steps to preserve old songs – at their November 1816 meeting they:

. . . awarded Five Guineas to Mary McDonell, wife of John McAllan, for having sung distinctly a *very ancient Gaelic song*, of peculiar merit, which, *but for her*, would certainly have been lost. [34]

At the same meeting they decided to issue guidance on the vexed matter of appropriate tartans and competing claims to tartans. A letter had been received from the Highland Society of London:

. . . calling upon them (through their President) to take up the case of the Clan Tartans in hand, *as otherwise at a stand* from the inconsiderate specimens given in; where several

> Clans had claimed certain Regimental Tartans, the right of
> neither; accordingly the Society of True Highlanders
> *deciding themselves perfectly competent to the task* have agreed
> to assist *those difficulted* in the achievement of this desirable
> object; for which purpose a day *will be set* with such as may
> apply either to the President or Resident Secretary.

The next year, Duncan Stewart advertised the third anniversary meeting of the Society at Inverlochy on 10th June 1817 and added:

> It is earnestly requested both by the Highland Society and
> The Society of True Highlanders that Members may be
> pleased to fetch with them swatches of their district
> Tartans, as well as those they claim as their own, or suspect
> to be unnamed, so that the confusion now complained of,
> and not without reason, may be immediately removed. [35]

Social issues also came under the consideration of the True Highlanders. The Highlands, like other parts of Britain were affected by a post-war economic depression. With demobilisation of the armed forces there was a reduction in cash wages coming into the area. Added to this there was a fall in the price of cattle and sheep and the kelp industry, producing potash for chemical processes, collapsed with the re-opening of imports from Europe. The Society appointed a committee in 1816 to examine the best means of alleviating the distress among the poor in the Highlands with the hope of preventing, as far as possible, emigration. In 1817 a donation of £5 was made towards the poor of Fort William and the Society, in addition, resolved to use their funds to purchase grain for sale at cost price in all the areas covered by their members.

Glengarry was the first President or *Ceann Suidhe* and later rejoiced in the title of *Fear Bunachar* – or Founder. Whatever office he occupied the Society was very much his creation and his creature. His and its opinions were swiftly communicated to the waiting wider world when occasion arose. In 1819, at the height of the Parliamentary Reform agitation which had seen the Peterloo Massacre in August of that year, Macdonell wrote to Robert Dundas, Viscount Melville, in typically forceful terms:

> My Dear Lord
> I am far from considering the present a moment for
> hesitation or indecision, I have therefore called a meeting

of the Society of True Highlanders at Inverlochy, in order
to address the Prince Regent on the present aspects of
public affairs in the South, for Thank God, in the
Highlands, we are Loyal and Staunch to a man – Having
only returned from Perthshire and Edinburgh on
Thursday last our Address will be among the last of
reaching St. James's, but were matters to go beyond
words the True Highlanders should, you may rest
assured, with their wonted hardyhood and gallantry be
found so Martial in the Van; at a time when every thing
dearest to Britons seems to be assailed by an
unprincipled set of designing demagogues. [36]

The True Highlanders also believed in enjoying themselves
and a highlight of their calendar was the annual Highland Games,
held in September to coincide with Glengarry's birthday on the
15th. The 1817 announcement is typical:

The True Highlanders Fete will be given in 'Straiden-
Garry' as last year, by the Fear Bunachar upon Saturday
13th day of September, when all True Highlanders are
welcome. The ancient Garb of Caledonia, and the
pastimes of her Mountain Race, the order of the day. [37]

The pastimes of the 'Mountain Race' were to raise certain problems
for the Society. The traditional running and trials of strength were
not controversial, except perhaps when, as in 1822, the competition
to lift an 18 stone boulder and throw it over a five foot high bar
was won by what the *Inverness Courier* called ' a mere stone-mason',
after having foiled all the 'pretty-men of Glengarry.' What
provoked criticism was the competition to tear the carcass of a
cow apart. The frequently critical *Courier* went into satirical mode
describing:

. . . another of our ancient sports, namely falling upon a
cow, in the deadthraw, and manfully tearing the still
reeking animal limb from limb, by dint of muscular
strength. Some people were, we saw, squeamish enough
to be shocked by this exhibition, and did not scruple to
use the epithets, 'brutal' 'disgusting' and so forth. . . .
Even the most expert of the operators took from four to
five hours in rugging and riving, tooth and nail, before
they brought off the limbs of one cow. [38]

This distasteful event, the responsibility for which must surely lie with Glengarry, attracted the severe disapproval of David Stewart of Garth, who had been one of the founding members of the True Highlanders. Writing to Sir Walter Scott in 1822, in the aftermath of George IV's visit to Scotland, he observed:

> I see Glengarry continues his attempt to bring odium on the Highland character by instituting premiums for such brutal feats as that of twisting off the leg of a cow. With a tolerable knowledge of Highland customs I declare I never heard even a hint of such a savage and useless exhibition of strength. [39]

Such displays cast doubt on the Society of True Highlanders, as indeed did Glengarry's conduct at the Royal Visit. A society which had started off with good intentions and which had friendly relations with the Celtic Society and the Highland Society of London became compromised, largely, it would seem, because of what Sir Walter Scott would describe as the 'wild and fierce' side of Glengarry's character.

There seems little doubt that Alasdair Ranaldson was at his happiest around his ancestral lands, near Creagan an Fhithich, the Raven's Rock, where his Highland spirit could find full play for its expression. Sadly he seemed not to have the gift of being able to live at peace with his neighbours, and, as we shall see in the next chapter, this involved him in a long-running and ludicrous feud with his neighbour and fellow chief of Clan Donald, Macdonald of Clanranald.

CHAPTER 10

Peerage and Precedence

'. . . being possessed of that ancient and ample
inheritance of a family heretofore ennobled. . .'

A lasdair Macdonell had been brought up to have a profound
belief in his own significance, in the role of clan chiefs and in
his family's leading place in Highland affairs. An obituarist was
to write of him that because of his early succession to the estate
and his isolation from the company of equals:

> . . . his youthful mind acquired early and exaggerated
> impressions of the dignity of a Highland chief. [1]

There is ample evidence that he inherited from his mother Marjory
a high-handed and autocratic manner – she certainly, on the
testimony of the letter books of the family solicitor William
MacDonald of St Martins, was not an easy woman to deal with.
Her Gaelic sobriquet of *Marsalaidh Bhinneach* or 'light-headed
Marjory' perhaps gives some idea of her character. A nineteenth
century historian of the Highlands, Charles Fraser-MacIntosh
argued that young Glengarry had been:

> . . . alternately crossed and petted, so that before his
> mother's death, and especially thereafter before attaining
> his majority, young Glengarry's temper and disposition
> showed itself as most overbearing. [2]

Glengarry combined a haughty sense of his own and his
family's worth with a temper that did not take well to being
thwarted. Although he was in his thirties before the question of a
peerage and of the precedence of the House of Glengarry came
publicly to the fore there is no doubt that these matters had run in
his mind many years earlier. Lord Minto, the British Ambassador
at Vienna, during the period of Glengarry's insanity there in 1800,

noted that Macdonell had, during one of Minto's visits, entered upon a long digression on the genealogy of Glengarry.

Undoubtedly Glengarry had more than a fair measure of the traditional Highland enthusiasm for the history and traditions of his family, clan and race. Writing, at some length, to Walter Scott about the history of Clan Donald and the rival claims to pre-eminence of Clanranald and Glengarry he assured the 'historical Bard of Scotland' that he could:

> . . . tell the origin of every other Branch and House
> sprung from the Clan, just as circumstantially, as I have
> given you the history of these, or as I can explain to your
> perfect understanding and I should trust conviction any
> questions or points you may consider requisite to
> elucidate either of those two. [3]

The first evidence of Glengarry's campaign to re-establish his family in the hereditary peerage of Scotland comes in 1812 when he wrote on this subject to Lord Melville, the son of Henry Dundas his early patron, and to Lord Liverpool, the newly appointed Prime Minister. Why, having come of age in 1794, he had waited eighteen years to broach this subject is unclear. Perhaps it might simply be that by 1812 the work of the Militia Regiment he commanded had settled down into something of a routine and there was now time and energy available for settling his family affairs. The fact that his application came so quickly on the heels of the appointment of Liverpool as Prime Minister – Liverpool took office in June 1812 and Glengarry had a letter on his desk by mid September – may suggest that he felt that the change of administration was in some way propitious for his plans. Although no trace of an earlier application now appears to survive in the archives it is, of course, also possible that earlier applications on this subject had been made.

Glengarry made his preparations with some care. He obtained the support, if perhaps not the entirely enthusiastic backing, of the great Highland magnate the Marquis of Huntly. He also mobilised the Dundas interest, as personified by Robert Saunders Dundas, 2nd Viscount Melville. Melville was at this time First Lord of the Admiralty, but, like his illustrious father Henry, he clearly still kept a finger in any number of Scottish pies. Glengarry had

travelled to London, the better to prosecute his case and wrote
enthusiastically to Lord Melville on 28th August from St Alban's
Street. There is in the first paragraph of his letter perhaps just the
suggestion that Melville was not particularly anxious to see
Macdonell, although the letter does bear a note indicating that
Melville did make an appointment with him for Wednesday 2nd
September:

> My Lord
> I was on Tuesday last honoured by a letter from the
> Marquis of Huntly of date the 20th Curt. from Gordon
> Castle; and in consequence, immediately called down
> at the Admiralty for your Lordship who had just then
> stepped into a carriage with some friends: I resumed,
> with no better success, my visit yesterday morning:
> And from the contents of the Marquis's letter, I have
> reason to be proud of the steady suppport of my Noble
> Friend! as it thereby appears he has interested himself
> strongly in my behalf and has written again to your
> Lordship on my account. Under these circumstances I
> use this freedom, and beg the favour of an Audience, at
> your Lordship's earliest convenience, with permission
> to lay, at that time, the draft of my Intended Petition
> before you, and to give your Lordship such
> explanations on the nature and grounds of my Claim,
> and the Object I aspire to, as will, I trust, <u>at least</u> justify
> in impartial Eyes, the Efforts I am now about to make
> for having the Honours of my Family, which became
> Extinct Ao. 1680 revived in My Person.
>
> And I will even add, with becoming Boldness and with
> <u>proper</u> Gratitude to His Respected Memory that had
> the late Worthy and ever to be lamented Viscount
> Melville, your Lordship's Venerable Father been in
> existence! <u>I could not now have doubted</u> but that my
> matters would <u>speedily</u> assume a very prosperous
> aspect – I beg forgiveness of this digression and I have
> the honour to be My Lord,
> Your Lordships Most Obedient & Humble Servt.
> A Macdonell[4]

Melville evidently agreed to recommend Glengarry's cause to
Lord Liverpool and the Marquis of Huntly wrote to Liverpool on
6th September in what seems to be a somewhat guarded and terse
manner:

> My Dear Lord
> Mr. Macdonell of Glengarry who writes me that he has
> some claim to lay before Government has requested
> that I should mention his name to your Lordship. I can
> most certainly recommend him as a very loyal man,
> indeed his zeal for Government, as well as in the cause
> of our friends is at all times most conspicuous. I am, my
> Dear Lord, with perfect regard
> Yours most sincerely
> Huntly [5]

What Lord Liverpool took from this recommendation is uncertain – Glengarry's zeal for the Government and his sound political affiliations were certainly vouched for but the letter hardly stands as a ringing endorsement of his claim. Glengarry's own letter to Liverpool, dated from Edinburgh on 15th September 1812, argues his case on grounds of the public good, although he fails to explain exactly what the public benefit would be:

> My Lord
> Having mentioned to your secretary before I left Town
> my intention of writing your Lordship from the country
> on the subject of your letter of the 9th inst. I beg leave
> now to enclose a letter from the Marquis of Huntly,
> which I trust will have the desired effect of obtaining
> for me your Lordship's countenance: Particularly as
> Lord Melville promised me he would recommend my
> case to your Lordship.
>
> I beg permission to subjoin my address – and trusting to
> your Lordship's urbanity for a favourable reply in a
> matter which may not only increase the powers, but, if
> possible heighten the desire, so early evinced of making
> myself further useful to my King and Country. [6]

Glengarry's petition to the King (or more precisely to the Prince Regent – George III being at this time in his long final period of illness) was drawn up at the College of Heralds by the Norroy King of Arms (whose unfamiliarity with Scottish matters perhaps explains the somewhat unorthodox spelling of 'Glengarie' throughout the document) and commences with the historical claims of his family to a peerage:

> To His Royal Highness the Prince Regent
> The petition of Alexander Macdonell of Glengarie in the

County of Inverness Esquire, sometime Colonel
Commandant of the late Glengarie Highlanders, or 1st
British Fencible Regiment, afterwards Colonel
Commandant of the late 4th Inverness Shire or Glengarie
Volunteers, and now Colonel Commandant of the 2nd
Regiment of Inverness Shire Local Militia

Most humbly showeth

That your Royal Highness's Predecessor King Charles
the Second was pleased to ennoble your petitioner's
family in the person of Æneas Macdonell of Glengarie
aforesaid, by advancing him to the Peerage of Scotland
in the Name, Style and Title of Lord Macdonell and
Arross to hold to him and the heirs male of his Body by
Letters Patent under the Great Seal, being dated at
Whitehall on the 20th of December 1660 in the 12th year
of his said Majesty's Reign.[7]

The petition showed that Æneas Macdonell had died in 1680
without issue and the Macdonell and Aros peerage had died with
him, although the barony and lands of Glengarry had passed on
to a second cousin and hence down to the present day. The term
baron, which in English custom indicated the lowest rank of the
peerage, did not in Scotland carry the same meaning. There it
indicated that the bearer held his land directly from the Crown.
Glengarry in a later petition, described himself as the 16th Baron
of Glengarry, without pre-empting the royal decision on a peerage.
What Glengarry's ancestor had enjoyed was the rank of a Lord of
Parliament and Glengarry now sought either the revival of the
ancient Scottish peerage or an equivalent rank in the British
peerage. In short:

. . . the dignity of a Peer of Parliament, in such manner
and by such Title as to your Royal Highness's Wisdom
and Goodness shall seem meet . . .

Glengarry went on to assert both the historical precedence of
his family and their loyalty to the Crown. Æneas had been an active
supporter of the Royalist cause during the Civil War and had
fought on to the final defeat of the Royalist forces in Scotland at
Lochgarry in July 1654. The more recent and awkwardly embarrassing fact that Alasdair the 11th Chief had been active on the
Jacobite side in the 1715 Rising was simply ignored. Alasdair,

indeed, had been so active that the Old Pretender had ennobled him as Lord Macdonell in 1716. Glengarry was of course, in the eyes of any remaining Jacobites, the 5th Lord Macdonell of this creation – as a loyal subject of the House of Hanover and a King's officer he could not use the illegal and officially unrecognised Jacobite title. Equally embarrassing was the fact that the Glengarry men had been out in force in the '45 under the command of Æneas the second son of the 12th chief. He dealt with these issues by blandly passing over this whole troublesome period of history and referring instead to a loyal address *Alasdair Dubh,* the 11th Chief, had submitted to George I on his accession in 1714.

Glengarry attached a copy of the loyal address to George I. He noted that due to 'court intrigue' the address had never been presented and that the 'Clans, in resentment of this supposed neglect, raised Rebellion in the following year.' This might not appear to be a totally convincing explanation for the 1715 Rising but it did at least blur any image that might exist in official circles of the Macdonells of Glengarry as inveterate opponents of the House of Hanover by raising the spectre of some nameless and long dead court intriguers whose hostility to the Highland clans had provoked them to arms.

Liverpool wrote back to Glengarry after some further correspondence assuring him that his petition would be laid before the Prince Regent but that he felt unable to interfere in any way in the business. The petition failed but Glengarry continued to believe strongly in his claims to the restoration of the family peerage and returned to the subject in 1820, when George IV came to the throne and the prospect of a new creation of peers to mark his accession seemed likely.

In May 1820, he once more approached Lord Melville, still in office as First Lord of the Admiralty:

> It has long since been reported and very generally believed that His Majesty has it in consideration now to create a new Badge [batch?] of Peers. But till the day of Coronation seemed drawing nearer I could not think of troubling your Lordship. However now I hope that I may confidently rely upon your Lordship's not seeing me passed over in the approaching List.

All I ask is only what was in my Family before and merely lost (as formerly stated to you) from the Patents being drawn out to the 'Heir Male of His Body lawfully begotten' whereas Lord Macdonell died without issue of any kind and was succeeded in his estates by his cousin Alexander Macdonell of Glengarry my immediate predecessor.

Therefore the title I now humbly crave is that of a Baron of the United Kingdom, and to be styled (as formerly) Lord Macdonell and Arross.

Your Lordship's hours must be so much occupied at present that I cannot think of intruding longer. but, with every reliance on your good wishes I have the honour to remain. [8]

George IV's coronation was long postponed. He came to the throne in January 1820 but was not crowned until July 1821 due to a combination of illness and the King's desperate desire to divorce his estranged Queen, Charlotte of Brunswick, before the coronation. This delay however did provide Glengarry with ample opportunity for letter writing and string-pulling. In June 1820 he advised the long-suffering Melville that he had written to Prime Minister Liverpool but had not yet had an answer. Ever optimistic he noted that:

I presume, under your Lordship's powerful auspices to judge favourably of the delay from the confidence I repose in the sincerity of your friendship. . .

and reminded Melville of his long-standing relationship with the House of Dundas:

Meantime I place entire confidence in your friendship's bearing my claim thro', for which you shall never have cause to be sorry – And begging the favour of such a communication from your Lordship, as I should expect from your worthy and venerable father's son, the patron of my youth. [9]

When, at last, the coronation was arranged, Glengarry left for London to witness 'that interesting ceremony' and advised Melville that he would call on him at the Admiralty to pay his respects:

. . . under a full conviction that your Lordship's friendly promise will now be realised, if any Title of Honour be granted at His Majesty's Coronation. [10]

Glengarry duly attended the 'interesting ceremony' of George IV's coronation, splendidly arrayed in the full panoply of Highland dress, including a brace of pistols. A nervous lady seeing him standing with one of these pistols in his hand assumed that he planned an assassination and raised the alarm. The story swiftly circulated in Society and the press and Glengarry was obliged to write a long letter to *The Times* giving his account of events:

> Sir
> The alarm expressed by a lady on seeing me in
> Westminster Hall on the day of His Majesty's
> coronation, and the publicity which her ladyship
> judged it becoming to give to that expression of
> alarm by means of your paper, I should have treated
> with the indifference due to such mock heroics in
> one of the fair sex, but that it has been copied into
> other papers with comments and additions which
> seemed to me to reflect both upon my conduct and
> upon the Highland character. I trust, therefore, to
> your sense of justice for giving the public the real
> history of the 'mysterious circumstance,' as it is
> termed. I had the honour of a Royal Duke's ticket for
> my daughter and myself to see his Majesty crowned,
> and I dressed upon that magnificent and solemn
> occasion in the full costume of a Highland Chief,
> including, of course, a brace of pistols. I had
> travelled about six hundred miles for that purpose;
> and in that very dress, with both pistols mounted, I
> had the honour to kiss my Sovereign's hand at the
> Levee of Wednesday last, the 25th. [11]

The coronation procession was to assemble at 10.00 a.m. in Westminster Hall and process at 11.00 a.m. to Westminster Abbey where the actual coronation would take place. Glengarry had seats in the gallery of Westminster Hall. He explained that, after taking his daughter for refreshments, on returning to their seats he had found one of them occupied and had gone to stand some way away to get a better view. He had been standing for some time and to relieve his chest of the weight of his breast pistol (he had been up and dressed in full Highland costume and accoutrements since 4 a.m.) he took it into his hand:

> It was at this instant that a lady within a short distance
> exclaimed, 'O Lord, O Lord, there is a gentleman with a

pistol!' To which I answered, 'The pistol will do you no harm, madame.' But a second time she cried out, 'O Lord, O Lord, there is a gentleman with a pistol!' This last I answered by assuring her that the pistol was not loaded, but that I would instantly retire to my place, since it seemed to give her uneasiness . . .'

Three men then approached Glengarry and asked him to hand over his pistol. Macdonell's response could have been predicted:

Need I say that, as a Highland Chief, I refused his demand with contempt?

A further gentleman, identified in Glengarry's letter only as a Knight of the Grand Cross, 'Sir Charles', then approached and asked Glengarry to hand the pistol over. Eventually a compromise between Glengarry's susceptibilities and the need for public calm was worked out. Glengarry's answer was:

'No, Sir Charles: you, as a soldier, may have it, as the honour of an officer and a man of family will be safe in your hands; but positively no other shall – so take it or leave it, as you please.'

Glengarry then handed the pistol over, retaining the second one which was still holstered, and rejoined his daughter. After examining the pistol 'Sir Charles' restored it to its owner and the rest of the day passed off uneventfully.

This, sir, is the whole story of the absurd and ridiculous alarm. Pistols are as essential to the Highland courtier's dress as a sword to the English courtier's . . .

With respect to the wild fantasy that haunted Lady A's brain of danger to his Majesty, I may be permitted to say that George IV has not in his dominions more faithful subjects than the Highlanders; and that not an individual witnessed his Majesty's coronation who would more cheerfully and ardently shed his heart's blood for him than your humble servant,

Ard-Flath Siol-Chuinn Mac Mhic-Alastair

The signature 'Ard-Flath Siol-Chuinn' is highly significant. Ard-Flath may be translated as 'chieftain' and Siol-Chuinn as 'seed' or 'descendants of Conn'. The Conn in question is the 'Conn of the Hundred Battles' – high king of Ireland and one of the semi-legendary progenitors of Clan Donald. This coded, but all embracing, claim to the headship of Clan Donald, however obscure it may have been to the readers of *The Times*, reflected a controversy which Glengarry had been enthusiastically pursuing for some years. The other part of the signature 'Mac Mhic-Alastair' – 'the son of the son of Alastair' – was simply, and uncontroversially, the patronymic of the heads of the house of Glengarry.

A few days after the excitement of the coronation, and of being suspected of having designs on the person of his Majesty, Glengarry submitted a petition to the King requesting the granting of a peerage. There were a number of differences between the 1812 petition and the 1821 submission. One of these was that he signed himself as Glengarry and Clanranald – a title related to his use of the designation 'Ard-Flath Siol-Chuinn'. The other significant difference was that while in the 1812 petition he had started with the award of the peerage to Æneas in 1660 and later noted his descent from the Earls of Ross and Lords of the Isles, in the 1821 petition he starts much further back, indeed in the fourteenth century.

> That John Lord of the Isles the VIIth in lineal male descent from Somerled Thane of Argyle and King of the Western Isles enjoyed the place stile and dignity of Lord Baron of Scotland from 1344 to his decease in 1387. That previous to the year 1344 the said John Lord of the Isles was acknowledged as a Sovereign Prince and your Majesty's Royal predecessor Edward the III[d] King of England entered into a Treaty on the 3[d] October 1357 with the said John in which Treaty the said John is stiled Lord of the Isles and faithful Allie and adherent of the said King Edward. [12]

The Lords of the Isles' habit of conducting an independent foreign policy, and a policy which was often inimical to that of the Scottish Kings, was one of the main reasons why the Lordship was suppressed by James III and James IV and the title incorporated into the honours held by the Crown. The title of 'Lord of the Isles' is still held by the heir to the British throne, along with his other Scottish titles of Duke of Rothesay, Earl of Carrick, Baron Renfrew and Prince and Great Steward of Scotland which collectively reflect the Crown's Bruce and Stewart ancestry.

The petition goes on to outline how the said John of the Isles had married Amy, the heiress of Roderick or Ruari of the Isles, and had by her a son Reginald (or Ranald). This Ranald was the progenitor of both the Clanranald and the Glengarry branches of Clan Donald and is a significant figure in Alasdair Macdonell's parallel campaign to be recognised, peerage or no peerage, as the head of Clan Donald.

The petition went on to trace the complex descent from the 1st John of the Isles, covering the peerage granted to Æneas by King Charles II in 1660 and the loyal address organised by Alexander in 1714 and bringing the story up to the present date. The petition adds in for extra weight and as a demonstration of the contemporary merits of the family and their loyalty and service to the Crown, a brief biographical sketch of Glengarry's younger brother James:

> . . . a Colonel in the army, Lieut. Colonel commanding the 2nd Battn. of the Coldstream Guards . . . who as Major led the 78th Highlanders to the decisive charge in the battle of Maida and repeatedly distinguished himself both in Egypt and Waterloo,

before noting:

> That the title of Lord of the Isles was suppressed by James the Vth † King of Scotland under the pretext of civilising the Highlanders, but in truth to deprive the family of your Petitioner of a great portion of that power which your Petitioner's ancestors then enjoyed.

> That your Petitioner's family notwithstanding that they were thus deprived of the Lordship of the Isles possessed ample property and being descended from the most ancient and most noble families of Scotland have on divers memorable occasions been distinguished for important military and civil services and for loyalty and attachment to the Crown . . .

and concluding, tactfully, with a loyal denial of any wish to strip the newly crowned King of one of his own titles,

---

† Actually the suppression was carried out by James IV in 1493

> That the Title of Lord of the Isles being one of those
> included among the numerous august Titles of your
> Majesty, your Petitioner humbly declines asserting the
> presumed right which he has been induced to believe he
> has to the said dignity and most humbly prays your
> Majesty will be graciously pleased in consideration
> thereof to take the peculiar delicacy of your Petitioner's
> case into your Royal consideration and revive in the
> person of your Petitioner who is chief of the name and
> clan of Macdonell the dignity of Lord Macdonell and
> Arross heretofore enjoyed by his cousin whose Barony
> and other estates your Petitioner now inherits or grant
> your Petitioner such other title as to your Majesty's
> wisdom generosity and goodness shall seem meet . . .

His Majesty's wisdom, generosity and goodness did not extend to creating Glengarry a Peer of the Realm, nor indeed are Glengarry's claims for such an honour entirely persuasive.

He did indeed represent a family which had once had a peerage which, by reason of the limited terms of the original award, could only descend through direct male heirs and, due to the failure of such male heirs, had become extinct. This was, however, hardly a unique circumstance. Although the petitions were addressed to the Crown as the fount of all honours the reality was that the King would act on these matters on the advice of his ministers and there is no particular aspect of public service which might have put Glengarry on the list of those who might expect preferment. Admittedly he had raised and commanded a Fencible regiment in the 1790s – but scores of such regiments had been raised in Scotland alone. He had commanded volunteer and militia regiments – but again this was hardly enough to merit a peerage. His claims on these grounds might well, in any case, have been offset by his somewhat murky legal history – to be tried for murder (even if acquitted) or to assault Caledonian Canal workmen are hardly the best recommendations for a gentleman seeking elevation to the peerage. Glengarry's political affiliations were, from the Government's point of view, sound and solidly loyal, but there was little evidence that anyone took his political standing or aspirations particularly seriously. As far back as February 1796 he had written to Henry Dundas guaranteeing his support for whatever candidate the Government (or Dundas) proposed to run at the forthcoming election but also, in case a candidate had not been identified, offering his own services:

> Knowing my Interest in the County to be as strong as most I beg leave to add that I shall not hesitate to declare myself a Candidate for that Honor if I find it meets with your approbation and that I might expect your support, but without that I have not the most distant idea of starting and you may rely on my supporting your friend at all events . . .

There was a further reason why his chances of a peerage were slender – there was an expectation that a candidate for an honour should be able to support his title; to live in a manner appropriate to the rank he bore. Glengarry's chronic financial difficulties would in themselves have been a persuasive argument against his ennoblement. He did attempt to address this issue by saying in both the 1812 and 1820 petitions that he was 'possessed of the ancient and ample inheritance of a family hitherto ennobled', which was indeed true; but broad acres, if burdened with debt, would not necessarily provide the support for the lifestyle expected of a peer.

Two petitions having failed, many people would have abandoned the quest. Not so Glengarry. His campaign continued and, although the subject of the interview is not stated, a letter in April 1824 dated from Gordon's Hotel, London to Home Secretary Robert Peel is almost certainly related to this cause:

> Col. Ranaldson Macdonell of Clanronald and Glengarry would feel obliged to Mr. Peel by favouring him with an interview on Monday first, the 19th curt., being anxious for an interview upon business (the objects of which he presumes has already been communicated to him) previous to his outset for Cheltenham with the ladies of his Family, where they intend dining on Tuesday. [13]

Home Secretary Peel proved no more helpful than his Prime Minister, Lord Liverpool, had been.

The Royal Visit of George IV to Edinburgh in 1822 must have raised his hopes – after the success of that visit Sir Walter Scott was among those who persuaded the King to lift the Act of Attainder against a number of the descendants of Jacobite peers who had lost their family property and titles after the '45.

Glengarry's family title had of course long gone into extinction by that time and he was not to be, despite his ostentatious devotion to the Crown displayed during the King's visit, the recipient of the Royal favour at that time. Four of the titles lost in the Jacobite cause were restored in June 1824 – those of the Earl of Mar, Viscounts Kenmure and Strathallan and Lord Nairn – by an act of royal grace and favour. Lord Liverpool introducing this measure in the House of Lords observed:

> In that visit which his majesty had graciously been pleased to make to Scotland . . . it was natural that those persons whose ancestors had been attainted, but who were themselves of irreproachable fidelity and unshaken loyalty to the illustrious house of Hanover, should humbly petition his majesty to be restored to those titles and honours which their ancestors had possessed. [14]

In the House of Commons Robert Peel welcomed the duty which fell upon him to propose the reading of the bill and noted that some of those who were descended from the holders of attainted titles did not:

> . . . on considerations of property, wish for the extension of the bounty to them. In making a choice, government found the necessity of selecting those respecting whom no doubt existed regarding the original patent, as well as those who were desirous of preferring their claims. [15]

It is hard to imagine that Glengarry could have read these comments without feeling that he was being ill-used. He too had petitioned for the restoration of a title held by an ancestor, he too considered himself to have demonstrated 'unshaken loyalty to the illustrious House of Hanover' and he, at least, felt no problems existed on 'considerations of property'. Peel's reference was of course to those potential claimants who no longer felt that their property, finances or manner of living would honourably support a peerage.

In 1825 Glengarry was, once more, anxiously seeking the support of the First Lord of the Admiralty, the 2nd Viscount Melville. Writing from Lower Brook Street in Mayfair on 27th April he pled:

My Dear Lord

I give you this trouble to request the honour of an appointment with your Lordship, at your earliest convenience. I hear from good authority that Lord Liverpool acceded to two more of the Scottish peerage (viz. ye Titles of Duffus and Carnwath) being restored to the representatives of these Honours, in Sutherland and Dalziel. You had the goodness to acknowledge the justness of my claim upon the British Peerage, as to say that when a Batch came out my name would be included as you 'considered the Representative of a Scotch Peer to have a fair claim upon the British Peerage' – Pardon me for bringing that circumstance now to your friendly consideration, when the world is impressed with the favourable disposition of His Majesty, as I am undoubtedly the Representative of several Titles of Honour in Scotland (the two highest of which Dignities have been vested by its Parliament in the Royal Family previous to the Union) a district of the Realm not disregarded by the King: And having since 1794 regarded your house as my patron which (during the lifetime of your worthy father) never failed; I am unwilling to attribute a less friendly disposition to his Noble Son, the present Viscount. [16]

This letter perhaps needs a few points of explanation. Melville's quoted remark that he 'considered the Representative of a Scotch Peer to have a fair claim upon the British Peerage' (presumably meaning an extinct Scottish Peerage) is perhaps an accurate reflection of his opinion but one can hardly help feeling that Glengarry has built too optimistically and indeed over-presumptuously on what surely can have been no more than a polite and politic response from a Government minister. It seems very unlikely that an accomplished politician of Melville's vast experience would have committed himself, his Government colleagues or the Throne, with the sort of categorical assurance that Glengarry attributes to him – 'when a Batch came out my name would be included'.

The honour Glengarry notes as being formerly held by the chiefs of Clan Donald and now vested in the Crown was, in addition to the Lordship of the Isles, the Earldom of Ross. This title reverted to the Crown in 1475 at the time of the first forfeiture of the Lordship and was not restored to Clan Donald when the Lordship was temporarily reinstated in 1476. The Ross peerage, as a Dukedom, had been granted to younger sons of James III and James IV and had been held from his birth in 1600 until his accession in 1625 by Prince Charles, the second son (and eventual heir) of James VI and I. Glengarry also reminds Melville of George IV's interest in his Scottish realm (as demonstrated by the 1822 Royal Visit) and concludes with a reassertion of the patronage link between Glengarry and the Dundas family.

Like all the earlier requests and petitions this, too, failed.

•

If Glengarry had no success in persuading the Crown or its Ministers to restore the peerage which Charles II had given on his Restoration to Æneas Macdonell he had little more success in persuading anyone outwith his own immediate circle that he could rightfully claim the title of Clanranald as well as Glengarry, and that he was, for whatever it was worth after the forfeiture, the heir to the Lordship of the Isles and the headship of all Clan Donald. Undeterred by his lack of success he persistently inflated his claims. In his 1812 petition he describes himself as simply Macdonell of Glengarry, in 1821 he uses the form Glengarry and Clanranald and in his letter to Robert Peel in 1824 he is using the form Clanronald and Glengarry.

The origins of this problem lie in the fourteenth century with Ranald (*fl.*1380 – c.1386) the son of John of the Isles and Amy MacRuari. Ranald's eldest son and heir was Allan and his family formed the main line of the Clan Ranald branch of Clan Donald. Allan's second son was Donald, the founder of the Glengarry branch of Clan Donald. Primogeniture thus would ensure that, assuming no failures of heirs, the Glengarry family would be a cadet branch of the main stem.

Glengarry's case would thus seem to be hopeless. However it was part of his argument, carried on at some length with anyone who was prepared to listen, that the succession of Clanranald was flawed, by descent by tanistry rather than primogeniture, compounded by illegitimacy, in the sixteenth century. Tanistry was the ancient Celtic practice of selecting an heir from among a kinship group rather than automatically granting the succession to the oldest son. Accordingly he claimed that the title should revert to the house of Glengarry as the senior legitimate male heirs of John of the Isles. In all the flurry of letters to the press, pamphlets, lawyers' opinions and so forth which surrounded this controversy it is difficult to disentangle the truth of the case. Glengarry's view was that as he had evidence that John of Moidart (or Iain Moidartach) had been, by act of the King's Council, legitimated in 1531 he was thus proved to have been born out of wedlock. This complex matter is made more complicated by a variety of official documents which Glengarry cites, such as an Act of the Privy Council as late as 1672, describing the Glengarry of the day as 'chief of the name and family of Macdonald.'

Perhaps the most sensible summing up comes in Sir Walter Scott's Diary for 14th February 1826, where, discussing Glengarry he writes:

> He has of late prosecuted a quarrel, ridiculous enough in the present day, to have himself admitted and recognised as Chief of the whole Clan Ranald, or surname of Macdonald. The truth seems to be, that the present Clanranald is not descended from a legitimate Chieftain of the tribe; for, having accomplished a revolution in the sixteenth century, they adopted a Tanist, or Captain – that is, a Chief not in the direct line of succession, a certain Ian Moidart, or John of Moidart, who took the title of Captain of Clanranald, with all the powers of Chief, and even Glengarry's ancestors recognised them as chiefs *de facto* if not *de jure*. The fact is, that this elective power was, in cases of insanity, imbecility and the like, exercised by the Celtic tribes; and though Ian Moidart was no chief by birth, yet by election he became so, and transmitted his power to his descendants, as would King William III, if he had had any. So it is absurd to set up the *jus sanguinis* now, which Glengarry's ancestors did not, or could not, make good when it was a right worth combating for. [17]

Scott, who was by profession an advocate and was Sheriff of Selkirkshire and a Principal Clerk of the Court of Session, was doubtless correct in his summation. He was also wise in his judgement that the issue was no longer worth fighting for. Scott had enjoyed the benefit of a number of letters from Glengarry on the subject of the Lordship of the Isles – Scott's epic poem *The Lord of the Isles* and his research for it, including a trip round Scotland on the *Pharos* with the Commissioners of the Northern Lights, seem to have been the catalyst for this correspondence. In October 1814 Glengarry wrote:

> Did I not feel I was too late for your present work I would willingly hand you an acknowledged anecdote of one of my ancestors, a Lord of the Isles, trusting to your indulgence, if it has already reached your well-informed ears. Tho' I will first observe my regret that you seem impressed with a belief that Clanranald (i.e. MacDonald of Moidart 'The Captain of Clanranald') is of legitimate extraction, and no less so that it does not appear to have reached you that the Glengarries were the Chiefs of Clanranald wh. is the oldest branch of the whole clan. [18]

In November of the same year he wrote a long letter to Scott on the Lordship and on Clan Donald's traditional privilege of forming the right of the line in a Scottish army – a privilege Glengarry claimed had extended from Bannockburn down to the Battle of Falkirk in 1746.

However long this claim to primacy among the Macdonalds and with it *Ceannas nan Gaidheal* – the headship of the Gael – had been burning in Glengarry's mind it seems first to have come to light in the perhaps rather improbable context of a Gaelic birth announcement in the *Inverness Journal*. This read:

> Ann 'n Lun'uin air a chuigeadh la' do n' mhios so, rug gu sabhailt, Ban-Tighearn' ceart onarach Caroline Ann Mhac-Dhon'uill, Bean Cheann-Feadhna', no Cheann Chinnidh Chlann-Raon'uill, nioghan laddir shlanteil. [19]

which may be translated as 'In London on the 5th day of this month the Right Honourable Lady Caroline Ann MacDonald, Wife of the Chief or Head of Clan Ranald, safely bore a strong healthy daughter'.

The problem, for Glengarry, lay in the terms 'Ceann Feadhna' and 'Ceann Chinnidh' . Among the possible translations of both words is 'chief' but Ceann Chinnidh carries the sense of the head of a family or clan while Ceann Feadhna is also used to denote captain or commander. In a letter to the *Inverness Journal* of 31st October a correspondent signing himself *Fear-Raonuillich* or 'Kin or follower of Ranaldson' (in reality probably Glengarry himself) pointed out that Ceann Feadhna and Ceann Chinnidh were not synonyms and that:

> Glengarry's ancestors stand upon record, as Ranaldsons, at a period when the Lairds of Moidart, as their proper mark of cadency, appear in the same authentic record as Allanson! [20]

This letter provoked a lengthy response by a correspondent signing himself 'Also Fear-Raonuillich.' The current 'Laird of Moidart' or Chief and Head of Clan Ranald (depending on one's point of view) who had submitted the birth notice to the *Inverness Journal* was Ranald George Macdonald MP. While neither principal ever quite publicly admitted responsibility for the correspondence Glengarry wrote to Ranald Macdonald in 1821:

> I shall hold myself responsible to you for the future silence of Fior Raonuillach; and, in like manner, I hope you will not refuse to answer for the silence of 'Also a Fior Raonuillach' [21]

For some reason the name of the correspondents had changed from Fear Raonuillach (Kin of Ranaldson) to Fior Raonuillich (True Ranaldson) but there is little doubt that the same two pens were behind the sets of letters. The details of the controversy are of little interest to any but the most devoted genealogist or clan historian – the manner of conducting it however reveals much about Glengarry's personality and obsessive nature.

The Raonuillich controversy ran on in the *Inverness Journal* until August 1818. In 1819 Glengarry raised the issue again in a new forum. The *Inverness Courier* reported in October 1819 that at the Michaelmas Head Court, held in Inverness to draw up the roll of free-holders and electors for the County, Glengarry rose and read a protest against R G Macdonald being described as 'of Clanranald' as he had no charters or lands that entitled him to this designation and that his true title was Macdonald of Moidart or 'Captain of Clanranald'. Glengarry was of the opinion that the title of 'Captain' properly indicated R G Macdonald's lower status and distinguished him from a genuine clan chief. The *Courier* (founded in 1817 and which proved to be somewhat more critical of Glengarry than the older-established *Inverness Journal*) went on:

> To prove this averment, Glengarry entered into a detail of the genealogical history of the Family of Moidart, explained the etymology of the word Clan, and concluded (with an accompaniment of some animated remarks) that he would consider it personal to himself if any gentleman should henceforward mention Mr. Macdonald otherwise than as Captain of Clanranald. Mr. Mackenzie of Woodside having, on behalf of his clients, answered the gentleman's objections, and some observations having been made thereon by several other members, it was rejected as incompetent to be entertained by the meeting. Glengarry here intimated that he would bring the question before the Court of Session, and thence, if necessary, to the House of Peers. [22]

Whatever the merits of Glengarry's case the wisdom of raising so delicate an issue in such a meeting and declaring that he would be offended if anyone referred to Ranald Macdonald other than as 'Captain of Clanranald' is questionable – particularly when accompanied by 'animated remarks'. However when Glengarry's heart and mind were engaged in a subject he frequently found difficulty in retaining a sense of proportion and balance.

In 1821 he took matters further by seeking Counsel's opinion on 'the material points of discussion in the Ranaldian Controversy.' John Jardine and John Riddell, advocates, duly submitted their opinion (and doubtless their fee note) which supported Glengarry's position. Glengarry also privately published the correspondence he had had with Clanranald and the record of the interventions by friends of both chiefs attempting to reconcile matters. John Macdonald of Borrodale, Clanranald's factor, wrote to Glengarry in March 1821 suggesting that some friends of both men should meet and examine some of the documents in the case, particularly a document which had been submitted to the editor of the *Inverness Journal* but not published by him:

> . . . to discover the merits or demerits of the paper, and of the present correspondence relating to it, and endeavour to come to such a clear understanding of it as may be the

> means of preventing the continuance of such
> disagreeable personal controversy between you and
> Clanranald. . . [23]

going on to observe:

> . . . a correspondence of such nature cannot possibly be
> to the credit of the parties concerned, but, on the
> contrary, will, as formerly, afford amusement to the
> enemies of both (if any they have), and to the public, at
> their joint expense.

Four men met on 12th March, two linked to Clanranald's cause and two to Glengarry's, (including Coll MacDonald of Dalness, Glengarry's lawyer). They concluded that Clanranald had been unacquainted with the offensive material in the submission to the *Inverness Journal* :

> . . . which in our opinion removes him from all
> responsibility thereanent; and in consequence, as real
> friends of the parties, recommend to them both to
> abstain in future from correspondence . . .

Other than Clanranald's assurance, presumably conveyed by his representatives, of his ignorance of the document, their evidence for this opinion is not stated but the perfectly reasonable wish that the matter should be let rest was not to be fulfilled.

Glengarry had published his correspondence with Clanranald in the Edinburgh and London papers and this breach of confidence annoyed Clanranald who instructed Borrodale to publish in the Edinburgh papers the minute of the meeting of the 12th March. Perhaps predictably, Glengarry was not happy with the outcome. In a letter dated 26 March 1821 he took his supporters Coll Macdonald and Captain Æneas Macdonell to task for acting *ultra vires*. He claimed that he had had no objection to Macdonald of Borrodale's proposal for a meeting of friends which would have given Ranald Macdonald the chance to disavow any connection with the anonymous publication of which Glengarry had complained but he objected to them having gone into matters for which he had given no authority and which he suspected Ranald Macdonald (or Macdonald of Castletirrum or Moydart as he designates him in this correspondence) had not authorised either.

Obviously he would never have authorised any discussion of the merits of his case, nor would a man as proud and sensitive as Glengarry have relished the public admonishment as to the foolish and discreditable nature of the controversy. Matters were made worse by his representatives having departed from the authorised Glengarry line. His letter to Coll Macdonald and Æneas Macdonell concludes:

> I most formally protest against your recognition of the title of Clanranald, in reference to the respectable person for whom the two gentlemen on the other side have acted.

Coll Macdonald replied the same day confirming that he had been asked to meet with Borrodale 'to ascertain whether or not Mr. Macdonald of Moydart . . . had a participation in the unpublished letter to the editor of the *Inverness Journal'*. Coll Macdonald was evidently a quick learner:

> What else followed was my conception of the consequential arrangement that ought to be adopted, on finding it attested that he never read the offensive letter.

The 'offensive letter' may indeed never have been seen by Clanranald, although the expenses of printing it were acknowledged to have been met by the office of Macdonald Buchanan, Clanranald's agent (and one of the four men who drew up the minute of 12th March.)

The fourth party to the meeting of 12th March, Captain Æneas Macdonell, responded to his clan chief's strictures with a more robust defence than Coll Macdonald had attempted. He asserted that his authority came from Glengarry's request to meet with Dalness and the Clanranald supporters:

> . . . you certainly cautioned us against entering into the main subject of your controversy; but that was unnecessary, as we neither did nor intended to do so. Our minute or award, points, in the first place, to the principal subject of reference, namely, the umbrage taken by you at some matter contained in a pamphlet assumed to have been offered for publication to the printer of the *Inverness Journal*. In the next place, we offer our recommendations to our principals in a temper that

explains itself. For myself, had I been aware that you had sent the letters to the press, I should have declined interfering in any shape, as I could not, under that circumstance, have deemed it a consistent thing to have offered my mediation in the temper I did.

Captain Macdonell is pointing out, as politely as circumstances allow, that Glengarry's publication of the private correspondence between Clanranald and himself had put the four negotiators in an untenably false position. He went on:

As to designating the Captain of Clanranald as Clanranald simply, that I will admit was unauthorised by you, and proceeded from me as an act of courtesy, to shew the spirit of peace and conciliation in which I acted, having at that time received the colourable disavowal, on the part of that gentleman, as to the offensive matter complained of by you.

Captain Macdonell concluded his defence, which had some of the qualities of a rebuke, by saying:

It is a pity you did not condescend in writing upon the exact matter and limit that was to govern me and Mr. Macdonald, Dalness, in that transaction; for, had you confined us, I should certainly either have declined your commission, or have kept strictly within it. You undoubtedly do me no more than justice in ascribing my motives of acting in this affair to good intentions, though these intentions unluckily have not coincided with yours.

It is strange that Glengarry was so confident in his own rectitude and in the strength of his case that he published such letters which, to an impartial observer, must have raised more questions than they answered. However, common sense and good judgement were never counted among Glengarry's strongest qualities and, as the *Inverness Journal* was to write in its obituary tribute, he had an open-hearted and generous character which however:

. . . scorned all restraint and reserve, and gave full vent to the impetuosity of its feelings. Whenever displeased, he never concealed his resentment. . .[24]

The 'Raonuillich' affair drew a wide range of people into the controversy. Even one of the advocates who had given an opinion on the matter at Glengarry's instruction, John Riddell, went into print. He seems to have moved from being an objective professional to being a committed partisan with considerable ease. The title of his 1821 pamphlet gives a perfectly clear indication of its tone – *Vindication of the Clanronald of Glengarry against the attacks made upon them in the Inverness Journal and some recent printed performances; with remarks as to the descent of the family who style themselves 'of Clanronald'*. Its typographically flamboyant judgement, after rehearsing the complexities of family histories, was that:

> It is now perfectly clear that Glengarry is *the true* Ranaldson, being the only one who can legally instruct a right to that epithet; and hence is Chief of the Clanronald, and necessarily of the Macdonalds. *In this status also, it must have been observed, that his male predecessor was solemnly recognised by* THE HIGHEST AUTHORITIES OF THE KINGDOM *in the Year 1672 – since which period there has been no* LATER *recognition of it in any other family.*

The 'his' and 'he' of course refer to Glengarry:

> Before the year 1810, the arms of his opponent were matriculated in the Registers of the Lion Court, simply as those of the Family 'of Moydart' and 'Captain of Clanranald' (a title he might also claim, but of which he is little solicitous) and WITHOUT SUPPORTERS. [25]

Riddell's emphasis on the lack of supporters in Ranald Macdonald's family arms is, in his view, another indication that his title as Chief of Clanranald was questionable. Heraldic supporters; the figures on either side of a coat of arms (such as the Lion and Unicorn on the Royal Arms); are augmentations granted only to certain designated categories of armigers. Peers of the realm and clan chiefs are among those who, in Scottish practice, can claim heraldic supporters. The arms of the current chief of Glengarry have, for example, as supporters two bears, each pierced by an arrow. That Ranald Macdonald's coat of arms did not have such supporters did not in itself prove that he was not the true chief of Clanranald but it did suggest that the Lyon Court were unconvinced of his title and taken with the description in the matriculation of the family arms as being Macdonald of Moydart and Captain of Clanranald would indeed suggest that Glengarry's claim had some foundations. However Scott's verdict is still to the point:

> . . . it is absurd to set up the *jus sanguinis* now, which Glengarry's ancestors did not, or could not, make good when it was a right worth combating for . . .

Scott's comment was written February 1826 and in January of that year the Court of Session had ruled on Glengarry's suit against Ranald Macdonald'. Glengarry had asked the Court to overturn Macdonald's matriculation of arms recorded in the Lyon Court on 9 August 1810 on the now familiar grounds that the defender was not chief of Clan Ranald and that the arms were not such as the defender was entitled to bear. The four judges of the 2nd Division of the Inner House were unanimous in rejecting Glengarry's case. Lord Robertson's opinion pointed out the basic flaw in Glengarry's suit:

> The pursuer [Glengarry] had his own arms matriculated in 1797, and he does not say that they are erroneous; nor does he set forth in his summons that he is the true chieftain, or that he has right to the arms of the defender. There is no conclusion in favour of his right to these arms; so that, were he to obtain decree in terms of his libel, he could take nothing under it. Popular actions are unknown in our law, and no one can bring an action to take from another what he himself has no right to. [26]

Glengarry was represented by one of the leading counsel at the Scottish Bar, Francis Jeffrey, one of the founders of the *Edinburgh Review*, with, as Junior Counsel, John Riddell, who had been for a number of years engaged on this cause of Glengarry's. Quite how much money Glengarry sank in this obsession is incalculable but the Ranaldian controversy must have significantly contributed to the enormous debt with which Glengarry burdened his estate.

Glengarry did not just invest money in this quest to have himself recognised as the true Clanranald, nor did he simply engage lawyers, he carried out fieldwork on the project himself. Writing in January 1825 to John Riddell, after asking for a sight of the advocate's first draft of the memorial for the court action and rehearsing some of the historical evidence in the case, he goes on to say:

> I shall sleep tonight in Fort William on my way to
> Sunart and Kinloch Moidart, in order to determine
> who are the evidence we shall bring forward <u>as an
> indubitable fact</u> of the bastardy of 'Eoin Moidartach'
> from their early years, and long before the
> commencement of our controversy: and I think that
> while so near the spot (tho' much pressed for time) I
> must try to get a glance at Castle Tyrum. [27]

In other words, Glengarry was going into Clanranald country to
interview potential witnesses who would testify that they
understood the line of the Clanranald chiefs to be descended
illegitimately. It is not entirely clear what value could be put on
such hearsay evidence but the visit does underline Glengarry's
passionate commitment to his cause.

Over eighty years after Alastair Ranaldson's death the question
of the precedency of the various branches of Clan Donald was, if
not legally resolved, at least harmoniously accommodated in an
agreement between the then heads of the houses of Clanranald,
Glengarry and Sleat.

> We the undersigned, Angus Roderick MacDonald,
> otherwise Mac Mhic Ailein, Chief and Captain of
> Clanranald, Æneas Ranald McDonell, otherwise Mac
> Mhic Alastair, of Glengarry, and Sir Alexander
> Wentworth Bosville MacDonald, otherwise MacDhonuill
> na'n Eilean, of Sleat, Knight Baronet

> conclude

> 1) That following upon the forfeiture and death of John
> Lord of the Isles and Earl of Ross and the death without
> issue in 1545 of his grandson Donald Dubh, the various
> branches of Clan Donald, of which the Lord of the Isles
> was supreme and undisputed chief, separated from and
> became independent of one another.

> 2) That although claims to the supreme chiefship of the
> whole Clan Donald have been maintained by our
> predecessors, and are still maintained by ourselves, there
> is no evidence that the whole Clan has ever admitted or
> decided in favour of one of the said claims. [28]

The Chiefs went on to note that because of the scattering of the
clan there was now no chance of reaching such a decision and that

the controversy had been the cause of great jealousy and dissension. They agreed that they would, while not abandoning the traditional claims of their houses to primacy, would not pursue these claims. The question of precedence would, when more than one of them was present, be settled on each occasion by lot, and that the Chiefs of Glengarry and Clan Ranald would not, hereafter, object to the use by the Chief of the House of Sleat:

> . . . of the designation 'N'an Eilean' or 'of the Isles' not because we, the Chiefs of the said Houses of Glengarry and Clan Ranald, admit that I, the Chief of the said House of Sleat, am the nearest and lawful heir-male of the said John, Lord of the Isles and Earl of Ross, but solely in respect of the fact that the said designation has by custom come to be generally associated with my said House of Sleat'.

This eminently pragmatic agreement was drawn up in a legal document signed by the three Chiefs between June and September 1911 and announced at a dinner held in Glasgow at the 1911 Scottish Exhibition of National History, Art and Industry. Sir Alexander Bosville Macdonald of Sleat replying to the toast to the Chiefs of Clan Ranald, Glengarry and Sleat, was reported by *The Times* as saying that:

> . . . at any time during the past 400 years it would have been impossible for one chief to respond to the toast of the two others. [29]

Certainly Alasdair Ranaldson had done more than his fair share to keep the dispute alive.

The agreement between the three Chiefs gives an interesting sidelight on the changes that had affected the Highlands since the days of Alasdair Ranaldson. Their signatures to the document were witnessed in Bridlington, Yorkshire in the case of Sleat, in Bordeaux, France in the case of Clanranald, and in Tuapsé, Southern Russia, in the case of the Chief of Glengarry. Æneas Ranald Macdonell, 21st Chief of Glengarry, was working for a company in the Russian oil centre of Baku on the Caspian Sea. He later became British Vice-Consul there and and had an adventurous career during the First World War and in the conflict between the western powers and the Bolshevik forces after the Russian Revolution. Following the death of Alastair Ranaldson and the eventual extinction of his male line the Chiefship had passed to the family of Macdonell of Scotus and the 21st Chief was a descendant of this line.

CHAPTER 11

The Last of the Chiefs

'Land of the Gael, thy glory has flown!
For the star of the North from its orbit is thrown . . .'

The expansive and traditional lifestyle to which Glengarry aspired and which indeed he had enjoyed with remarkable success from attaining his majority was, in reality, far beyond the resources of his property to sustain. A more modest manner of gentlemanly living could certainly have been supported by the extensive and aggressively managed Glengarry estate, but three houses, European travel, regular visits to England, lavish hospitality and frequent litigation all bit deeply into his income. Nor was Glengarry's personality one which would take easily to concepts such as restraint, retrenchment or economy. After Glengarry's death the debts which had accumulated on the estate were found to amount to around £80,000.

This debt represented a sum of perhaps £6 to £8 million in present day values. Another way of looking at this level of debt is to consider that in 1802 the annual rental income of the entire Glengarry estate was only £5072, in itself a very significant increase on the rental of some years earlier. However much the profitability of the estate had since been increased by clearances, sheep farming, the feuing of property and other developments it seems unlikely that it would have produced as much as £10,000 a year rental by 1828. The accrued debt thus represents somewhere between eight and sixteen years total rental income, a purely theoretical concept, as the Glengarry household obviously had to be fed and clothed from this income. Indeed, a high proportion of the estate income must have gone on servicing this enormous debt.

However, eventually it would seem that the realities of the situation were borne in upon him. An anecdote from a contemporary, Duncan Macdonell of Aonach, reports that when Glengarry was visiting him in the summer of 1827 the chief said:

> 'Duncan, I have been thoughtless; I have been, as I thought, sustaining the honour of my ancestors; but now I see that I have been wasting the heritage that generations of them have left me. I must turn over a new leaf, I am determined to do it; I am going south bye-and-bye to have this business definitely arranged'; it was on this very expedition he was going, it was said, when he met with his untimely fate. [1]

It was thus to meet with his lawyers and to find some means of putting the affairs of his deeply mortgaged and debt-burdened estate in order that Glengarry, accompanied by two of his daughters, Marsali, then aged fifteen, and Jemima, aged thirteen, set out from Glengarry House to travel to Edinburgh in January 1828. Glengarry's wife was ill at the time and stayed behind with the five younger children. Æneas was already at Edinburgh, a student at the University after receiving a year and a half of polishing at Eton College. It may well be significant that the family was wintering in Inverness-shire rather than moving for the season, as was their custom, to Garry Cottage in Perth. Living costs would be lower in the country and the tempting opportunities to spend money on entertainment and hospitality significantly reduced. Louise Macdonell in her memoirs of her father noted that for the children, at least, there was little or nothing to spend money on at Glengarry and the household budget would similarly be based, not on a cash economy, but on the crops and produce of the home farm and the estate.

Despite his many disputes with the Caledonian Canal Company, and his action for damages and complaints against the invasion of his privacy caused by the noisome 'smoking steam boats' which were set sailing on Loch Oich, Glengarry's choice of transport was the steam boat *Stirling*. The *Stirling* (sometimes called the *Stirling Castle*) had been built at Kincardine in 1814 for service on the River Forth. She was 68 foot overall and measured just over 69 tons. [2] She had been re-registered at Inverness in 1824 for service on the Canal and the west coast route to the Clyde. She was owned by a co-partnery of twenty owners – a mixture of local business men and landowners and others. The two most interesting owners were perhaps Thomas Telford, the consulting engineer for the Caledonian Canal and one of the great engineers of the age, who owned 2/64ths of the vessel, and Henry Bell, the pioneer of commercial steam navigation in Scotland, with 4/64ths.[3] In 1825 Bell sold half his interest – 2/64ths – to a Glasgow iron merchant, Moses McCulloch. The *Stirling* was, by 1828, quite an old steamship, and rather overtaken by progress. Larger steamers, of 100 foot length, and 100 tons measurement and with suitably powerful machinery were now in service on the Clyde and on the West Highland routes.

The Macdonell party boarded the *Stirling* at Laggan Locks, between Loch Oich and Loch Lochy, on Wednesday 16th January 1828. The ship sailed down Loch Lochy, the last of the chain of lochs forming the Great Glen, and entered the southernmost section of the Caledonian Canal at Gairlochy. She completed her passage of the Canal and because of the adverse weather spent the night at Corpach – the western extremity and sea-lock of the Canal. The next day, Thursday 17th January, the weather was no better, indeed press reports speak of 'a perfect hurricane', of the wind blowing with 'awful violence, accompanied by showers of sleet', but despite this the ship left harbour and set off down Loch Linnhe on her way to the Firth of Lorne, Crinan and the south. However only about six miles south of Fort William the engines failed and without power she drifted on to the rocks in Inverscaddle Bay on the western or Ardgour shore of the loch. A local landowner, a Mr. H McDougall, saw the event and its aftermath and wrote a report for the vessel's agent – a report which was published in the Glasgow papers:

> 17th January 1828
> Sir,
> I am sorry to be obliged to intimate the melancholy account of the loss of the *Stirling* Steam-boat, under my house, six miles after leaving Fort William this morning. As far as I can learn, every exertion on the part of the captain and crew had been done to save the vessel and passengers, but the gale had been such as rendered every exertion vain. All on board have been got on shore in life, except one man, an Englishman,

who had been a butler with Mr. Macdonald of Clanranald, and on his way to Edinburgh, as Mr. Macdonald of Glengarry, with his two daughters were on board, on their way to Edinburgh. Mr. Macdonald had been so much hurt on landing, that he died at nine o'clock this night, in consequence of a contusion on the head. All the rest of the crew and passengers are in a fair way of recovery; all that was possible has been done for the comfort of the shipwrecked sufferers, as well as the saving of property. The vessel is a total wreck.

H. McDougall [4]

A correspondent to the *Glasgow Herald*, who excused Captain MacLean and his crew for any responsibility for the loss, wrote:

The *Stirling* was a very small boat, of no great power, and had been for several years employed on this passage. Her size being such as to admit her to pass through the Crinan Canal, she was of course of too little power to contend against the winds and currents down the Highland lochs. [5]

The *Caledonian Mercury*'s report of the loss, copied in the same issue of the *Glasgow Herald*, stated:

Glengarry's attention was naturally directed to the safety of his daughters; and a boat having been procured, one of them was safely conveyed to the beach, the rest of the passengers and crew endeavouring in the mean time to escape as best they could. But, unfortunately, while the second Miss Macdonell was conveying ashore, Glengarry, alarmed by her danger, leaped from the steamboat on to a rock; and his foot slipping, he was precipitated into the water, his head striking with great violence against a ledge of the rock.

After sustaining this blow to the head he made his way ashore and went with his daughters to McDougall's house. The *Glasgow Herald* of 25th January reprinted an account from the *Edinburgh Courier* which stated:

Glengarry was much hurt in the face and head and he was brought to the shore, as well as some other. He was able, however, to walk to the farm-house of

Inverscaddel, where he had his wounds dressed, and did not appear to be in a dangerous state. He was put to bed; and in the evening was seized with convulsions which terminated his life at ten o'clock.

Louise Macdonell's version of the event, which she would have had from her older sisters who were on board the *Stirling*, does not quite convey the impulsiveness and fatherly concern which seem to have motivated Glengarry:

All the people got out on the rocks; in leaping from the steamer papa knocked his head on the rock, but it was bound up with various cotton neckties, then used by gentlemen, and nothing serious was expected. . . One of my sisters wrote to tell mamma that they were all safe. After they were in bed my sisters were roused. My father had taken brain fever, and expired that night. [6]

Presumably what had killed Glengarry was what is now known as a subdural haematoma, a gathering of blood formed as a result of the blow to his head, pressing on the brain.

A curious and poignant reminder of the loss of the *Stirling* and the death of Glengarry is still to be found on the larger scale Ordnance Survey maps of Ardgour, where a half-tide rock in Inverscaddle Bay bears the name 'Glengarry's Rock' or 'Sgeir Mhic 'ic Alasdair', commemorating the death of the 15th chief of Glengarry.

News of Glengarry's tragic and almost certainly unnecessary death – his daughters were, after all, safely ashore – was swiftly conveyed back to Invergarry and to his widow. The first letter from Marsali Macdonell, announcing the shipwreck and the family's safety, came on the 18th January, to be followed a few hours later by a second letter with news of Glengarry's death. Word came to send the coach (for the girls) and the barge (for the body) but, according to Louise Macdonell, the estate factor did not seem to have been able to face Rebecca Macdonell with the news and hid himself. Louise relates that her mother, who it will be recollected was ill at this time, was eventually told the news of her husband's death in such an abrupt manner that 'it was months before she recovered'.

Marsali and Jemima returned home on Friday 19th and in the evening of the same day the barge brought Glengarry's body back up the Caledonian Canal, through Loch Oich to Invergarry House. A letter was sent to Æneas who returned from his studies at Edinburgh University to take on, at the age of 19, the role of clan chief and landlord of vast, but debt-burdened, estates.

The funeral of Mac Mhic Alasdair was a major event in the Highlands. It would attract large numbers and would require considerable preparation and arrangement, and no little diplomatic skill, to ensure that all passed off with appropriate dignity. Time had to be taken to allow word to be sent to all concerned and adequate time provided for the mourners to travel to Lochaber.

The family's traditional burying-place was in the graveyard at Kilfinnan, overlooking the north end of Loch Lochy, where a plain roofless mausoleum still stands, sheltering the remains of the chiefs of Glengarry. Macdonell's burial did not take place until Friday 1st February, a fortnight after news of his death had reached Invergarry. Louise, in her reminiscences of her father, gives an account of it:

> It was wonderful what mamma did, in spite of her weakness: all had to be arranged – where men from the various districts were to walk, so as to prevent any quarrels or fighting. I remember the large quantity of cheese which was procured from two farms at a considerable distance, as food, cheese, oatcakes, and whisky had to be provided for about one thousand common men. A cook came from Inverness to prepare food for more than fifty gentlemen in the offices in the square.
>
> And truly the funeral was a considerable one. Hosts of men gathered on the lawn, to whom cheese cut in squares and oatcakes were handed round in hampers, followed by a man with bottles of whisky and a glass, during which time some rain fell, but not much fortunately, as no shelter could have been found for such a number. At last the funeral started; no hearse or carriages of any sort were at it. The coffin was carried on men's shoulders – the piper playing in front; our only brother, in full Highland dress, his arm covered

with crape, at the head; papa's only brother, Sir James,
in plain clothes, at the foot; mamma's two brothers,
Lord Medwyn and Uncle George, Charles Stuart Hay,
and others, at the side. Mamma had given strict
instructions that no whisky was to be offered till after
the body was under ground. [7]

Rebecca Macdonell's ban on pre-interment whisky was a wise
one. The *Inverness Courier* in its report of the funeral noted:

By the judicious arrangements made, those scenes of
drunkenness and quarreling which in former days,
and we are ashamed to add, in more recent times, had
disgraced similar occasions in the Highlands were
prevented. The whole was conducted with the utmost
order, decorum and solemnity, suited to the
mournfulness of the occasion, and the better sense of
propriety which begins to prevail in the Highlands. [8]

The *Courier* adds some interesting details to Louise's account. It
puts the attendance, the 'common men' in Louise's phrase, at 1,500
and the gentry at 150. The procession left Invergarry at 2 p.m. and
reached Kilfinnan, five miles distant, between 4 and 5 p.m.:

The body enclosed in a double coffin, lead and wood,
was borne breast-high by 18 Highlanders, who were
relieved at regular intervals. The day was
uncommonly tempestuous; and the procession had to
pass through a swollen burn, reaching above the
knees of the people in the procession.

The death of Glengarry was marked by poets and musicians. His
personal piper, Archie Munro, composed a lament *Cumha Mhic 'ic
Alasdair*, as did the blind household bard, Allan MacDougall, *Ailean
Dall*. This, echoing the marbhrannan, the classical Gaelic form of
elegy or lament, extended to seventeen verses in praise of the late
chief's qualities, his heroic virtues, generosity and gave expression
to the sorrow of the Highlands. The Gaelic original is printed in
his collection *Orain, Marbhrannan agus Duanagan Ghaidhealach*
(Inverness, 1829). Three verses from this 'Lament for Mac 'Ic
Alasdair', translated by R W Renton, give the feel of the poem:

The Last of the Chiefs

Lament for Mac 'Ic Alasdair
To the air: 'The Lament of the Mull women'

1
It is poor in the morning my waking,
Without joy without mirth,
Sore is the arrow which has stabbed me,
Which has wounded me from behind.
A tale which has come fresh to us
Has left my heart crushed –
The death of the hero of most renown to the Gaels,
The death of the hero of most renown to the Gaels.

7
Vexing to me is the state of your girls,
Your dear young princesses,
Who encountered you in your room
While the others stretched you on the boards.
Your two girls were kissing you,
The one who was older hopefully
Blowing a gentle breath on your pores
Expecting that she would bring you alive to your natural self,
Expecting that she would bring you alive to your natural self.

12
Lying in Kilfinan
We left a generous host,
A hand that could avenge,
A foot that could range the deer forest.
You were a hunter of venison
With your thin straight rifle.
Since your end has come
The royals will get peacefulness,
Quiet sleep and their enemy will not climb up to them.
Quiet sleep and their enemy will not climb up to them.

In Edinburgh Sir Walter Scott was moved to compose *Glengarry's Death Song*, an undoubted expression of his genuine affection for the dead chief, if not perhaps a work of the greatest literary quality:

Land of the Gael, thy glory has flown!
For the star of the North from its orbit is thrown;
Dark, dark is thy sorrow, and hopeless thy pain,
For no star shall e'er beam with its lustre again.

Refrain   Glengarry – Glengarry is gone evermore,
Glengarry – Glengarry we'll ever deplore.

O tell of the warrior who never did yield,
O tell of the chief who was falchion and shield,
O think of the patriot, most ardent and kind;
Then sigh for Glengarry in whom all were joined.

The chieftains may gather – the combatants call,
One champion is absent – that champion is all;
The bright eye of genius and valour may flame,
But who now shall light it to honour and fame?

See the light bark, how toss'd! she's wrecked on the wave!
See dauntless Glengarry on the verge of the grave!
See his leap! see that gash, and that eye now so dim!
And thy heart must be steel'd, if it bleed not for him.

Arise thou young branch of so noble a stem,
Obscurity marks not the work of a gem;
O hear the last wish of thy father for thee
'Be all to thy country, Glengarry should be.'

Why sounds the loud pibroch, who tolls the death bell,
Why crowd our bold clansmen to Garry's green vale?
'Tis to mourn for their chief – for Glengarry the brave,
'Tis to tell that a hero is laid in his grave.

O! heard ye that anthem, slow, pealing on high!
The shades of the valiant are come from the sky,
And the genii of Gaeldoch are first in the throng,
O list to the theme of their aerial song.

It's 'welcome Glengarry, thy clansmen's fast friend.'
It's welcome to joys that shall ne'er have an end,
The halls of great Odin are open to thee,
O welcome Glengarry, the gallant and free.

> Glengarry – Glengarry is gone evermore,
> Glengarry – Glengarry we'll ever deplore. [9]

This is a rather remarkable poem, which might almost be thought excessive in its sentiments had it been written in praise of a great warrior such as Glengarry's brother Sir James, the hero of Waterloo. It is worth recalling that Glengarry's closest approach to active service was when the Glengarry Fencibles garrisoned Guernsey. While a post of danger, close to France and theoretically threatened, the island did not see combat during Macdonell's service there and his successor petitioned the War Office for the Regiment to be transferred to a more active station. When the Glengarry Fencibles transferred to Ireland and saw service in the rebellion there

Macdonell had relinquished command and was quarreling at Fort George and travelling on the continent. Whether as a company commander in the Strathspey Fencibles, as Colonel of the Glengarry Fencibles or Colonel of the Inverness-shire Volunteer and Militia regiments he never actually saw a foreign enemy in the field or heard a bullet fired in anger. Indeed his closest approximation to combat was his duel with Lieutenant MacLeod. Walter Scott, who knew Glengarry's history well, and who knew his strengths and weaknesses equally well, would nonetheless seem to have accepted and buttressed the heroic image of the warrior chief that Glengarry presented. Indeed, as has been noted previously, it is truly remarkable how many people were prepared to accept Glengarry at his own valuation.

When obituaries are being written a nice balance has to be struck between truth and piety, candour and respect for the dead. The *Inverness Journal,* in which many of Glengarry's battles had been fought, possibly best approached that diplomatic balance. It was not afraid to say:

> It must not be denied that he had faults which threw a shade over his better qualities, but they chiefly arose from the force of early impressions. . . [10]

The paper explained that:

> . . . his youthful mind acquired early and exaggerated impressions of the dignity of a Highland Chief, which remained with him till the hour of his death, and were the source of much that was delightful, as well as nearly all that was harsh and unpleasing in his character. His defects were for the most part the result of education – his virtues and excellencies were the genuine produce of his own heart.

They had, however opened their appreciation, with a historical contextualisation of Glengarry which would probably have pleased the late chief:

> Glengarry was all that history records, or imagination paints, of the ancient Highland Chieftain. His mind, his manners, his form, his gait, his habits, his pursuits were all suited to his character. The same bold and enterprising spirit – the same rash contempt of danger –

the same enthusiastic attachment to the soil, the people, the customs of his native country – the same frank, generous, openhearted disposition which had been displayed by the ancient Chiefs, shone with conspicuous lustre in the life of their last representative. No one could look at Glengarry without saying, 'this is no common man;' and there were few who had seen or conversed with him once, who did not retain a lively recollection of him during the remainder of their lives . . .

The *Journal* obituarist went on to write:

His peculiar characteristic was a noble open-hearted generosity which scorned all constraint and reserve, and gave full vent to the impetuosity of its feelings. Whenever displeased, he never concealed his resentment, or ever used any underhand or dishonourable means to gratify it; when he felt kindness towards any person, he obeyed the ready dictates of his heart, and expressed himself with all that warmth and ardour which his feelings inspired. His attachment to his friends was warm, disinterested and lasting – he would go to any lengths, and make any sacrifices, to serve them.

Their conclusion was the eminently fair one, which can be confirmed by other evidence:

Those who best knew him will allow him to have been a true patriot, a warm friend, an affectionate husband, an indulgent parent, and it will be long – very long – before those who had the happiness to enjoy his friendship and knew the generous qualities of his mind and heart will cease to remember and lament the early loss of Mac Mhic Alister.

This sentiment was echoed by Sir Walter Scott, writing two years after Glengarry's death, to the Irish novelist Maria Edgeworth. He writes of 'poor Glengarry':

. . . who, with all wild and fierce points of his character, had a kind, honest, and warm heart. [11]

His death marked the passing of an age. It signalled the end of the centuries old Macdonell possession of the mountains and moors, farms and deer forests lying between the lochs of the Great Glen and the sea-bound peninsula of Knoydart. The end did not come at once, but it came with inexorable certainty. The trustees on the estate, Æneas the 16th Chief not of course being of age when his father died, found the estate burdened with an impossible debt. Retrenchment was the order of the day.

Garry Cottage in Perth was sold for £2,900 to the Duke of Atholl. The family moved from Glengarry House in the summer of 1828 and settled for a couple of years in Merchiston Castle, near Edinburgh, thus making Glengarry House available to be let to sporting tenants. To judge from the registration of banns in the Parish of Rhu, Dumbartonshire, for a spate of family weddings in 1833, (Æneas, Marsali and Jemima all married that year) the family would then seem to have moved to a house in Rhu or in the new and fashionable watering-place of Helensburgh, which lay in Rhu Parish.

In August 1829 Æneas came of age and a celebratory dinner was held in the Macdonell Arms Inn, Glengarry. His twenty first birthday could not have been an entirely happy event. Part of his inheritance was a series of court cases which his father had initiated and the trustees on the estate had advised him that it would be necessary to sell most of the property to clear the debt burden. In 1836 it was announced that the Earl of Aboyne (the heir to the Marquess of Huntly) had bought the Glengarry property. In 1840 it was sold on for £91,000 to Lord Ward and in the same year the Glenquoich part of the estate was sold for £32,000 to Edward Ellice. In 1853 the last remnant of the family lands, Knoydart, was sold, leaving the once vast territories of Mac Mhic Alasdair reduced to the ruined castle on Creagan Fhithich and the mausoleum at Kilfinnan.

But by this time the links between the Glengarrys and their land had become more tenuous. Æneas, who had married Josephine Bennett, the niece of an Irish bishop, took the decision to move to Port Philip, near Melbourne, Australia with his family and dependents. The *Inverness Courier* noted in January 1840 that:

> He is constructing timber houses and furnishing himself
> with various agricultural implements and other
> conveniences for residence in that distant region. Mr.
> Macdonell was compelled some time since to dispose of

the property, which was heavily mortgaged and encumbered by his father . . . We cannot regard the expatriation of the head of an old Highland family, with its clan associations, its pipe music, and its feudal associations, without some regret and emotion. [12]

Æneas exported something of his father's spirit to Australia and there is an account of a St Andrew's Day fête in his honour in 1841 at Port Philip at which all the participants were Scots and the grace before dinner was said in Gaelic. However pioneering life in Australia seems not to have been to his taste and Æneas and his family returned to Scotland and settled on the last of the Macdonell lands, at Inverie in Knoydart. Here he died at the early age of forty three in 1851.

His heir, the 17th Chief, Alexander Ranaldson, a youth of eighteen when his father died, found the family affairs in a poor state. His trustees sold Knoydart and, as a part of the arrangement, cleared the crofters and cottars from the estate. The Knoydart clearances were much criticised for their ruthlessness and featured in many of the works on the Highland Clearances, with the role played by his mother, Josephine Macdonell, attracting particular censure.

Alexander, seeing nothing to hold him in Scotland, emigrated to New Zealand, where he was to be joined by his only surviving brother Charles. Alexander died, aged twenty eight, in June 1862 in Dunedin, of rheumatic fever. He was succeeded as 18th Chief by Charles.

Charles continued to farm in New Zealand, married in 1865, but had no children. Returning to Britain in 1868 he died at sea, bringing to an end the direct line of male descent of the house of Glengarry.

With the failure of the direct line of Chiefs the succession reverted to a distant relative from the Scotus branch of the family who traced his descent from Angus the younger brother of Alasdair Dubh, the 11th Chief. The Chiefs of Glengarry have continued in this Scotus line to the present day. The current Chief, Ranald, 23rd of Glengarry, succeeded his father Air Commodore Æneas Ranald Donald Macdonell in 1999.

Alasdair Ranaldson's widow, Rebecca, died in Edinburgh in 1841. Four of the daughters married. However the longest-lived of them, Louise, to whom we owe the two brief memoirs of her father, died unmarried at Rothesay in 1900.

•

Alasdair Ranaldson Macdonell of Glengarry is a contradictory and complex figure and a hard man to sum up.

In many ways he was as Scott suggests 'wild and fierce' and he was roundly condemned by knowledgeable contemporaries like David Stewart of Garth who despised his hypocrisy in preaching about the old Highland virtues and customs and at the same time callously depopulating his estates in the interests of higher rents and greater profitability. Writing to Sir Walter Scott, Stewart put his views in unvarnished form:

> Glengarry is held up as a model of the Highland chieftain, altho' he stands by himself without another individual of similar principles, conduct and general behaviour. So far is he from being a model that I know no man like him and he does infinite injury to his poor countrymen in the false and cholerous views he offers to the public of what he is pleased to call a True Highlander, while he is no more of a true Highlander than the last Lord Lovat to whom he has a most striking affinity of character and feeling. [13]

The 'last Lord Lovat' to whom he so unflatteringly compares Macdonell was Simon Fraser, the 11th Lord Lovat, who was executed for his part in the '45 Jacobite rising. In a long life Lovat managed to betray Hanoverian and Jacobite with equal facility.

In a letter to Sir John MacGregor, Stewart was equally forthright:

> Glengarry farms contained 1500 souls. Those farms have now 35 persons. Is not this extirpation? and yet Glengarry with a consistency only to be equalled by the rest of his character goes about the country attending public meetings and making speeches in his own praise as a true friend to the Highlanders. [14]

In his *Sketches of the Character, Manners and Present State of the*

Highlanders of Scotland published in 1822 Stewart was more circumspect in his language but equally scathing about the practice of clearance, of which Glengarry was a noted proponent. As a soldier Stewart would perhaps have had a particular concern for Glengarry's treatment of the men he enlisted into the Strathspey and later the Glengarry Fencibles. Their attachment was expressed in the most effusive terms by his company of Strathspeys who asked only to serve him as they had served his ancestors. The Chaplain, Father Macdonell, wrote in 1794:

> . . . so soon as he has it in his power he says he'll show to the whole world that he prefers men to sheep. All the men that are with him in the Fencibles rest perfectly satisfied that he'll make good his promise to see them comfortably settled in Glengarry. Their attachment to him is beyond anything you can conceive. [15]

Ten years later Father Macdonell had to organise a mass migration to Canada of hundreds of these now landless ex-soldiers when Glengarry proved unable or unwilling to live up to his promises and proved to prefer sheep to men.

High sounding phrases were indeed Glengarry's stock in trade – writing to Henry Dundas in February 1796 he postured:

> Whoever thinks that I will give up my Regiment must be very ignorant indeed of the consequences derived from the inviolable attachment of a numerous tribe of faithfull Highlanders – especially when their service may be rendered so very useful to Government as at the present critical juncture – no consideration on Earth will separate me from my men or make me forfeit the confidence they repose in me. [16]

Six months later, in August 1796, he resigned his commission as Colonel of the Glengarry Fencibles.

The close bond between Glengarry and Father Macdonell – so close that Glengarry at one point was even taking instruction from the Chaplain with a view to converting to Roman Catholicism, so close that the Chaplain was prepared to travel half way across war-torn Europe to repatriate Glengarry from Vienna – broke down in acrimony and legal action. Perhaps Lord Adam Gordon, the Commander in Chief in Scotland during the period of the mutiny of the Strathspey Fencibles, was shrewd in his summation – 'a young chieftain composed of vanity and folly.'

However there is another side to the story. To put the other side does not condone the violent, unprincipled and vainglorious dimension to Glengarry's character but it may shed some light on the darker side of his character, even if the final summing-up may be unfavourable.

Many knowledgeable contemporaries blamed the defects of Glengarry's character on his mother – and few can be found with much to say in her favour. From family lawyers to the editor of the *Inverness Journal* and later historians the opinion is consistent that the young Glengarry was badly raised and developed an overbearing temper and an unreasonably high view of his own importance. Circumstances or better guidance might have corrected this but succeeding to his estate at fourteen and gaining command of his own regiment at the age of twenty-one put him, in day to day matters at least, beyond outside control.

Yet he could be a good friend, a fond father, a loving husband, a kindly master, an enthusiastic patriot, a devoted promoter of Highland manners and customs. People who had nothing to gain from a relationship with him were happy to be counted his friend. Even the rightly censorious and strictly honourable David Stewart of Garth was willing to enlist in the Society of True Highlanders. Sir Walter Scott, whose prestige and national status it is hard to overestimate, while acknowledging the 'wild and fierce' elements in his friend's nature also recognised his 'kind, honest, and warm heart.' Perhaps Scott had the clearest view when he wrote in his *Journal*, two years before Glengarry died:

> Warm-hearted, generous, friendly, he is beloved by those who know him, and his efforts are unceasing to show kindness to those of his clan who are disposed fully to admit his pretensions. To dispute them is to incur his resentment. . . [17]

Scott also wrote that Glengarry was:

> . . . a kind of Quixote in our age, having retained, in their full extent, the whole feelings of clanship and

chieftainship, elsewhere so long abandoned. He seems to
have lived a century too late . . .

Which is indeed the case.

Robert Louis Stevenson, writing about the subject of another
Raeburn portrait, and of an equally ambiguous and complex
character, Robert McQueen of Braxfield, said:

> . . . sympathy is a thing to be encouraged, apart from
> human considerations, because it supplies us with the
> materials for wisdom. It is probably more instructive
> to entertain a sneaking kindness for any unpopular
> person . . . than to give way to perfect raptures of
> moral indignation against his abstract vices. [18]

Perhaps the writer in the *Inverness Journal* was filled with a similar
attitude when he wrote:

> No one could look at Glengarry without saying, 'this is
> no common man'.

Whoever first attached the sobriquet 'The Last of the Chiefs' to
Glengarry found a handy and accurate label for the man. The credit
for this title in fact seems to be due to John Galt. In his novel *The
Steam-Boat* (1822) his hero, Thomas Duffle, describes the incident
of Glengarry and his pistols at George IV's coronation and says:

> The gentleman was Glengarry, than whom, as is well
> known, there is not now-a-days, a chieftain of a more truly
> Highland spirit; indeed it may almost be said of him, as I
> have read in a book it was said of one Brutus, the ancient
> Roman, that he is one of the last of the chieftains . . . [19]

The phrase recognises, what Scott also recognised, that he was the
end of a line, born out of his proper time – but it also surely
recognises the tradition and lineage which he represented – gone,
supplanted, but not without value and significance. Weak, violent,
untrustworthy and improvident he may have been but The Last
of the Chiefs, Alasdair Ranaldson Macdonell of Glengarry, Mac
Mhic Alasdair, descendant of Conn of the Hundred Battles, of
Somerled and of the Lords of the Isles was indeed 'no common
man.'

Macdonell Mausoleum at Kilfinnan, Loch Lochy
(Burial place of Alasdair Ranaldson Macdonell)

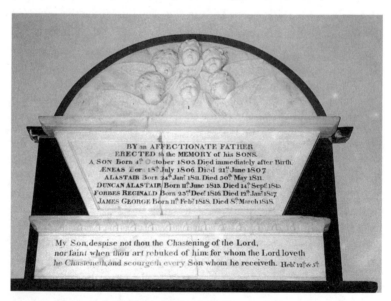

BY an AFFECTIONATE FATHER
ERECTED to the MEMORY of his SONS.
A SON Born 4ᵗʰ October 1805 Died immediately after Birth.
ÆNEAS Born 18ᵗʰ July 1806 Died 21ˢᵗ June 1807
ALASTAIR Born 24ᵗʰ Janʸ 1811 Died 30ᵗʰ May 1811.
DUNCAN ALASTAIR Born 11ᵗʰ June 1815 Died 14ᵗʰ Septʳ 1815.
FORBES REGINALD Born 23ʳᵈ Decʳ 1816 Died 12ᵗʰ Janʸ 1817
JAMES GEORGE Born 11ᵗʰ Febʸ 1818 Died 8ᵗʰ March 1818

My Son, despise not thou the Chastening of the Lord,
nor faint when thou art rebuked of him: for whom the Lord loveth
he Chasteneth, and scourgeth every Son whom he receiveth. Hebˢ 12ᵗʰ & 5ᵗʰ

Memorial to Glengarry's six infant sons
in South Laggan Chuirch

Chapter 1 The Royal Visit

1. Lockhart, John Gibson *Memoirs of Sir Walter Scott* London 1914, Vol 4 p.33

2. *Inverness Journal* 15 June 1815

3. Lockhart *op. cit.* p. 34

4. *Glasgow Herald* 12 August 1822

5. *The Scots Magazine* October 1822

6. Lockhart *op.cit.* p.38

7. Crabbe's *Diary* quoted in Lockhart *op.cit.* p.41

8. *The Scots Magazine* October 1822

9. Lockhart *op.cit.* p.44

10. *The Edinburgh Observer* 2 September 1822

11. *The Scots Magazine* October 1822

12. *The Edinburgh Observer* 2 September 1822

13. *The Scots Magazine* October 1822

14. *The Scots Magazine* October 1822

15 Lockhart *op. cit.* p.54

16. National Library of Scotland (NLS) Abbotsford Correspondence MS3895 f77

17. NLS Abbotsford Correspondence MS3895 f148/151

18. *The Edinburgh Observer* 5 September 1822

19. *The Edinburgh Observer* quoted in the *Glasgow Herald* 13 September 1822

20. *The Edinburgh Observer* quoted in the *Glasgow Herald* 13 September 1822

Chapter 2 Mac Mhic Alasdair

1 Scott, Walter *Journal* Edinburgh 1890, Vol.1 p.120

2 Scott, Walter *Letters* 1816 March/April

3 Fraser-Mackintosh, Charles *Antiquarian notes. . .* Second series. Inverness 1897 p.125

4 Scottish Record Office (SRO) GD1/8/22 Methven Collection William MacDonald WS Letter Book

Chapter 3 Oxford

1. Macdonell, Louise C.R. 'A Highland Chief and his Family' in *Blackwood's Magazine* April 1895 p.520-536

2. Macdonell, Louise C.R. 'Glengarry and his Family' in *Blackwood's Magazine* September 1893 p.323 – 339

3. Quoted in Anson, Peter F. *Underground Catholicism in Scotland 1622–1878* Montrose 1970 p.213

4. Scottish Catholic Archive (SCA), Blairs Papers

5. SCA, Blairs Papers quoted in Toomey, Kathleen M. *Alexander Macdonell, the Scottish Years 1762-1804* Toronto, 1985

6. University College Archives, Information from Dr. R Darwall-Smith, College Archivist

7. Mackintosh, H B. *The Grant, Strathspey or First Highland Fencible Regiment 1793-1799* Elgin 1934 p.23

8. SRO GD1/8/22 Methven Collection, William Macdonald WS Letter Book

9. Quoted in Fraser-Mackintosh, Charles *Antiquarian Notes* 2nd series Inverness 1897 p.129

10. Fraser-Mackintosh *op. cit.* p.129

11. Macdonell, Louise C.R. *A Highland Chief and his Family op. cit.*

Chapter 4 Colonel of Fencibles

1. Mackintosh, H.B. *The Grant, Strathspey or First Highland Fencible Regiment 1793-1799* Elgin 1934 p18/19

2. Public Record Office (PRO) Muster Roll Strathspey Fencibles WO13/3944

3. Information from University College Archivist

4. PRO WO13/3944

5. An act for requiring a certain Form of Oath of Abjuration, and Declaration, from his Majesty's Subjects, professing the Roman Catholick Religion, in that Part of Great Britain called Scotland. (33 George III Cap. 34)

6. Macdonell, Rev. Alexander 'A page from the history of the Glengarry Highlanders' in *The Canadian Literary Magazine* April 1833 p.5

7. Letter as printed in *The Tablet* 24 November 1928

8. SCA Blairs Papers, Macdonell to Hay c.1/5/94

9. Mackintosh *op. cit.* p.46

10. Macdonell *op. cit.* p.5

11. Bulloch, J.M. *The Scots Fencibles and English Service, an episode of 1794* XX

12. Mackintosh *op. cit.* p.50

13. PRO WO 13/3944

14. Quoted in Toomey, Kathleen M. *Alexander Macdonell, the Scottish years 1762-1804* Toronto 1985 p.112

15. SCA Blairs Papers Chisholm to Hay 10 November 1794

16. Macdonell *op. cit.* p.5

17. SRO Melville Papers GD51/1/831

18. SRO Melville Papers GD51/1/839

19. Mackintosh *op. cit.* p.57

20. SRO Melville Papers GD51/1/844/1

21. SRO Melville Papers GD51/1/193

22. SRO Melville Papers GD51/1/844/3

23. SCA Blairs Papers Macdonell to Hay 12 February 1794

24. Mackintosh *op. cit.* p.58

25. Fraser-Mackintosh, Charles *Letters of two centuries. . .* Inverness 1890 p.328/9

26. SRO JC26/282

27. SRO Melville Papers GD51/1/864

28. SRO Melville Papers GD51/6/189/1

29. SRO Melville Papers GD51/6/189/4

30. SRO Melville Papers GD51/6/189/3

31. PRO Muster Roll Glengarry Fencibles WO17/237

32. SRO Melville Papers GD51/6/189/1

33. SRO Melville Papers GD51/6/189/7

34. SRO Melville Papers GD51/6/246/1

35. SRO Melville Papers GD51/6/246/2

36. PRO CinC's Memoranda August 1796 WO31/50

37. Macdonell *op. cit.* p.5

38. PRO CinC's Memoranda August 1796 WO31/50

39. PRO CinC's Memoranda September 1796 WO31/51

40. SCA Presholme Letters, Macdonell to Margaret Fraser 26 August 1803

41. SCA Presholme Letters *op. cit.*

42. SCA Blairs Letters Chisholm to Cameron 26 December 1803

43. SRO Seafield Papers GD248/192/2/16

Chapter 5 The Duel and the Trial

1. *The Scots Magazine* September 1798

2. Quoted in *The Scots Magazine* September 1798

3. *Edinburgh Evening Courant* 9th August 1798

4. *The Scots Magazine* September 1798

5. Cockburn, Henry *Memorials of his Time* 1856 p.122

6. *The Scots Magazine* September 1798

7. Fraser-Mackintosh, Charles *Antiquarian Notes* 2nd series. Inverness p.139

8. Fraser-Mackintosh, Charles *Antiquarian Notes* 2nd series. Inverness p.139

9. Fergusson, Alex. *The Hon. Henry Erskine. . .* Edinburgh 1882 p397

10. Fraser-Mackintosh, Charles *Antiquarian Notes* 2nd series Inverness p.292

Chapter 6 The Grand Tour

1. PRO FO 610 Passport Register

2. NLS Minto Papers MS11248

3. NLS Minto Papers MS11263

4. Minto, Countess of *The Life and Letters of Sir Gilbert Elliot, 1st Earl of Minto. . .* Vol.3 p.73

5. *op. cit.* p.119

6. NLS Minto Papers MS11263

7. Gordon, Pryse Lockhart *Personal Memoirs, reminiscences of men and manners at home and abroad* London 1830 Vol.1 p.177-9

8. The Angelica Kauffmann portrait of Montgomerie is in the possession of the Earl of Eglintoun and was exhibited at a

Kauffmann exhibition at Bregenz in 1962. The Glengarry portrait is now in the possession of the Clan Donald Centre and is on loan to the Scottish National Portrait Gallery.

9. Fraser-Mackintosh, Charles *Antiquarian Notes . . .* second series. Inverness 1897 p.132

10. NLS Minto Papers MS11263

11. NLS Minto Papers MS11254

12. NLS Minto Papers MS11263

13. Minto, Countess of *The Life and Letters of Sir Gilbert Elliot, 1st Earl of Minto. . .* Vol.3 p.114

14. NLS Minto Papers MS11263

15. NLS Minto Papers MS11255

16. NLS Minto Papers MS11263

Chapter 7 The Volunteers

1. *Glasgow Courier* July 6 1802

2. SRO Home Office Scottish Correspondence RH2/4/87 ff151/2

3. PRO Home Office Militia Correspondence 1803 HO50/59

4. PRO Home Office Militia Correspondence 1804 HO50/94

5. PRO Home Office Militia Correspondence 1805 HO50/125

6. British Library, Major General Mackenzie Papers, Add. Mss 39197 f103

7. PRO Home Office Militia Correspondence 1809 HO50/209

8. PRO Home Office Militia Correspondence 1811 HO50/256

9. PRO Register of Courts Martial WO92/1

10. PRO Home Office Militia Correspondence 1814/15 HO50/312

11. PRO Home Office Militia Correspondence 1810 HO50/235

12. PRO Home Office Militia Correspondence 1811 HO50/256

13. PRO Home Office Militia Correspondence 1813 HO50/292

14. PRO Home Office Militia Correspondence 1813 HO50/292

15. PRO Home Office Militia Correspondence 1814/15 HO50/312

16. *Inverness Journal* cited in Barron, James *The Northern Highlands in the nineteenth century* Inverness 1903–13

17. 48 George III Cap. CL 'An Act for enabling His Majesty to establish a permanent Local Militia Force in Scotland, under certain Restrictions, for the Defence of the Realm.'

18. SRO Melville Papers GD51/1/1000-1

19. Scott, Sir Walter *Journal* Vol.1 p.120 Edinburgh 1890

20. *Inverness Journal* 17 July 1812

21. PRO Home Office Militia Correspondence 1813 HO50/292

22. PRO Home Office Militia Correspondence 1813 HO50/292

23. *Inverness Journal* 25 August 1814

Chapter 8 Glengarry at Home

1. Boswell, James *Boswell's Journal of a tour to the Hebrides* . . . 1936 p13

2. Scott, Sir Walter *Journal* Edinburgh 1890 Vol.1 p.120/121

3. Macdonell, Louise C.R. 'Glengarry and his family: some reminiscences of a Highland Chief' in *Blackwood's Magazine* September 1893 pp323-339

4. Beith, Alexander 'The Parish of Glenelg' in *Second Statistical of Scotland*

5. Macdonell 1893 *op.cit.*

6. Macdonell Louise C.R. 'A Highland Chief and his family: some reminiscences' in *Blackwood's Magazine* April 1895 pp 520– 536

7. Beith *op. cit.*

8. Macdonell 1895 *op. cit.*

9. Beith *op.cit.*

10. Clan Donald Centre Library MS034 Alasdair Ranaldson Macdonell to Æneas Ranaldson Macdonell 28/7/1824

11. Macdonell 1893 *op. cit.*

12. Macdonell 1895 *op.cit.*

13. Macdonell 1895 *op.cit.*

14. Macdonell 1895 *op.cit.*

15. MacIntyre, John 'The Parish of Kilmonivaig' in *Second Statistical Account of Scotland*

16. Macdonell 1895 *op.cit.*

17. Macdonell 1895 *op.cit.*

18. Macdonell 1895 *op.cit.*

19. Macdonell 1895 *op.cit.*

Chapter 9 Creagan an Fhithich – the Raven's Rock

1. SRO RH2/4/87 ff151/2 (Home Office Scottish Correspondence)

2. Somers, Hugh Joseph *The Life and Times of. . . Alexander Macdonell . . .* Washington DC 1931 p.23

3. Quoted in Robertson, James Irvine *The First Highlander* East Linton 1998 p.89

4. Second Statistical Account of Inverness-shire, Parish of Kilmonivaig 1842

5. *Inverness Journal* 19 February 1813

6. *Inverness Journal* 30 September 1814

7. First Statistical Account of Inverness-shire, Parish of Kilmanivaig c.1792

8. NLS Richardson & Co. Letter Book MS20844 p.504

9. NLS Richardson & Co. Letter Book MS20845 p.45

10. *Inverness Courier* 23 September 1819

11. SRO GD176/1833

12. SRO GD51/5/606/2

13. Lindsay, Jean *The Canals of Scotland* Newton Abbot 1968 p.152

14. *ibid p.159*

15. Shaw, Patrick & Dunlop, Alexander *Cases Decided in the Court of Session* 1830 p.881-889

16. Quoted in Fraser-Mackintosh, Charles *Antiquarian Notes . . .* Second Series Inverness 1892 p.141–142

17. SRO SC/29/53 Attested copy precognitions

18. *Inverness Courier* 31 October 1822 as printed in *20th Report of the Commissioners for the Caledonian Canal* pp1823 VII 412

19. Fraser-Mackintosh, Charles *Letters of Two Centuries . . .* Inverness 1890 p.355–357

20. Fraser-Mackintosh, Charles *Antiquarian Notes. . . op. cit.* p139–142

21. Fraser-Mackintosh, Charles *Letters of Two Centuries op.cit.* p.359–361

22. *Inverness Courier* 14 July 1818

23. *Inverness Courier* 11 January 1821

24. Barron, Evan Macleod *Inverness and the Macdonalds* Inverness 1930 p.110

25. Fraser-Mackintosh, Charles *Antiquarian Notes. . . op.cit.* p.154

26. *ibid* p.145–146

27. NLS Abbotsford Correspondence MS3887 f11

28. NLS Abbotsford Correspondence MS3889 f81

29. Letter to Walter Terry in Lockhart, J.G. *Memoirs of Sir Walter Scott* London 1914 Vol. 4 p.56

30. NLS Abbotsford Correspondence MS3899 f187

31. NLS Abbotsford Correspondence MS3900 f252

32. *Inverness Journal* 23 June 1815

33. *Inverness Journal* 13 October 1815

34. *Inverness Journal* 22 November 1816

35. *Inverness Journal* 23 May 1817

36. SRO GD51/9/393

37. *Inverness Journal* 5 September 1817

38. *Inverness Courier* 10 October 1822

39. NLS Abbotsford Correspondence MS3895 f148/151

Chapter 10 Peerage and Precedence

1. *Inverness Journal* 25th January 1828

2. Fraser-MacIntosh, Charles *Antiquarian Notes. . .* Second Series Inverness 1897 p.129

3. NLS Scott Correspondence, Received MS866 f60

4. SRO Melville Papers GD51/9/371

5. British Library, Liverpool Papers, Add Mss 38249 f173

6. British Library, Liverpool Papers, Add Mss 38249 f172

7. British Library, Liverpool Papers, Add Mss 38378 f107

8. NLS Melville Papers MS1056 ff94/95

9. SRO Melville Papers GD51/1/1000-2

10. NLS Melville Papers MS 1056 ff96/97

11. Macdonell, Louise C.R. 'Glengarry and his family' in *Blackwood's Edinburgh Magazine* September 1893

12. British Library, Liverpool Papers, Add Mss 38289 f200

13. British Library, Peel Papers, Add Mss 40364 f98

14. Parliamentary Debates, House of Lords 24 May 1824

15. Parliamentary Debates, House of Commons 14 June 1824

16. SRO Melville Papers GD51/1/193

17. Scott, Walter *Journal* Edinburgh 1890 Vol.1. p120/121

18. NLS Abbotsford Correspondence MS3885 f176

19. *Inverness Journal* 19 October 1817

20. *Inverness Journal* 31 October 1817

21. Correspondence between Colonel Macdonell of Glengarry & R.G. Macdonald, Esq. M.P. Glengarry [?] 1821

22. *Inverness Courier* quoted in Barron, James *The Northern Highlands in the nineteenth century* . . . Inverness 1903–13 Vol.1

23. Correspondence between Colonel Macdonell of Glengarry & R.G. Macdonald, Esq. M.P. Glengarry [?] 1821

24. *Inverness Journal* 25 January 1828

25. Riddell, John *Vindication of the Clanronald of Glengarry* . . . Edinburgh 1821

26. Shaw, Patrick & Dunlop, Alex. *Cases decided in the Court of Session* . . . Vol.4 Edinburgh 1826 p.372

27. Clan Donald Centre Library. MS034 Letter from Alasdair Ranaldson Macdonell to John Riddell 29 January 1825

28. NLS Letters of Certification and Agreement between the Chief and Captain of Clanranald, Macdonell of Glengarry and Macdonald of Sleat.

29. Cited in Notes & Queries 11 S IV 14 October 1911.

Chapter 11 The Last of the Chiefs

1. Mackenzie, Alexander *History of the Macdonalds and Lords of the Isles* Inverness 1881 p.358

2. PRO BT107 113

3. PRO BT107 408

4. *Glasgow Courier* 22 January 1828

5. *Glasgow Herald* 25 January 1828

6. Macdonell, Louise 'Some Reminiscences of a Highland Chief' in *Blackwood's Magazine* September 1893

7. Macdonell, Louise 'Some Reminiscences of a Highland Chief' in *Blackwood's Magazine* September 1893

8. *Inverness Courier* quoted in *The Glasgow Herald* 11 February 1828

9. This poem was given by Scott to Glengarry's widow and was in the possession of the family for many years. Many editions of Scott's poetry omit it. The text printed here appears in MacDonald, Norman H *The Clanranald of Knoydart and Glengarry* 2nd ed. 1995 p.156

10. *Inverness Journal* 25 January 1828

11. Scott, Walter *Journal* Edinburgh 1890 Vol.1 p.120

12. *Inverness Courier* quoted in Barron, James *The Northern Highlands in the Nineteenth Century. . .* Inverness 1903–13 Vol.1

13. SRO Abbotsford Correspondence MS3895 ff148/151

14. SRO GD1/53 David Stewart of Garth Transcripts of MacGregor of MacGregor MSS David Stewart of Garth to Sir J MacGregor quoted in Robertson *The First Highlander*

15. SCA Blairs Papers Macdonell to Hay 12 February 1794 quoted in Toomey, Kathleen M. *Alexander Macdonell, the Scottish Years 1762-1804* Toronto 1985

16. SRO Melville Papers GD51/6/246/1

17. Scott, Walter *Journal* Edinburgh 1890 Vol.1 p.120

18. Stevenson, Robert Louis Some 'Portraits by Raeburn' in *Virginibus Pueresque and other papers* London 1912 p.145–6

19. Galt, John *The Steam-boat* Chapter X

BIBLIOGRAPHY

The notes to each chapter show the sources used for specific references and quotations. Early nineteenth century Scotland has a huge literature but the following books were particularly useful in providing detailed information or background information.

Barron, Evan Macleod *Inverness and the Macdonalds* Inverness 1930

Barron, James *The Northern Highlands in the Nineteenth Century* Inverness 1903–1913

Browne, James *A history of the Highlands and of the Highland clans* Glasgow 1838

Bulloch, J.M. *The Scots Fencibles and English service, an episode of 1794* Banff 1915

Bumsted, J.M. *The People's Clearance: 1770-1815* Edinburgh 1982

Clyde, Robert *From Rebel to Hero: the image of the Highlander 1745-1830* East Linton 1995

First and Second Statistical Accounts of Glenelg and Kilmonivaig

Fraser-Mackintosh, Charles *Antiquarian Notes. . .* Second Series Inverness 1897

Fraser-Mackintosh, Charles *Letters of Two Centuries* Inverness 1890

Fry, Michael *The Dundas Despotism* Edinburgh 1992

Kelly, Bernard William *The fate of Glengarry, or, the expatriation of the MacDonells. . .* Dublin 1905

Lenman, Bruce *The Jacobite Clans of the Great Glen 1650-1784* Aberdeen 1995

Lindsay, Jean *The Canals of Scotland* Newton Abbott 1968

MacDonald, Angus & MacDonald, Archibald *Clan Donald* Inverness 1896–1904

MacDonald, Norman H. *The Clan Ranald of Knoydart and Glengarry* 2nd ed. Edinburgh 1995

Macdonell, Alexander Correspondence between Colonel Macdonell of Glengarry and R.G. Macdonald ? 1821

Mackintosh, H.B. *The Grant, Strathspey or 1st Highland Fencible Regiment* Elgin 1934

McLean, Marianne *The People of Glengarry: Highlanders in Transition 1745-1820* Montreal 1991

Prebble, John *The King's Jaunt, George IV in Scotland, 1822* London 1988

Reid, John *Bibliotheca scoto-celtica* . . . Glasgow 1832

Riddell, John *Vindication of the 'Clanronald of Glengarry'* . . . Edinburgh 1821

Robertson, James *General view of the agriculture in the county of Inverness.* . . London 1808

Robertson, James Irvine *The First Highlander: Major General David Stewart of Garth.* . . East Linton 1998

Somers, Hugh Joseph *The life and times of.* . . *Alexander Macdonell, DD, first bishop of Upper Canada* Washington DC 1931

Stewart, David *Sketches of the character, manners and present state of the Highlanders of Scotland.* . . Edinburgh 1822

Toomey, Kathleen M. *Alexander Macdonell, the Scottish Years 1762-1804* Toronto 1985

INDEX

For information about other books from Argyll Publishing
Tel 01369 820229
Fax 01369 820372
email: argyll.publishing@virgin.net
write to Argyll Publishing, Glendaruel, Argyll PA22 3AE Scotland
or visit our website: www.deliberatelythirsty.com